They Left Us
Everything

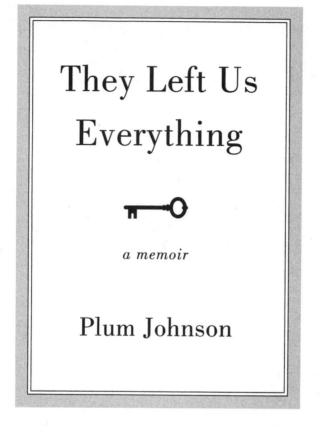

They Left Us Everything

a memoir

Plum Johnson

G. P. PUTNAM'S SONS

New York

PUTNAM

G. P. PUTNAM'S SONS
Publishers Since 1838
An imprint of Penguin Random House LLC
375 Hudson Street
New York, New York 10014

ISBN 978-0-399-18409-3

Printed in the United States of America
1 3 5 7 9 10 8 6 4 2

Book design by Gretchen Achilles

For my children

Contents

PART III

Dispersal

Never Mind the Dog

The night before I turn sixty-three, I'm looking in the mirror, pulling my sagging jawline up to my ears, listening to voice mails on speakerphone. Three are from Mum:

"Happy birthday, m'darlin'!"

"Promise you'll drive out first thing tomorrow!"

"Damn this machine! Call me!"

Mum is ninety-three, and these are her messages just since dinner. Nineteen years, one month, and twenty-six days of elder-care have brought me to my knees. But first thing next morning, I crawl to my car, hack at the ice on my windshield, and slump into the front seat with the heater cranked up.

Mum lives in Oakville, forty-five minutes from my home in Toronto, so I follow the curve of the highway west around the shores of Lake Ontario, watching the lid of brown smog recede in my rearview mirror, and exit south down a tree-lined road—to the slower, more remembered pace of my childhood. Just ahead, the lake rises up, beckoning me with its liquid shimmer.

Even now in late November, the icy water sparkles.

Our old clapboard house is rooted here in this prime location overlooking the lake, a place Mum calls "the most beautiful spot on earth." This is where my four younger brothers and I were raised. This is where one of my brothers died. Dad died here, too.

I pull in to the driveway and step up to what we euphemistically call "the boathouse door." None of us uses the front door anymore; we all use the boathouse. Dad used to store his sailboat here, between the garage and the house, and eventually roofed it over as a kind of carport to keep off the snow. There hasn't been a boat here in more than forty years.

They say you can never go back, but the people who say that haven't seen this house. Nothing's been changed since Mum and Dad bought the house in 1952—not even the dining room wallpaper—and the family who sold it to them had owned it since 1917. You come through the door and think you're in a time warp.

A movie scout for Walt Disney Pictures once walked in here and his eyeballs almost fell out of his head. "Get here quick!" he screamed into his cell phone. "You don't understand . . . we won't even need props!" Which is why there's a framed picture of me in the living room scene of *The Ref* with Kevin Spacey.

As I step into the mudroom, the first thing I see is the cast-iron woodstove with HOME COMFORT etched on the front. Teetering on top is a tin of powdered dance wax and a potholder with Mum's Southern message: Y'ALL SPOKEN HERE! Dangling from the window latches are long metal flyswatters. I hear a faint humming—the summer flies are long dead, so it might be the pipes, or it might be the furnace, or I might just be imagining things. Hanging from wood pegs near the ceiling, next to waterlogged canvas life jackets and stiff straw boaters, are old wooden tennis rackets, screwed by wing nuts into their square wooden presses. Stuck into one of the windowpanes is a plastic sign of a gun aiming straight at your heart: NEVER MIND THE DOG: BEWARE OF THE OWNER!

Then I see Mum.

She's in the kitchen, plumped into a chair at the long harvest table, wearing black polyester pants, a red turtleneck sweater, and large white plastic earrings. Her round cheeks are pink and her lips are enlivened with Revlon Red. She has no wrinkles, even in her nineties, and no eyelashes—or at least none that we've ever been able to see. She has never plucked her eyebrows or had a facial, something she's always considered vain and a waste of money: "Men never have facials, they never use face creams . . . just soap and water . . . and do *they* have wrinkles? *No!*" Her fingernails are painted red, though, because she will, from time to time, have a manicure. She also dyes her hair brown because, she says, "There's already too much gray in the world . . . why would I want to add to it?" Mum loves glitz, so above her diamond engagement ring she wears a gaudy pile of sparkly beads on an elasticized band. On the table are her favorite red sunglasses, shaped like a pair of wide laughing lips.

The cowbell on the door handle jingles as I let myself in. Mum looks up expectantly and smiles.

"Hi, Mum," I say as I kick off my boots. "How are you?"

"What?"

"I SAID, 'HOW ARE YOU?'"

"You don't need to shout!"

"I wish you'd get a hearing aid," I mutter.

"Going deaf is the best thing that ever happened to me!" she says. "Everything's too loud anyway."

The kitchen table—her command central—is piled high with newspaper clippings, Sears flyers, church leaflets, and Christmas cards. Letters from the Publishers Clearing House announce that she's won a million dollars, and Mum's already stamped those brown reply envelopes. At the far end of the table, loose photographs of grandchildren and great-grandchildren are propped up in a motley reunion around a vase of plastic flowers, and kitschy feathered roosters perch near the fruit bowl, competing for space with her salt and pepper shakers, which are shaped like little pink pigs in waiters' uniforms. There's an open tin of homemade shortbread from some well-meaning neighbor and a stack of *Biodiesel Smarter* magazines, published by one of her grandsons—Mum is a loyal subscriber. Her long-handled magnifying glass lies atop the editorial page of today's newspaper.

The only obvious hint that Mum has a problem is her oxygen tubing. It winds around her ears, across her cheeks, and into her nose, emitting a constant *pock-hiss . . . pock-hiss*. Sometimes the tubing falls off her ears. Sometimes she gets so mad she Scotch-tapes it to her hair.

I walk across to give her a hug, but she throws up her arms like steel rods to keep me at a distance.

"Don't hug me—it's flu season!"

I bend down and kiss the air beside her cheek. She's recently had cataracts removed, and I notice that her eyes are covered with a gooey film of gel.

"How are your eyes, Mum?"

"The same." She shrugs.

"What did the doctor say yesterday?"

"The same old thing, I told you! Why do you want to know?"

Mum says she can't stand "old people who discuss their ailments." Everybody's got problems, she says; it's just what happens when you get old, so why talk about it?

4

From the top of the fruit bowl she takes a persimmon—my favorite fruit—and shoves it toward me.

"Here!" she says. "This is for you—happy birthday!"

She's drawn a smiling face on it with Magic Marker and tied a ribbon around its middle. I'm pleasantly surprised, because usually Mum gives me cheap, gaudy jewelry, just like hers, and doesn't even wrap it—she leaves the receipt in the bag. This is the first year she's given me a *consumable* . . . and I *like* it, which suggests I'm no longer in acquisition mode—I'm happier with gifts that won't clutter . . . things I can eat. I look at the brightly painted eyes and upturned lips of the persimmon and think, *I must be getting old.*

"I'd give anything to be your age again!" says Mum.

"Really, Mum? Thanks—that puts everything in perspective."

"Do you have any plans to celebrate?"

How could I, when I have to be here? Mum couldn't possibly know how I'm feeling—anchored by aging parents. By the time she was thirty-six, both her parents were dead. My resentment bubbles over, so I sidestep her question and try a little dig.

"What were you doing when you were sixty-three?" I ask her.

"Let's see," she says, oblivious, "I guess I was taking that wonderful cruise up the Nile!"

She turns to her pile of newspaper clippings. "Now," she says excitedly, "I have some things to show you!" She points to an article on Barack Obama. "I want you to read this—the best thing the Nobel Committee ever did was give that intelligent man the Peace Prize. If the world would just listen to what he has to say, we might stop trying to blow each other up!" Then she plows through her stack and hands me more, one after another. "Recognize her? Our oldest ancestor in Ethiopia—she's a fossil named Ardi, over four million years old! And look—the Leonid meteor shower! Imagine, two hundred comets an hour!"

"The Leonid what? Where?"

"Over Southeast Asia—this afternoon! The Earth is going to pass through all this cosmic debris that was produced when Christopher Columbus was alive! Don't you wish we could see it?"

My brain is spinning. I'm still thinking about her ophthalmologist.

"And I want you to help me with this!" she says. "Remember when I told you about the festival?"

"What festival?"

"Stratford! It's pathetic—they're losing money! They need to mount an advertising campaign!" She bangs the kitchen table with her fist and grabs a pen. "So I've come up with a new word . . . *Shakesperience* . . . Isn't that the greatest word?"

Her old advertising copywriting experience has come flooding back and she's written a letter to the director, laying out a marketing plan to help him out. I'm reading her draft, scribbled on the back of an old grocery list, imagining some young assistant rolling her eyes before dumping it in the trash. "I sent this weeks ago!" Mum says. "Why hasn't he written me back?"

"People don't know what to do with handwritten letters anymore, Mum. They only use e-mails."

She purses her lips, shakes her head, and tosses her draft back into her pile of debris. I get the feeling she's shocked by her own lack of power to effect change.

"He's just rude, if you ask me! No manners whatsoever." She adjusts her oxygen tube and gasps for breath. "*Damn* this thing!" Mum's mind can access facts faster than Google—her memory is prodigious. She remembers more about current events than most people and can rattle off an astonishing array of historical data. But politics has always interested her most; her family in Virginia was steeped in it. Her ancestors include Edmund Randolph, who was the first attorney general of the United States, and Bartholomew Dandridge, who was George Washington's brother-in-law. She has ancestors buried at Thomas Jefferson's home, which entitles her to access the cemetery, so she's delighted she doesn't have to pay admission when she visits Monticello.

When Mum was growing up, Richmond, Virginia, and Washington, D.C., were populated by many of her relatives in positions of power. Two of her cousins later became U.S. ambassadors, and her oldest brother was director of Germany's industrial reconstruction after World War II for the Marshall Plan—which he helped draft. He also served on various councils advising several presidents, from Truman to Kennedy, so Mum felt privy to the backroom dealings of the world stage. She was used to getting the inside scoop.

I don't think Mum realized how unusual this was. She simply believed that if you wanted to change something—anything at all—you just had to make one phone call. To the person in charge. Who was probably a cousin. Which is why her unanswered letter to the director of the Stratford Festival in rural Ontario has, quite literally, taken her breath away.

Mum has been on oxygen for years now, ever since she quit smoking (and playing tennis) at the age of eighty-five. Thin, clear plastic tubing—miles of it—snakes through this four-thousand-square-foot house, tethering Mum to a loud, belching, institutional-sized machine located in the upstairs hall. The tubing trails after her wherever she goes, like a long, loopy extension cord. Sometimes she forgets she's tethered and walks one too many times through the front hall, into the dining room, through the pantry, back into the front hall, past the living room, and into the dining room again, encircling herself in an impossible tangle.

"Damn this thing!"

If she sits on the chairlift to ride up the main staircase, she hauls the tubing into a coiled lasso and slings it over the armrest, as if she's out to strangle a bull.

"Damn it to hell!"

The dials on the machine are now cranked up to what the doctors say is their highest level of oxygen output, but when this becomes inadequate, Mum plans to get two machines. "Who says I can't? That's ridiculous!"

You'd think her predicament would make anyone swear off smoking for life, but all I want when I'm with her is a cigarette.

After Dad died, Mum felt lonely and began talking about moving into a retirement home. She complained that most of her good friends were dead. Others had moved into swank retirement homes nearby, like the Churchill, but Mum refused to join them in what she called "those hoity-toity places named after dead politicians." She didn't understand how anyone could arrive at old age and still be a snob. "Didn't they learn anything in all those years?" She wanted interesting people around her, from all walks of life. Eventually she found a place more to her liking—"more down to earth." It was miles away.

My brothers and I tried to talk her out of moving. We couldn't imagine how she could shrink her expansive nature into one room. But when she insisted, and a two-room suite became available, my brother Victor put down the hefty deposit.

The week before Mum was due to go, I'd been home with her, sitting in the TV room. She was wedged into the upholstered recliner with her feet up. To ease the circulation in her swollen ankles she'd cut open the elastic tops of her nylon knee-highs, and they drooped like cuffs over her shoes. I pointed to a picture on the wall. It was a hunting scene of hounds chasing a fox to ground.

"You've always loved that picture," I said to Mum. "Why don't you plan to take it with you?"

Her face turned purple. "How dare you!" she shouted.

"What?"

"How dare you tell me what I can and cannot take!"

"Mum!" I said. "I was only making a suggestion."

She pounded her fist on the armrest. "You all can hardly wait to get me out of here! You all want to send me away so you can sell this house!"

I was astonished. "That's not true! We've begged you not to go."

"How dare you!" she screamed again.

A strange voice thundered up from my soles, the first time I ever remember raising my voice to my mother. "How dare YOU!" I roared. "How dare you suggest that we want you out. This was your idea! We had nothing to do with it! We've done nothing but bend over backward . . . for *years* . . . to do what you ask . . . to try and make you happy . . . and all you do is turn on us!" Then I fled the room in tears. I ran into the living room, sank into the sofa, and wept and wept—loud, heaving sobs. "I miss Dad! I miss Dad!"

Dad's slow fade had consumed most of my forties and fifties, but I had more patience then, and sweetness. Now I was convinced that Mum would make it into the *Guinness World Records* as the Longest Living Mother. Friends of mine who'd lost their mothers early kept telling me, *"You don't know how lucky you are . . . I'd give anything to have my mother back for even one minute!"* But I just couldn't relate. All I wanted was my freedom. I looked into the future and thought, *Will I ever get my life back?*

Almost an hour went by before Mum shuffled into the room, trailing her oxygen tubing. She looked defeated, standing there unsteadily in the middle of the hall. She waited until my sobs subsided.

"Do you think we should talk to somebody?" she asked.

I looked at Mum, surprised. "Talk to somebody? You mean, like a therapist?"

"Uh-huh."

I stared out the window, wondering where we'd ever begin. I could spend a lifetime on a therapist's couch trying to untangle my complicated relationship with Mum.

"I think it's too late."

"I think so, too," she said, and sounded relieved.

I knew Mum was facing a cruel choice for an extrovert—to either live in isolation here, "the most beautiful spot on Earth," or be stimulated by crowds of people in a sterile environment—but she'd made her decision: she wanted to give the retirement home a try. So a week later I called in the troops and we all drove her over there for a two-week test run.

I was proud that we'd come together, presenting a united front. It happened more frequently now, although it hadn't always been that way—some of us had managed years earlier to escape. When Sandy was starting his career, he'd moved as far away as possible—to Hong Kong and then Saudi Arabia—and rarely came home; Robin went to the University of Virginia as a young man and never moved back; and Chris had lived in Saskatoon for almost twenty years. That left Victor and me—the youngest and oldest—holding the fort. For years he and I had rolled our eyes as Mum praised the others for their short weekly phone calls. "It's remarkable! Do you know they call me *every* Sunday?" But whenever she'd laugh and say, "All mothers love best those children who live farthest away," Victor and I would joke about moving to Fiji.

Each of us provided a unique kind of solace to Mum, and together we made up a whole: I provided efficiency; Robin, diplomacy; Chris, empathy; and Victor, practicality. If Sandy had been alive, he would have provided dignity. She knew we all loved her—it was just hard to show it with any patience these days. Her demanding, domineering personality seemed to gather force with each passing year—it was her way or the highway—and we were at our wits' end.

At the retirement home, the boys had looked tall and strong and handsome, dressed in their best. Robin was in his tweed jacket and brown brogues, Chris in his green argyle sweater and Birkenstocks, Victor in his leather bomber jacket and Blundstones. They all sported beards and ties.

We checked in with the director, wandered with Mum through all the common areas, nodded to people in wheelchairs silently watching TV, inspected the garage where all the scooters were parked, and gazed at the pots of violets and ferns in the small alcove they called the "garden room." It scared me. It was like looking into my own future, into a warehouse full of abandoned parents waiting to die. No potted plants could soften the image. Where was the hope? Where was the noise and clutter of grandchildren? I felt sorry for Mum—her apartment looked so empty, silent, and white. The only thing close to an animated object was her little black overnight bag perched on the edge of the bed, and she stood beside it, looking lost.

But then we took her to supper.

The dining room was hushed. Subdued lighting and wall-to-wall carpeting sucked the life out of conversation. Metal walkers were parked at the entrance. Waitresses glided back and forth with trays of rice pudding. A sign by the potted palm told us to wait for the hostess, so Chris took a menu and studied it.

"Hey, Mum, this looks good . . . Look—cottage cheese, your favorite!"

"Where's the damn hostess?" said Mum. "That's what I want to know!"

"I believe she'll be here shortly," said Robin.

Mum peered into the dimly lit room. "Why is everyone so silent?"

"They're eating," said Chris.

"But nobody's talking to each other!"

"Maybe they don't know each other," said Victor, shrugging.

"Then why are they sitting together?"

"The hostess seats you . . ." I said. "I think she puts you at a different table each meal."

"You mean we have no choice? That's the stupidest thing I ever heard of!"

"*Shhhh*—not so loud, Mum!"

"Well, I certainly don't want to sit beside that woman over there—look!" Mum pointed to a woman eating alone at a table for six near the window. "She looks boring as hell."

"*Shhhhhhh*, Mum!"

Eventually, the hostess led us straight to the window. The neatly dressed woman was eating dessert. She didn't look up. Robin pulled out Mum's chair.

"Why do we have to sit here?" But by then we were already seated.

"Bring me a glass of water," said Mum to the hostess.

"Your waitress will be with you shortly, ma'am."

"I don't want a *waitress*," said Mum. "I want *water*. Can't you get me water? Surely there must be *some* water in this place!"

The woman at our table patted her mouth with her linen napkin, laid it neatly at her place, reached for her cane, and limped away.

"Thank goodness!" said Mum.

We eyed each other over our menus. This wasn't going so well. But we stayed until bedtime, made sure Mum's TV worked, and reminded her how to use her portable oxygen tanks. She wouldn't be able to wander all day as she could at home, hooked into a steady supply. If she wanted to leave her bedroom she'd have to use portables that lasted only two hours, and this new reality was causing her anxiety.

We said good night and promised to phone regularly.

Robin drove back to Virginia. Within three days, I got a call from the administrator.

"I'm sorry," she said. "Your mother isn't settling."

Mum refused to contemplate any other places, so Victor and I knew what this meant: we'd have to continue to supervise her care and make sure that loyal friends continued to visit . . . for weekly bridge games, Bible study, tea parties, DVD screenings, and doggie playtimes—a bigger social calendar than most institutions. Victor and I had been synchronizing our calendars months in advance for years, ever since Dad was diagnosed with Alzheimer's, but whereas Dad had been sweet and grateful,

Mum was so caustic and demanding that she was tipping us over the edge.

We picked Mum up and took her back home.

Inside the mudroom, we were greeted by rows of extra oxygen tanks all leaning up against the woodstove.

"Anyone got a lighter?" joked Victor, laughing.

I hear soft slippers on the back staircase. Our kindly Tibetan caregivers, Pelmo and Tashi, who've been with us for more than a decade, still live in the three-room apartment we created at the back of the house when Dad got Alzheimer's. They've dedicated part of their space as a shrine to the Dalai Lama. His Holiness peers down from a gigantic poster, surrounded by plastic flowers, incense, and gold-fringed banners.

Pelmo comes down to say hello. She's slim and graceful in a simple dark shirt and trousers, her long black hair parted in the middle and caught in a bun at the nape of her neck. I'm hoping to have a conversation with her about her hours: she starts work earlier now, to attend to Mum's personal care, so by three in the afternoon, she's already worked a seven-hour shift. I want to make sure she's properly paid and gets enough time off.

"How can we make mealtimes easier?" I ask Pelmo. "Should we try ordering Meals on Wheels?"

"Don't talk about me as if I'm not here!" says Mum. "I don't need food. I've got a freezer full of chicken."

I open her freezer and survey all the unidentified plastic tubs. Each one holds a congealed mass. "Pelmo, this all has freezer burn—you need to throw it away!"

Pelmo's eyebrows shoot up and she looks to Mum.

"Pelmo does not throw my food away!" says Mum. "This is *my* kitchen!"

"Sorry . . . sorry . . ." says Pelmo. "I go upstairs."

As she's leaving, Mum says to me, "You don't understand how horrible it is having *strangers* living in my house!"

Pelmo and Tashi are hardly strangers; in fact, I consider them saints. Later I catch Pelmo in the pantry, out of Mum's earshot, and apologize for Mum's rudeness.

She smiles broadly. "It's okay," she says. "Your mum, I know she has good heart. These things she says, she does not mean."

"Look!" Mum calls from the kitchen, gasping for breath and stabbing a manicured fingernail at one of her newspaper flyers. "Sears is extending their Christmas sale—they're practically *giving* things away! Let's go look at sweaters."

"Mum, you've already got three million sweaters upstairs."

"I know," she says, "but this is irresistible! It's your birthday. Let's just go . . . just for a few minutes."

The lack of oxygen has turned her fingertips blue. I ask if she really has the energy for a shopping mall.

"I don't think you understand," she pants. "I can't *stand* being cooped up here all day!"

I want to say *I don't think* you *understand,* but I bite my tongue. I call to the pantry, "Pelmo? I'm taking Mum to Sears!"

After helping Mum switch to her portable oxygen supply, I collect her purse, sunglasses, and walker, and we totter arm-in-arm toward the boathouse door. There are three steps we have to get down. Holding the door open with my shoulder, I lower first the walker, then her oxygen tank. Mum's arms are outstretched like a figurehead on the bow of the *Titanic*, her hands clinging to the door frame, the tubing stretched taut from her nose to the tank on the ground. As she descends the steps, she leans on me heavily, as if I'm a solid oak banister, and I wonder if the chiropractor can see me tomorrow. Mum is not thin.

"Just a minute . . . just a minute!" she shouts. "I need to catch my breath."

We stand in the darkened garage for a few minutes. I stare at the tubing that connects us and think of umbilical cords.

"Breathe through your nose, Mum."

"I am!"

While she inches her walker toward my car in the driveway, I trundle the oxygen tank in tandem. A few yards seem like hundreds of miles. Every few steps, she has to stop for breath. Getting Mum into the car is a whole other thing. She has to disengage from the walker and turn seat-first into the car, holding on to the car frame without getting tangled in the tubing. She's exhausted. I'm exhausted. She heaves onto the seat.

"Who made this car?" she shouts. "They ought to be shot!" Now I lift the heavy tank with its metal wheels into the front seat with her. We must find space for it somehow, wedged between her legs, because the tubing won't reach her nose if I put it in the back. By now my patience is spent, so I slam her door a little too pointedly. I fold the walker and heave it into the backseat, cursing the flyer from Sears. *Hell*, I think, *they ought to be shot*.

Driving raises my blood pressure a notch. I haven't bothered to strap Mum in. The seat belt won't fit over this explosive cargo and, surely to God, at some point, does it really matter? As we approach each intersection, she leans forward, grips the dashboard, and shrieks, "It's a stop sign!" or, "It's a red light!"

"I know, Mum," I say calmly. "Breathe through your nose."

"I am!"

At the mall I have to repeat all these steps in reverse. I unload the walker, the oxygen tank, and my mother, and guide all three to a bench inside. Then I trundle the walker back to the car and drive to find a parking spot. This is usually about three miles away. By the time I reunite with Mum, she's anxious and worried.

"Where have you been?" she bleats.

"I had to park the car, Mum. And now I have to get a wheel-chair."

I've learned by now where the wheelchairs are—and they're nowhere near Sears. At the kiosk the rental is free, but they take my car keys as hostage. Why can't they take my mother instead? Then they hand me what looks like a heavy, Soviet-era wheel-chair that's folded flat like origami. It takes all my strength to spring it open. It has no holder for oxygen tanks, no basket for purchases. Just a flat leather pocket on the back, to hold what . . . my driver's license? I wheel it over to Mum on the bench.

She looks defeated. "I don't think I have the energy," she says.

"Energy for what, Mum?"

"For this!" she says angrily, waving at the wheelchair.

"This is a *wheelchair!*"

"I know that!" She glowers at me. "I *said* I don't have the energy!"

"You want to go home, then?" I say this with a low, threatening growl. She considers it for a moment while I stare at the ceiling.

"No!"

"Well, breathe through your nose, then."

"I am!"

"I'll be pushing," I say, a little more gently. "You won't have to do anything except sit there."

The bright lights of Sears beckon at the other end of the mall and soon her excitement mounts. I bend like a pretzel to push her. Combined with the oxygen tank, I figure I'm pushing more than two hundred pounds.

"Damn!" she says suddenly.

"What?"

"I don't have my glasses."

"You won't need your glasses, Mum. I'll read things for you."

"Not my reading glasses!" she snaps, as if I'm an imbecile. "My *sunglasses*. The lights hurt my eyes!"

"Where are they?" I say, reaching for her purse.

"In the car! Where else would they be?"

I want to weep.

The car is locked. I can't get my keys back unless I return the wheelchair. And I can't return the wheelchair without taking Mum out and putting her back on the bench.

"That's too bad, then," I hiss. "Don't look at the lights, look at Sears!"

We brush past the perfume counters. Clerks stand in the aisles, aiming atomizers like guns to our heads. I shoot them back a withering look. We get to the sweaters. Clothes are crammed in disarray, left in heaps on the carpet, surrounded by discount signs. Mum perks right up.

"Stop here!" she barks. "Bring me that one!"

In among the depressing sea of muddy colors—navy, gray, maroon, and beige—Mum has expertly picked out a pretty fleece jacket in pale pink. It's a sports model for joggers.

"Let's get it!" she says.

"You sure?" It's not even red.

"I'll get a lot of use out of this!" She turns to me. "Don't you think so?"

As I wheel her to the checkout counter, I wonder if the clerk can read Mum's shopping history on her monitor. If so, she knows that after Christmas Mum will be returning it.

By the time we get home, Pelmo is back on duty, cooking dinner, so I keep my coat on and one foot out the door.

"I have to go now, Mum."

"Oh, stay!" she pleads, suddenly smiling and clapping her hands. "Help me wrap presents!" As usual, Mum's bought all her presents at garage sales throughout the summer and heaped them in a closet in the spare bedroom. I know what's up there: sets of wooden salad bowls, out-of-date atlases, naked Barbie dolls, and books bought by the pound at the local library sale. There's enough junk to fill every recycling bin in town.

"Can't it wait?" I say, exasperated. "Christmas is still a month away."

"In case I don't live till Christmas."

"Really, Mum! You can't keep worrying about Christmas."

"Well, I do—I might die!"

"Mum, every Christmas you say this, and every Christmas you're *still here*! Are you going to wrap enough presents to leave behind for the next one hundred years?!"

She looks at me suspiciously. "Why do you have to rush off?"

"I'm not exactly rushing," I say through gritted teeth, checking my watch. It's dark outside and I've been here eight hours.

"Stay and have some supper—you have to eat *sometime*!"

"I have a date, Mum," I lie.

"A date?" She looks surprised. "With who?"

"Nobody special." How would I have the time or energy to add another relationship to my life? Since my divorce thirty years ago I've dated many men, but the thought of trying to blend yet another family into this one was always too exhausting to contemplate.

"When will I see you again?" she asks.

"I'll be out on the weekend," I say, *"just like always."*

Her mouth hardens into a tight, defensive line. "You make it sound like a fate worse than death."

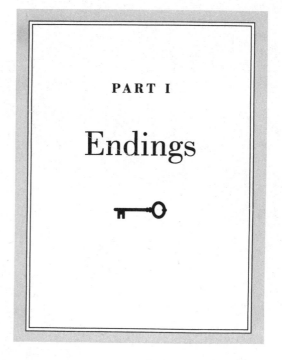

PART I

Endings

Mum's Will

Mum never did return that pink jacket to Sears.

She died three weeks after Christmas.

Tonight we're holding a Sibling Supper to read her last will and testament. The boys and I have been holding Sibling Suppers (no spouses allowed) to discuss Mum and Dad for almost twenty years. It's where we commiserate and strategize and conduct our own version of group therapy. Two or three times a year, Robin drives up from Virginia, Chris flies in from western Canada, and Victor and I book a good restaurant. We order filet mignon and the best bottle of wine and basically laugh all night.

Tonight's Sibling Supper won't be so funny. We all feel like we've been in a train wreck. Mum's funeral a week earlier has left us feeling drained and stunned. Instead of booking a restaurant, we're meeting at Victor's home in Riverdale.

We navigate our cars through the darkened, snow-covered streets and climb carefully up the salted wooden steps to his narrow yellow-brick row house. We take off our boots and sling our jackets over the coat tree inside the front hall. A cozy fire is lit in the living room to ward off the January chill. All the spouses know the rules, so, after drinks together, they go out and leave us to our business.

Six months before she died, Mum had leaned into my face with the steady pulse of her oxygen machine *pock-hiss*ing in the background and said, "Just think, as soon as I kick the bucket all your money troubles will be over!" She was thinking of her house. Mum figured its sale would put all of us on Easy Street, but what she didn't know was that we'd recently mortgaged it. Years of round-the-clock caregivers for her and Dad had sucked the life out of their nest egg. We'd just hoped that, with Victor's careful supervision of Mum's financial affairs, what was left would see her through. Tonight we're going to find out how close to the edge we came.

Our pecking order isn't what you might think—it has nothing to do with birth order. It has to do with perceived competencies and long-assumed role expectations. For example, when Dad was alive I felt he was emotionally open to me, so if something delicate had to be presented to him, I volunteered for the job. Robin is the wise diplomat, so we turned to him for a considered opinion. He inherited Mum's prodigious memory—mention something once and he never forgets it—so he's also been our collective memory bank. Mum felt emotionally open to Chris, so if we ever wanted to gauge her reaction to a sensitive topic, we asked Chris to do it. Victor is the smartest with money, so he's had power of attorney over Mum and Dad's financial affairs. Besides, Victor is the only one who could have wrested Dad's account books away from him, and he could stand up to Mum better than any of us.

After supper, we clear Victor's dining room table, pour extra wine, bring out the scotch, and hand around photocopies of the will. Victor and I have been named co-executors. We start the meeting with a prayer and a promise that we won't let the will or anything else tear us apart. We agree that material possessions aren't worth fighting over. But despite how much we've pulled together, we're processing this event separately. Our memories are all different, our experiences unique.

Tonight I want an ashtray, which drives Chris crazy. He quit smoking years ago. He moves to the far end of the table and makes a big fuss about me having a cigarette "here . . . in such a small, enclosed space." He's the socialist in the family and likes to operate by consensus—which is too bad for him tonight, because we're all looking for comfort. Robin and Victor haul out cigars.

"Get over it," says Victor. "Look, it's a vaulted ceiling . . . I'll open the front door."

Chris raises his arms in surrender and Victor starts reading the will out loud. It's only a formality, but it seems important to give this Sibling Supper some gravitas. We've been through wills before, on both sides of the family, and it's astonishing what ill will can be generated from a sheaf of paper.

At least Mum's will is straightforward. She never understood wills that showed favoritism—why bequeath a fight to the next generation? She believed that wills should treat all children equally, so everything is divided by four. Dad's will was straightforward, too. He'd left all his assets to Mum, which is why we didn't discover one small glitch until after Mum died: Victor found some old IOUs in Dad's safety-deposit box. Whenever we'd borrowed money in the past—to repay a student loan, perhaps, or to finance a property—Mum wasn't too bothered with accounting; we found notes she'd scribbled to herself on scraps of paper in her desk. But whenever we borrowed from Dad, he made us sign a formal IOU. Mum's will generously stipulates that all debts to her are forgiven, but the lawyer has explained that debts to Dad are not Mum's to forgive—she inherited his assets, not his debts. Debts to Dad should be deducted from our inheritance and repaid to the estate. Not everyone is happy. Obviously, in hindsight, Mum was the better bank.

Mum has also left each one of us a specific, treasured object. To me, she's left the German music box that has been in her family since 1878. To Robin, she's left the wooden prison ship, carved out of wood and fishbone by Dad's great-great-grandfather during the Napoleonic Wars. To Chris, she's left the elaborate sterling-silver punch bowl passed down by our Irish ancestors. And to Victor, she's left the silver water goblets that we always used on special family occasions. Each of the grandchildren has been left something, too. The girls get a piece of jewelry, and the boys one of Dad's war medals.

When Victor has finished reading the slim document, he asks if one of us will act as secretary to record the minutes for the many items we need to discuss. Everyone looks at me, but I keep quiet for once. There's an uncomfortable silence. Eventually Chris volunteers. Victor gives us an up-to-date summary of Mum's financial affairs—how much is left in the bank and what debts are outstanding.

The most important decision we have to make tonight is what to do with the main asset: the house. Mum had always worried about this. She asked me repeatedly, "What will you children do with the house after I'm gone?" I didn't want to give her false hope, but I'd been trying for years to come up with a plan. Could we duplex it? Turn it into a B&B? Could I live over the garage and rent out the main part? We poll the table to find out if any of us wants to buy the others out. Everyone looks at me again—they know how much I love it—and I'm filled with feelings of inadequacy.

How could I be in such a position as to not be able to afford this house? It means I'm relatively poorer in middle age than my father was when he was only thirty-six. It underscores all the mistakes I've made. I allow myself to wallow in so many "if onlys." If only I'd stayed married . . . If only I hadn't sold my company . . . If only I'd invested in real estate . . . If only I'd been smarter . . . or luckier. I'd already bought a lottery ticket—the Stupid Man's Tax—and not one of my numbers rolled out.

There's only one possibility left: finding a treasure under the floorboards. Isn't there something . . . *somewhere*? A priceless Roman coin, perhaps, or a dirty little Degas? I can't bear to give up my dream of keeping this house in the family.

Predictably, immediately following Mum's funeral we'd received several real estate inquiries, all disguised as sympathy notes. Some were from agents, but most were from private buyers. They rambled on at some length about how they had met Mum, found her so fascinating, sat on her veranda, loved the view, et cetera, et cetera, as if they'd been Mum's best friends for eons. We didn't recognize any of the names. They all ended with "So, if you're ever thinking of selling . . ." I'd wedged them into Mum's letter holder in the kitchen—a gold metal dachshund shaped like a Slinky.

We discuss what to do with these letters: should we choose an agent or just start negotiating with one of the private buyers? As co-executors, Victor and I have a fiduciary responsibility to get the best price. We know the house has dramatically increased in value—about three times what my Toronto home is worth, because lakefront is so highly prized now—but we need to get it professionally appraised.

The exterior wooden clapboard needs painting, something Dad did faithfully every seven years, and it's a costly and mammoth task. We pour more scotch and decide to have the house painted as soon as the weather's warm enough.

We've told Pelmo and Tashi that they can continue to live in their apartment at the back of the house until they find new jobs, but they're leaving for Tibet soon on a six-week holiday. We can't leave the house empty; there are too many valuable things there, and, more importantly, there's Mum's dog—a small, aging, black-and-white Shih Tzu. Mum called him Sambo—a name which always made me cringe. I'm sure my childhood book *Little Black Sambo* is now banned in most school systems, so whenever I'm out in public, I call him Simbo, so as not to offend anyone. He's deaf and almost blind, but he knows his way around Mum's house by heart. We all agree it would be cruel to board him.

"How would you like to inherit a dog?" Victor says to me.

"Very funny," I say. "You're the dog person, not me."

He looks at everyone else. "I vote Plum moves to Oakville!"

"Splendid idea!" says Robin.

Chris laughs.

"Seriously," says Victor. "It makes sense. You've always loved the house. Now's your chance . . . have a holiday!"

"Why don't *you* move out there?" I say.

"I have a business to run! Your kids have all moved out. It'll only be for six weeks . . . just until Pelmo and Tashi get back."

I feel like I'm getting railroaded, but Victor's right: it does make sense. I'm in the middle of a freelance assignment and can take my computer with me. I can also begin the process of clearing out sixty years' worth of clutter.

I think, *How hard can it be? I know how to buy garbage bags.*

For as long as I can remember, I've been time-deprived—overextended with elderly parents, children, grandchildren, and my own career—so I can't wait to empty Mum's house and put the role of dutiful daughter behind me. I rise to the challenge of a six-week deadline.

"Okay, look," I say, "if I move out there, the estate has to buy new mattresses."

"New mattresses?!" says Victor.

"You'll put the chiropractors out of business!" says Robin.

"The old mattress in the guest room is like sleeping on rocks in a hammock. Same with the one in my old bedroom," I say. "I'm not going to ruin my back."

"Okay . . . okay . . . we'll buy you two new ones."

"And a new toaster." I'm just getting started.

"Toaster?" says Victor.

"Can't you use the fireplace?" asks Robin.

"I'm not going to stand there holding down the lever every time I want a piece of toast! A new toaster or I don't go."

Victor sighs. "Anything else?"

I start ticking things off with my fingers. "Yeah, call display on the telephone . . . cable TV, so I can watch the BBC . . . Internet service for my computer . . . an espresso machine . . . and a bigger hot-water tank so I can wash my hair and take a bath on the same day."

Victor explodes. "There is no way I'm putting in a bigger hot-water tank. It's only going to be you there! How many baths do you need?"

Robin smiles. "Can't you go down to the public pool and get free hot showers like Father did? I'm sure his old tickets are around somewhere."

We're all laughing, but I'm feeling empowered with leverage. If we can make the house livable, maybe it *could* feel like a holiday. Victor refuses to budge on the water tank, but the boys agree to everything else.

The last thing on our agenda is a method for fairly dividing the contents. We decide on the method Mum's family had used at Rokeby, their family farm in Virginia. When Grandmother died, all her possessions were appraised and the value divided equally as "play money" among her many children. They took turns "buying" one thing at a time until they'd used up their portion. Before we can use the Rokeby Method, however, all of Mum and Dad's possessions need to be appraised, photographed, and cataloged. I volunteer for this task, too.

I think, *How hard can it be? I know how to take pictures.*

Robin offers to drive up frequently to help archive the documents and to catalog the books. Victor will be dealing with the finances, the probate, and the ongoing maintenance of the house. Chris is careful not to volunteer for anything. He tells us he's been in therapy for years, trying to divorce Mum, and I get the feeling that for him the house is radioactive. Maybe he's washed his hands of the whole mess already or maybe he's lived away for so long that he's learned to detach. I can't decide if I'm pissed off or jealous. Why didn't he teach *me* how to set boundaries? Finally,

Victor asks him if he'll get quotes for painting the house. Chris shrugs. "Okay."

We agree to sprinkle Mum's ashes in warmer weather. Victor will order her bronze memorial plaque. Some of us think her ashes should be sprinkled under the tree at the corner of the garden; others think she should be sprinkled in St. Jude's churchyard; others beside Sandy at St. Mary's Church in Virginia, so we'll ask the funeral home to divide her into three separate plastic Baggies, to make everyone happy.

I have an announcement to make. My daughter Virginia and her fiancé, Louis, have finally decided to get married. They'd like to use Mum's house for their wedding in June, if we haven't sold it by then. Victor has an announcement of his own. He and his girlfriend, Peni, have decided to get married, too, and they'd like to use Mum's house in September.

This is such great news after such a sad week! We whoop and holler. When Pelmo and Tashi return, we'll ask if they can stay on a bit longer. We'll postpone selling the house until October and enjoy one last summer.

"Two weddings and a funeral!" Victor says, laughing.

Mum used to have a *New Yorker* cartoon magnetized to her fridge. A middle-aged couple is seated on a sofa. The man looks at his wife and says, "Now we can finally relax . . . all our children are married, divorced, and remarried again." Mum put it on the fridge when Chris got divorced and remarried. We've all been divorced now except Robin. Robin has always behaved eccentrically, as though he belonged in a previous century—formal in his manners, tipping his hat, ordering detachable wing-tip collars from a specialty shop in England, quoting Greek and Latin, and building a scriptorium where he can write his books with quill pens. When he was twenty-five he followed the eighteenth-century tradition of marrying his cousin in the country. Relatives on both sides of the family had disapproved, but Robin and Kitty are the only ones still together.

The *New Yorker* cartoon that's been magnetized to my own fridge in Toronto is slightly different. It shows two women in Central Park, eyeing each other: they both have infant carriers strapped to their backs, but while the younger woman's carrier contains her baby, the carrier on the middle-aged woman contains her elderly mother.

I can laugh at the cartoon, but the person I've become has shocked me. It feels as though the last twenty years have leached out my patience, my empathy, my compassion—the best parts of me—until I feel unrecognizable, a person I don't like very much. I didn't much like Mum, either. Her cranky, grievous war against aging and my inability to cope decimated our relationship. It's possible this is what's making the loss bearable for me now. If she'd died when I was younger, when I still remembered how wonderful she was, perhaps grief would be overwhelming me. But Mum had suffered enough losses already. Why had I made her suffer the early loss of me? When had I become so selfish?

Now I understood my friends who missed their mothers:

I'd give anything to have her back—even for one minute.

One minute.

How hard could that be?

I tell the boys I've been unable to sleep well these past few nights. Mum's spirit has been hovering all around me. I can hear the steady ticking of her 8-mm movie camera grinding away in our childhood and see all the reels stored in their small, square yellow boxes. In my head, the grainy footage stutters out of Dad's projector in the playroom. Mum left us an extensive historical record of our childhood, but since she was the one holding the camera, she's rarely in the frame. Now she's the only one I want to see. Dad rarely played with us, yet there he is, running to hide behind a tree, swinging a baseball bat, pushing a swing. Where's the truth? In my dreams, scenes of my own childhood slide back and forth and overlap like theater backdrops.

What is happening to me?

Two months ago I couldn't wait for Mum to go, and now I'm searching for evidence of her.

"Someone should write a book about Mum's life," I say.

"Careful," says Chris. "Here you go again . . . doing Mum's work for her."

Hornet's Nest

Before going out to Mum's house for my six-week "holiday," I close up my own home in Toronto. I adjust light timers, empty my fridge, and pack lightly. I take only my computer, my paints, and a small overnight bag with me. It seems counterproductive to bring too many things into a house I'm trying to empty. My body feels invisible anyway, subjugated to my energy, hardly worth clothing. I can haul garbage bags for weeks in this same black T-shirt and jeans.

When I come through the boathouse door, I can't tell if Sambo is happy to see me or not. He's curled into a depressed ball in his wicker basket and only lifts his head, opening one sad cataract eye. When I reach down to pat him, he licks my hand. It's all he can muster.

Pelmo and Tashi greet me like lost relatives, but after they show me the mail and Sambo's new pills and how to put ointment in his eyes every night, we stand awkwardly in the kitchen, unsure how to share this space now that Mum has died. They offer me dinner, but I decline, and they retire up the back stairs to their apartment. They need to finish packing. They're leaving for Tibet tomorrow.

It takes me a while to adjust, as if I'm feeling my way in the dark after a light's been switched off, but I don't feel sad. There's too much to do.

Rummaging in the fridge, I look for food that's still edible. Sambo gets up and stumbles slowly around the kitchen. He noses the bits of dry kibble in his dish but then turns away, so I decide to make us both some scrambled eggs. I hide Sambo's pills in his portion, hoping I don't get ours mixed up.

After dinner I get his leash and take him for a short walk, even though he's reluctant. It's not a particularly cold night, but it's dark and damp, and I can tell Sambo's arthritis is acting up. He hobbles like an old man. I open the garden gate with its old iron latch shaped like a fox head, its ears flopping back down behind us with a familiar *chink-chink*, but we get only as far as Sandy's memorial tree at the bottom of the road.

I decide to sleep in Mum's bedroom for the first few nights. I don't know why I feel the need to do this—whether it's to feel embraced by Mum or to graduate into her place—but a cousin slept in her bed after the funeral, so I feel her ghost is gone. I carry Sambo upstairs with me, and he finds his usual place under her four-poster bed. The gathered bed skirt parts like a curtain as his long feathered tail disappears beneath.

As a child, when Dad was away, I sometimes slept with Mum, but never before on her side, near the window. I never knew until tonight that from her side you can see the lake and the stars and the lights of Niagara Falls without even lifting your head.

I hear the faint tinkling of Sambo's dog tags as he struggles to find a comfortable position, but eventually the gentle lapping of the waves lulls us both to sleep.

Mum's bedroom is directly over the veranda, and in the middle of the night something wakes me. I sit bolt upright in the dark. Below me, I hear the soft thud of the screen door against its hook-and-eye latch. Is it the wind? Or an animal, maybe? Sambo hasn't stirred, so it couldn't be an intruder . . . or could it? I remind myself that Sambo is deaf. Without turning on any lights, I pad down the carpeted staircase to the living room and peer out the veranda door. I see nothing but a dark, moody night. I go into the kitchen, where the stove clock is illuminated: 4:48.

The waves lap incessantly now—a faster, urgent beat—and I hear the patter of rain; dark drops glisten on the windowpanes. I pull open one of the kitchen windows. It's almost as tall as I am, and a cold wind rushes through the screen, making paper on the kitchen table flap and lift. A fat gray lake stone is nestled on the ledge, so I grab it to use as a paperweight, but something about its shape gives me pause. I flip on the light so I can see. A heart is in my palm. Someone has written on it in indelible red ink.

I am reaching for your hand. Please reach back.

I turn it over.

Divine Love is written on the back.

I turn it over and over. Where did this heart-shaped stone come from? Pelmo's always bringing flotsam up from the lakefront—did she find it washed up on shore? I'm sure that whoever tossed it into the waves didn't have me in mind as the final recipient, but it's found its way to me nevertheless.

I'm taking it as a sign.

I feel comforted—connected to the lake and the rain and the universe—and fully awake. Lightning slices the sky in the distance. A rainstorm is unusual in February, but it matches my mood.

At daybreak I can hear Pelmo and Tashi stirring above the kitchen. Soon, Tashi is thumping their big black suitcases down the back stairs and piling them in the mudroom, ready for their departure. They'll be gone for two months, visiting family in a remote village in the Himalayas, so we'll be unable to communicate.

I ask Pelmo about the lake stone.

"Yes," she tells me. "Other day I find . . . on lake with Sambo!"

"Did you write this message on it?"

"No, no," she says. "From me is not . . . comes from gods, I think." Her smiling eyes twinkle. "Maybe is your mum?"

Yes, I think to myself, *I need to find you. Please reach back.*

Pelmo gives me a big hug and tells me to take good care of Sambo. I can tell she's worried. She bends down to stroke him behind his ears.

"I come back . . . you be here?" she asks him. "Yes?"

On the kitchen table there's a pile of Mum's mail for me to sort through. The largest stack is from charities. Mum contributed to more than thirty of them on a regular basis. She and Dad both followed the disciplined rule of donating ten percent of their income, and Mum had many favorites in addition to her church—usually having to do with teenagers in distress or homeless children around the world.

I can picture Mum sitting here each year before Christmas, trying to decide how best to apportion her money. I sit down with more coffee and begin to write "Deceased" across all the envelopes, then "Return to sender."

Dad listed all his charitable giving in his account ledgers; it came off the top of his income, before anything else. Even when Dad was in his thirties and struggling to support five children, he regularly sent monthly checks to both his widowed sister in England and his widowed sister-in-law in Portugal—five pounds each. Later, when he could afford it, he raised this to twenty-five pounds. Dad was frugal, but he was generous with what he had.

I look at a photograph of Mum and Dad, taken just before we moved into this house. They'd been born during the Great War, lived through the Great Depression, served in World War II, carved a life for themselves in the Far East, given birth to three of their five children, and were relocating to Canada. They look impossibly young to have done all this by their mid-thirties, the same age my children are now.

It's incredible to think that with only one income they could have afforded this house. Dad paid $12,000 for it—close to his annual salary. Today it's worth $2.5 million. This puts it out of reach for most young families and certainly out of my reach or that of any of my brothers. Gone are the days when the price of your home equaled one year's salary. How many of us have a salary of $2.5 million?

When Dad retired in 1978, after more than forty years as an insurance executive with the same company, his salary was only $37,000. He gave modest raises to those under him but rarely took a raise himself. Still, he'd managed to pay off the mortgage and save enough for him and Mum to live comfortably here during his thirty-year retirement until they eventually died in their beds.

But the land taxes were the real killer. In 1953, they were $500. Over the years they steadily increased until, in 1977, they were more than Dad had paid for the house. He was a pensioner by then, on a fixed income, and he accused the town of forcing him out of his home. Carrying a banner with his rallying cry of EXPROPRIATION THROUGH TAXATION! and armed with a long wooden pointer and more than twenty years of accounting ledgers, Dad staged a town-council filibuster. Nobody on council had ever seen account ledgers like Dad's. In his elegant cursive script he'd kept a record of every penny he'd ever spent; even ice-cream cones were listed.

Day after day, Dad trotted up to town council and interrupted their proceedings. Victor went with him as his "adviser." Eventually, the council got so fed up that they granted him a minor adjustment. When the house sells now, the land taxes will likely double.

There's a note from St. Jude's church about their upcoming spring rummage sale. They're looking for stuff. *Perfect timing,* I think. This gives me a deadline. This house is so big, I realize I'll need a master plan for clearing it out. I can't afford to get emotional. There are twenty-three rooms, so if I get caught up in the rigging, I'll go down with the ship.

I go into the library and open Dad's desk. All his stationery is there, in tidy piles. I take a few sheets of his paper, embossed with the family crest and its motto, HONOR ET VERITAS. I think about all the times Dad drummed "Honor and Truth" into us— it might as well have been carved into a permanent stone arch above our heads. Mum has a jar near the phone crammed full of pens, but none of them work. My first act of liberating the clutter is to dump the whole jar into the trash. I find a pencil and go out on the veranda to start my list.

The rain has stopped and the sun is out. The skies are clear and the tree branches are bare, the ground frozen with puddles of water on top. The lake shimmers in pastel shades of lilac and pink. The weather is unseasonably warm for southern Ontario at this time of year—warm enough to sit outside in the winter sun with only my jacket on. I start writing.

MASTER PLAN:

1. Lock up valuables.
2. Empty closets and dressers upstairs.
3. Empty cupboards and drawers downstairs.
4. Sort documents.

I'm beginning to feel optimistic. Maybe it won't even take six weeks.

There's a small closet upstairs where we can add a padlock. We'll use it to store all the obvious things—the silver flatware from the dining room, silver trays that Mum has scattered all over the pantry and kitchen, Dad's war medals, Mum's jewelry. It's not the greatest solution, but it's only temporary. And since it's mostly metal, we won't have to worry about it catching fire, if there is a fire. This house is made entirely of wood. Fire is a big concern of mine, and it was always a concern of Mum's, too.

Upstairs in their bathroom, Dad kept a mammoth coil of fat sisal rope, which sat thickly at the ready for decades. In the event of fire when Dad was away, Mum was to drag the monster pile to her bedroom window, tie one end to the leg of her four-poster, heave the other end outside to the ground—a distance of almost thirty feet—and shimmy down . . . presumably, in the early days, carrying a baby. Her bedroom window has a heavy aluminum storm window bolted on from the outside, but I assume Dad never considered this minor obstacle. I make a note to check all the batteries in the fire alarms.

My plan is to keep the framed photographs and books on the shelves to give the illusion that the house is still occupied when it's shown to prospective buyers, even though all the cupboards and drawers will be empty. By the end of the day I have a long list of items to buy, mainly garbage bags and storage bins.

By the time I have dinner ready and wine poured, my younger daughter, Jessica, has arrived. She's offered to spend the first week with me, commuting by train from work each day. All three of my children seem concerned about me staying alone in Mum's house. My older daughter, Virginia, is planning to bring her infant son out on the weekends and I'm receiving constant supportive e-mails from my son, Carter, in Turkmenistan. When I tell him I fall asleep apologizing to Mum, he writes,

Why are you apologizing to her?! Shouldn't she be apologizing to you? You have a very weird and complicated guilt relationship with your mother. You need to take a step back and look at both of you from a fresh angle. You'll see that she had everything to be grateful for, having a daughter like you!

Jessica is supportive, too, but she defends her grandmother. Whenever I discuss my tattered relationship with Mum, Jessica says, "She just felt misunderstood by you." I feel a twinge of recognition and regret. Jessica's right—and the truth hurts.

I warn Jessica that she and I might be headed down the same wrong track, as in a Greek tragedy, the Fates paying me back.

"Don't wait until you're sixty-three and lying on a therapist's couch," I tell her. "Tell me what I'm doing wrong now . . . Have the conversation with me while we still have time to fix it!" But tonight it happens all over again. In the dining room our conversation slides sideways and Jessica is exasperated with me.

"Why do you always color outside the lines?" she says. "We start talking about one thing and then you go off on these tangents that have nothing to do with what I've just said!" Then she stops. She sighs sympathetically. "It's just the way your mind works, I guess."

I used to be sweet and empathetic like Jessica—where did it go? Why couldn't I have been so accepting of my own mother?

After dinner, Jessica and I go upstairs. She puts on one of Mum's old flannelette nightgowns, I fill the hot water bottles, and we climb into Mum's four-poster canopy bed together. The house feels so cavernous and the rooms so lonely, it's as though we need to camp together on the same island tonight. The lake is quiet, but I sleep fitfully.

My sense of Mum feels as cluttered as this house, and I can't seem to get to the bottom of it. There were layers of misunderstandings on both sides, but I can only try to scrape away my own now. The ones that make me want to turn away are the very ones I know are the most important. I'd been horrified by Mum's growing infirmities—afraid of the road map she was showing me. I knew it wasn't easy for her to relinquish this life and slide into the next. For years she'd been hanging on like a forager vine, entangling her shoots around a grove of host trees. It took all her strength to let go. Now I wonder if I'll be as strong when my turn comes.

As if reading my thoughts, Jessica lifts her head from her pillow and says quietly, "You know, there's one thing everybody's born knowing how to do."

"What's that?"

"Everybody's born knowing how to die."

I awake before Jessica and carry Sambo downstairs. I try to clear a place on the kitchen table for breakfast, but Mum's clutter is everywhere. I replace her plastic daffodils with a glass bowl of mandarin oranges. With the dryness of the furnace, the mandarins will petrify after several weeks and stay hard and colorful for a long time. Dad always refused to add a humidifier. Instead, he placed pans of water on the floor beside every hot air vent, which only hydrated the dogs. We used to joke that the reason Mum and Dad looked so young was that the dryness had mummified them, but since Dad rarely turned up the furnace, it's also possible they were simply freeze-dried in the permafrost.

As I pop bread into the new toaster, I can hear Jessica stirring upstairs. I'll soon be driving her to the train. When she comes downstairs, I can tell she's been crying—her eyes are rimmed red. All three of my children had a unique bond with Mum: Virginia as the first grandchild she doted on; Carter through his shared love of politics and history; and Jessica through a mutual understanding. She seemed to bring out the best in Mum—perhaps the extra generation gave them space to breathe. Dad said they were "simpatico." Jessica was deeply affected by Mum's death, and small things can suddenly trigger her grief. This morning she's been ambushed by a photograph: Mum's head is tilted into Jessica's neck and the two of them are laughing with their arms around each other. I'd moved the picture onto the hall table, where she didn't expect to see it.

"Oh, sweetie, I'm so sorry," I say, and I fold her to me.

"It's okay," she says. "I just really miss her."

I look up at the windows. Every frame drips with icicles that thaw and freeze and thaw again in our wild, unpredictable winter. Sometimes they all melt away to nothing. Then, forty-eight hours later, the icicles are so long it feels like I'm imprisoned behind bars.

When I get back from the train station, I go upstairs to make the bed. I empty the hot water bottles into the sink and remember that Dad used to turn the furnace off at night. When we awoke, icicles had formed not only on the outside of the windows but on the inside, too. We slept in woolen socks, hats, sweaters, and nose cozies—my own invention that I started to knit as soon as I was old enough to hold knitting needles. They were cone-shaped affairs that covered our noses and had loops to hook over our ears. Dad supplemented with hot water bottles, but he'd pour in only a tablespoon of boiling water, and so they'd lie flat and floppy on our bellies. "Waste not, want not!" Dad would say. Then he'd climb into bed beside Mum, who he claimed was the best kind of furnace there was.

I pass by the open doors to all the bedrooms and reality finally hits. How am I ever going to untangle this mess? How am I ever going to separate the trash from the treasure in the overstuffed contents accumulated during Mum and Dad's combined lifetimes of more than 180 years? Some of the valuable items I know none of us will want, while junk of no apparent value has such memory-laden significance that we'll have to draw straws to see who gets it. All the grandchildren tell me they want the plastic sign of the gun on the mudroom window. I wonder where the nose cozies are?

I stomp down the wooden stairs to the basement with my load

of dirty towels, keeping my head down low so my hair won't brush up against any spiderwebs lurking in the ceiling. Light filters in through the laundry room windows behind pots of wispy dried geranium plants, casting splinters of cold morning sun on the concrete floor. A cat's cradle of empty clothesline zigzags across the room. The ironing board sits forlornly in the corner, an old flannelette cover clipped over it with wooden clothes pegs.

Then I look up. There's Mum's hornet's nest, which she saved in a brown paper bag to show to her grandchildren. It's gray and papery, about the size of a football. She'd found it in the garden, fallen from the eaves, and sliced it in half. She marveled at its architecture, its complex geometry, and the sheer intelligence of the hornets that built it.

"Isn't it fascinating? Look at all those compartments! All those thin layers of paper packed together! Did you know hornets spend their whole lives flying back and forth just to build nests like this for their children?"

Mum used to take it in her car to show members of her bridge group, her Bible study group, her belly-dancing class, and her Alzheimer's support group after Dad got sick. She even called the mayor's office to see if they wanted it for their education department. The rest of the time it hung in its bag from the basement ceiling, along with an envelope of Dad's hollyhock seeds.

What should I do with it?

I can hear Mum's voice: "You can't throw that away!" And it stops me in my tracks.

This house I am now slicing apart is *theirs*—the place that we'd taken for granted would always be here as a backdrop to our lives.

Where do I start? I worry that one piece of pocket litter will lead to another until I'm following flakes of memory so deep into the woods I may never get out.

On the other hand, maybe I have this opportunity—this temporary stay of execution—to sift through a half-century of stuff, to see what everything means. Maybe I'm looking for answers instead of exits.

What answers?

How could I still have questions?

Friends warned me of this. They said, "When your mother dies, you'll wish you'd asked her some questions." I had more than sixty years to ask questions, but they didn't form until after she'd gone.

Now there are questions I didn't even know I had.

Point O' View

Mum loved to name her houses. They all had spectacular views, so just as she'd named our Hong Kong house "Taipanorama," she named our new one in Canada "Point O' View."

When World War II ended, Dad finished his stint in the Royal Navy and returned to his old job in Hong Kong. As a young war bride, Mum eagerly followed him out there, with me in her arms. By 1950 we'd moved to Singapore and I had two little brothers. If Dad had had his way, we might have lived there forever—he loved the tropics—but during the final days of 1950, Singapore exploded into what the colonial government called "The Malayan Emergency." To Dad it must have seemed that the Anti-British National Liberation War had entered his own living room, because Mum packed us all up and left him. We landed at Rokeby—her family's historic home in King George County, Virginia.

Despite Dad's entreaties, Mum refused to return. Dad's British relatives had warned him about the folly of taking on an "American wife with independent spirit," and he soon found out what that meant. Mum dug in her heels, backed up by her formidable clan. Their separation lasted a year; it was Dad who surrendered.

I remember the night he walked in. Christmas festivities were in full swing at Rokeby and the massive front hall was packed with people laughing and drinking. In the music room, I and the other small cousins had just heard Leon, the handsome, young farmhand, clomp on the roof with horseshoes—a family tradition that signaled the arrival of Santa's reindeer. Suddenly, an uncle leaned down and said to me, "Your daddy's here! Your daddy's arrived!" The crowd seemed to move in a wave of excitement toward the front door and I was swept along with it. Through the forest of adult legs, I glimpsed in the distance a man in a gray fedora and a long, dark coat. He'd been gone for a fifth of my lifetime—a locked-away memory from a faraway place. I hung back and waited.

He moved into the downstairs bedroom with Mum and baby Robin, and early the next morning Sandy and I tiptoed in to find him dressed in a sarong, standing at the marble sink in their bathroom, using Oriental toothpaste from a little round tin. Mum lay in bed, snuggled under the quilt, smiling.

Over the next few weeks, they discussed where to go next. It became clear that Dad wouldn't live anywhere "American," and Mum wouldn't move to England, so after many discussions, they agreed that Canada would be their cultural compromise: it was close enough to Mum's America, yet part of Dad's British Empire. Canada seemed a vast unknown, appealing to their penchant for adventure, yet only a few days' driving distance. Mum's family worried we might get lost in the wilderness: they'd read the popular new book *Mrs. Mike*, so as far as they knew, the only things north of the border were Mounties and grizzly bears.

Dad took Mum on a train ride across Canada to decide where to settle. Mum took along her windup Bell & Howell movie camera and Dad filmed her in her coonskin coat, knee deep in virgin snow, waving to miles and miles of empty railway tracks with nothing but pine trees in the background. It was a far cry from the lush landscape we'd left behind in Singapore, but just outside Toronto, they met someone on the train who recommended a small town on the shores of Lake Ontario. They decided to call it home.

Oakville had the feel of an artistic summer-camp community—sleepy and rural, surrounded by farmland, not unlike Rokeby. It had one traffic light and a couple of gas stations. The short main street had a Woolworth's department store, a grocery store, a drugstore, and a candy store—Donna Lee's—where the owner's son sat in his wheelchair at the back, fixing clocks. Early each morning, horse-drawn wagons from Gilbrae's Dairy clip-clopped from house to house, rattling glass bottles. At the end of town, near the bridge, the police station had a friendly two-room jail that doubled as a homeless shelter.

Three blocks south from the main street sat an empty house: a rambling, unheated barn of a place surrounded by dirt paths and lilac hedges and overlooking a wild, pebbly beach that coughed up dead fish and driftwood. It had been used by out-of-towners as a seasonal cottage and had languished on the market after the war like a white elephant: a burdensome beauty, too costly to maintain. In a letter to his brother in England, Dad called it "a wreck." His uncle in Rome wrote, *My dear boy, do you mean to tell me that you have paid £5,000 for a house in . . . the colonies? Made of wood?* Who wanted an unheated barn of a place on cinder blocks, facing stiff winds off the lake, with high ceilings, twenty-three rooms, and eighty-four drafty windows?

Mum, that's who. The fact that it lacked a furnace didn't faze her: she was still unpacking mothballs and recovering from the heat. This house had two things that mattered to her most: cross-drafts and servants' quarters. Maids—and especially cooks—had always been part of Mum's household. Even as a young working girl in New York City, she'd been in the habit of sending her dirty laundry home to Virginia each week by train. Her mother's maid, Lucy, would return it freshly ironed, along with a home-baked meal prepared by the family cook, Edmonia.

The house suited Mum's southern disposition: its wide, white-columned veranda reminded her of her *Gone with the Wind* childhood: she claimed she could see New York across the lake from her bedroom window. The lake reminded Dad of rowing along the Thames in his student days and his war stint with the Royal Navy in the Indian Ocean.

It took Mum and Dad almost a year to shore up the exterior. Dad added insulation, storm windows, and central heating, and threw a few more cinder blocks under the veranda to carry our weight. To the four thousand square feet of interior space, Mum added closets, tennis racks, and miles and miles of bookshelves. She slapped up some wallpaper in the dining room, but she didn't bother renovating the kitchen—she didn't expect to spend much time there. The house came with some big old turn-of-the-century furniture that the previous owners had abandoned.

When Mum left behind our luxurious ex-pat lifestyle in Hong Kong and Singapore, she unwittingly left behind chauffeurs, houseboys, cooks, and gardeners. When Chris and Victor were born here in Oakville, Mum was shocked to discover that babies born in Canada didn't automatically come with amahs. But although the staff was missing, this house in Oakville approximated the size and shape of the houses they'd left behind. It was expansive and commanding, just like their personalities, with strong bones, too, able to withstand the storms generated by their frustrations. It saved their marriage: Dad quipped that it had so many rooms they could go days without seeing each other.

Of the twenty-three rooms, eight are bedrooms and many have two doors, each room leading into the next. There are rooms for everything: a mudroom, workroom, TV room, playroom, kitchen, pantry, trunk room, pool room, laundry room, dining room, living room, and an attic running the full length of the house. There are two staircases—one for the main part of the house with a solid oak banister and one in the back, off the pantry, for the maid.

Masses of tall windows open in on their hinges like doors, their panes rippling with handblown glass. Mum called them the shout-out kind, hearkening back to a friendlier time. The sight lines are extraordinary—the lake beckons from every window. Everywhere you turn, the sun streams in and the rooms are ablaze with light.

Facing the lake, the wide, full-length veranda is skirted by lattice and climbing wisteria vines. Fresh breezes waft through the screens, carrying the mingled perfume of hydrangeas and lilacs. Beneath the veranda there's an ancient floor of beach sand and shale where raccoons and squirrels take shelter from winter storms and where, in summer, the creative energy of the winds ebb and flow unobstructed.

Mum loved the fact that Point O' View had a limitless horizon. Big skies, like high ceilings and long horizons, allowed imaginations to soar, she told us, and looking up at the stars at night made you see how infinitesimal your problems really were. She hated to be boxed in by rules or structure of any kind.

The house had ample space for Mum's clutter and she filled it with their joint acquisitions: Dad's inherited British antiques, her Colonial American ones, their Malay busts, Chinese portraits, carved cedar chests, and the low opium bed that served as our coffee table. She set up her manual typewriter at one end of the dining room table and wrote copious letters to her friends and family, describing her new life in Canada. But her letters didn't stay away for long; friends found them so fascinating that they mailed them back, certain she'd want to save them. Mum stuffed them into plastic bags and chucked them in the trunk room, feeding her own personal compost heap that seemed to grow faster and steamier than Dad's in the garden.

Dad's bunker was the basement. This was where he escaped to putter: where he polished his shoes each morning on the long wooden bench; where he set up his pots of seedlings in a make-shift incubator under the windows; and where he kept his bird-seed, gardening tools, and plant encyclopedias.

Dad was handsome—some said a Cary Grant look-alike, tall and distinguished in his bearing—reserved, mannerly, disci-plined, and fastidious. He was a perfectionist, used the King's English, and lived the way he had during the Great Depression, with minimal possessions—only the bare necessities, each one neatly stored in its place: labeled, filed, shipshape. After surviving war in the jungles of Malaya, Dad saw self-denial as a matter of pride, a badge of honor; he learned to excel at it, and over time it became a lifestyle choice: cut the fat, stay lean.

Mum was beautifully buxom and vivacious—casual, irreverent, and full of common sense. After we finally acquired what Dad called "the idiot box," Mum's foxhole was the TV room, a cozy little room off the kitchen. This is where she listened to the nightly news from Walter Cronkite, read *Time* magazine, and drank gin out of her coffee mug. Mum was creative and artistic and lived in the world of ideas. She was gregarious, enthusiastic, spontaneous, and vitally curious about everything. But mess and clutter followed her like wake from a pleasure cruiser.

Her jackets, sweaters, bathing suits, tennis rackets, and running shoes were jettisoned behind her as she gushed through the house. Letters, books, and newspaper clippings spilled out onto every surface, and when she needed more space, she simply moved to a different room and began her piles anew.

Dad built dykes to stem the flood of Mum's untidiness, but she invaded his neat space anyway. He posted signs: ANNE! PUT BACK! . . . ANNE! DO NOT OPEN! . . . ANNE! KEEP OUT! But she just laughed and ignored his pleas.

Like Dad, Mum had been the youngest in a large well-to-do family, but where Dad had been orphaned and penniless in childhood and learned that life was harsh, Mum had been given everything and learned that life was fun. Her family adored her engaging personality; she was the baby who made everyone laugh. Her father owned a bank and her family owned multiple country homes to which all were invited during the long summer months. Securely surrounded by family and friends, she learned to be generous and inclusive: the world was her oyster.

Mum wanted us to think the impossible, question authority, have open minds, and stretch our imaginations—to "go for it." But Dad demanded that we stop daydreaming, obey authority, pay attention to duty, and create order out of chaos. His favorite expression was *"You can't make strong steel without a hot fire!"* He believed that if we learned how to weather hurricanes in childhood, we'd be able to survive any small storm as adults; if we learned to do without, we'd never be in need. He thought he was doing us a favor—he wanted us to be as strong as steel.

Mum and Dad were magnetized—we just weren't sure at which end. From the time they first met during the war, they fought for supremacy over each other, using wit and words as ammunition, sometimes funny, often scathing, until they'd produced a little army of their own. In many ways, we children were the glue that held them together: we strained their resources to the point where divorce was no longer an economic option. Instead they hunkered down to a lifetime of battle, full of tumult and the occasional truce, together a boiling cauldron that threatened to overflow but never did. The result for us was a rich, exotic stew of opposites—intense, confusing, and sometimes dangerous.

Like most fathers, Dad took the family car to work in the mornings and Mum did her shopping on foot—in her tennis dress. The Oakville Club was perched over the harbor, offering tennis courts, sailing berths, and the annual cabaret, but the main social hub, it seemed, was our house. Mum reached out to everybody.

I remember as a child thinking it perfectly normal that complete strangers joined us for meals. Sometimes, we were surprised to see they were even wearing our clothes. Mum would invite passersby in for tea. Dad would pick up hitchhikers and bring them home for dinner; if they'd been standing out in the rain, he'd give them a dry shirt. When the minister at church announced that a runaway teenager needed an adoptive home, Mum was the first to put up her hand. Suddenly, some sullen sixteen-year-old girl would be occupying our spare bedroom, stealing our things. Mum once tried to adopt a thirteen-year-old bike thief after she read in the paper that he'd been arrested for operating a gang. "Why would they put a child like this in jail?" she said. "If he can organize a gang of boys much older than himself, he's obviously bright and loaded with potential. He just needs to be redirected!" She thought nothing of inviting whole families to live with us if they were temporarily homeless, and one single mother with two young sons, whom Mum had befriended in England during the war, moved in for almost a year.

Our house overflowed with little boys—Mum seemed always to be pregnant with them—and she often had them on some kind of leash. At my grade-two Christmas party, I remember other mothers being dropped off at the school wearing stylish tweed coats with little mink collars, and thin rubber boots buttoned over their pumps. But Mum believed in exercise, so she had walked, massively pregnant again, trudging through the deep snow, wearing oversized galoshes and a mammoth white Borg coat that came down to her ankles. She looked like a polar bear. Around her middle she'd tied a long piece of yellow rope, and my two younger brothers clung to the ends like little farmers attached to a clothesline, trying not to lose sight of their barn in the blizzard. On her head Mum was wearing her brown leather World War II pilot's helmet, earflaps down, chinstrap dangling in the wind. She had dressed for what she considered was the main occasion—not the party, but the cold—and I was mortified. But Mum was practical and provocative. She challenged convention every chance she got. *She didn't give a damn.*

The days of our week had a prescribed rhythm, defined by

chores and meals. In our family, Sundays were for church, roast beef, and country walks; Mondays for grocery shopping and shepherd's pie; Tuesdays for clothes washing and chicken; Wednesdays for ironing and spaghetti; Thursdays for vacuuming and liver; Fridays for silver polishing and fish; and Saturdays for gardening, floor waxing, and dinner parties. There were no popular restaurants—parents created their own.

When we weren't in school, we children ran in packs with our unleashed dogs, into one house, out another, banging open screen doors, grazing in open kitchens, and briefly greeting other mothers who were in the middle of baking cookies or hanging their sheets out to dry. We wiped our hands on their aprons. Our parents didn't see us from dawn to dusk. We had the run of the town. Before the advent of television, we entertained ourselves. In the spring, my brothers and their friends wore toy guns in holsters and leather chaps over their corduroys, stringing up stuffed animals with clothesline nooses and exploding dead fish with firecrackers. My friends and I dug clay from the banks of Lakeside Park to make pottery, and went down to the pier at night to watch the local Portuguese fishermen with their glowing lanterns scoop up nets of flapping smelt. In the winter when the creek froze over we learned to skate by pushing chairs over the surface; in our garden we built elaborate snow forts complete with connecting tunnels, flags, and arsenals of snowballs.

But Saturday mornings were different. This is when neighborhood children scattered and watched from afar, morbidly fascinated by our father—and grateful he wasn't theirs. Dad had so many lessons to teach us that he could barely cram them all in. He never gave us a task without inspecting it afterward. He checked the flatness of our sheets after we made our beds, our fingernails after we washed our hands, the shine of our shoes after we polished them, our toy cupboards after we cleared up. He was always making us memorize poems and copy out maps, and correcting what he called our "lazy English."

"Stop saying 'Um'—think before you speak! . . . It's not 'yeah'—it's 'yes'! . . . It's not 'nope'—it's 'no'! . . . 'Kids' are baby goats—the word is 'children'!"

Saturdays were allowance days—when our chores expanded, but when we might also get paid. Dad kept a homemade ledger, called the "Wowance Book" by Victor, who was only two years old and unable yet to pronounce the word. Our allowances grew in penny increments, depending on our age; as the oldest, my allowance was a dime. After breakfast at the dining room table we'd stand at attention beside Dad's chair. He'd bring out his ledger, interview each of us, peruse our weekly offenses, and then tot up our fines. More often than not our fines would outstrip our wages and we'd owe Dad money, which we then had to work off with additional chores. If we were lucky we got a few pennies, which we had to sign for.

After assigning us our duties, Dad would march outside and turn his attention to his beloved vegetable patch. Tucked in behind the back of the house was a large plot of land where Dad grew tomatoes, pumpkins, carrots, lettuce, and rhubarb. He also grew marigolds, nasturtiums, and hollyhocks. Everything was planted in neat rows, staked with thin bamboo poles and long lines of white string. On hot days Dad removed his shirt, knotted his white handkerchief at the four corners, dipped it in water from the outdoor tap, and placed it on his head like a hat. While the boys helped Dad outside, my job was to clean the kitchen. Dad's detailed list was thumbtacked inside the door of the broom closet. It listed our chores and the time frame in which they were to be completed. Under "Plum" it read: "7:30–7:38 mop floor, 7:39–7:46 scrub sink, 7:47–7:52 clean counters . . ."

Periodically, Dad came in to inspect. He'd examine the sink in minute detail until he found a dot of grease I'd overlooked. "You call this clean?" he'd shout. "Do it again! If a thing is worth doing, it's worth doing well!"

By the time Mum got out of bed and drifted downstairs in her housecoat and furry slippers, looking for coffee and an ashtray, she'd find me heaving with sobs.

"Nothing I ever do is good enough!" I'd cry.

Out in the driveway she could see Sandy standing erect, his arms stretched up, holding a log over his head for five minutes—his punishment for not having cleaned the garage properly. When I think of it now, Dad's memories of POW camps must have been only ten years in the past, but what was Mum thinking?

One Saturday morning Dad came home with a man he introduced to us as Popeye, a homeless man he'd found sheltering at the police station. Popeye was old, arthritic, and unkempt, with matted hair, rotted teeth, a stubbled chin, and torn clothing. He smelled bad and spoke Dutch—which Dad knew a little of, too, from his days in Java. (Dad loved languages, and also spoke a smattering of Portuguese, Spanish, and Malay.) He told us he was employing Popeye to help him weed. Since we were Dad's regular laborers (the source of our pocket money), we viewed Popeye with a mixture of relief and skepticism. What did this mean?

Dad carried a wicker chair and a small table down to the bottom of the garden and placed them in the shade. Then he ordered me into the kitchen to prepare a tray of tea, complete with biscuits, jam, and our best silver cutlery. He sent Sandy to the mantelpiece to bring out a tin of Dad's best pipe tobacco—and there Popeye sat, smoking his pipe, sipping his tea, paid by the hour until lunchtime. Dad supervised our work in the garden until it was time to drive Popeye back to the shelter. This went on every Saturday, for years. Dad told us to be kind to Popeye, "because that could be you one day."

On Sundays after lunch, while Mum wrote her letters, Dad took the five of us for hikes in the countryside. Dad had a particular way of walking. He took long strides with a bounce in each step, claiming that with this method even young children should be able to walk four miles in an hour. He showed us how to do it and clocked our speed with a stopwatch. While he strode ahead, swinging his walking stick like an army major, our Dalmatian, Scrappy, raced after him and we tried to keep up.

During these walks, Dad taught us how to make water wheels. In his pocket he brought corks, bits of paper, toothpicks, and rubber bands, and he made elaborate contraptions that churned downstream in the Sixteen Mile Creek, rotating in the current like a Mississippi paddlewheel. He also taught us how to dig for worms, skewer them onto our hooks, and slosh around in the mud to catch crayfish in the watering hole.

When it came time to drive back, we piled into the station wagon. The road home was straight south, three miles down to the lake. Dad tied Scrappy to the outside of the car, knotting his leash to the back door handle. Then he started the engine. We fell silent and watched nervously out the back window as Scrappy began running as fast as he could. As Dad accelerated we saw Scrappy's black spots blur, his tongue lolling out of the side of his mouth, his leash taut against the handle, his body stretched like a greyhound. Robin and Sandy hung out the side window, gripping the ledges, their hair whipping straight back in the wind. In the front seat, Dad focused his view on the side mirror, checking Scrappy's stamina, but I was focused on Dad. His dark side fascinated me. He had the same expression I saw when we sailed: pushing the limits of endurance, his jaw clenched and a hard glint in his eye. When we all landed safely at the back door, my heart was beating as fast as the dog's. The rest of the day Scrappy lay in a heap on the veranda, Chris's arms cuddled around him.

We weren't allowed to use the telephone—a luxury that Dad insisted was reserved for adults—unless it was an emergency, and even then he stood beside us with an egg timer, shouting, "Say what you have to say and ring off!" Luckily my best friend, Diana, lived across the garden, so she and I strung a clothesline between properties—between her bedroom window and mine—and reeled across notes to each other, stuffed into empty soup tins. In our free time we created a theater in the basement, writing scripts and making props and auditioning neighborhood children for our cast of characters. If we ran out of girls, we made wigs and conscripted my brothers. For dramatic scenes, we cut up onions to make ourselves cry. When I was ten the local library asked to mount one of our plays, and Mum was so excited she urged me to start writing a few plays like Shakespeare.

"If he could do it, why can't you?" she said. "After all, you have the same twenty-six letters he had!" I heard Dad scoff behind his newspaper.

I hated to disappoint Mum, but nothing I wrote sounded like Shakespeare. I tried to imagine all his letters tossed out of my Parcheesi cup, scrambled like puzzle pieces onto the playground. What was his secret? It must have something to do with which letters he used . . . and how many of each. I spent months of frustration trying to count Shakespeare's letters, to crack his code. Mum continued her enthusiastic support, but I discounted her praise. It was Dad's I longed for, because his was so hard to come by.

People were always saying "You're so like your mother!" but I hated it when they said that. Dad hurled it at me like an insult, so I didn't want to be like Mum. Besides, I inherited Dad's shape— tall, lean, and flat—not Mum's soft, cuddly, big-bosomed figure. It's true that when I laughed my nose crinkled up, exposing crooked teeth exactly like hers, but I secretly hoped people might think I was more like Dad. I admired his reserve, his discipline, and his elegance—things Mum didn't have.

Mum was the life of the party. Others were titillated by her individualism, but I hated being sucked into the center of attention where she invariably stood. She was always pushing me forward, volunteering me for things as if I were an extension of her: *"Plum would be happy to babysit / walk your child to school / help at the church fair!"* If I complained, she'd say, "You need to reach out to people! Everyone feels shy, but shyness is a form of selfishness." Then she'd add, "I know you better than anyone! Remember, I'm the only one who's known you *all your life,"* implying that she knew me better than I knew myself.

Sometimes I used to cry on Dad's shoulder. "Oh, Dad, she criticizes everything I do . . . sometimes I think she just hates me!"

"You're wrong," he'd say gently. "She admires you . . . She loves you . . . She wishes she could be just like you." But I didn't believe him. Why would she want to be like me?

Dad never disciplined me—he left that up to Mum and her

silver hairbrush—but he occasionally disciplined the boys with a long, thin bamboo cane that he kept in his closet for this purpose. It was supposed to be holding up his tomato vines.

"You'll get three of the best!" he'd shout. "And if you cry, you'll get three more!"

For me, the worst of it was the calm before the storm. Dad would order the boys to go to his bedroom, take down their pants, bend over the four-poster, and wait for him. The cruelty of it seared my heart, yet I felt powerless to stop it. When I took a bath with my brothers afterward, I could see the angry blue stripes and red welts on their little backsides as they climbed gingerly into the tub. I remember the night when I'd finally heard enough.

I was eleven years old, hiding behind the curtains in my bedroom. I had my hands to my ears, trying to block out the screams of Sandy and Robin in the bedroom next door. Every swish of the cane as it whooshed through the air landed on the beat of Dad's forceful words.

"You—can'tmake—strongsteel—without—ahot—fire!" he bellowed, as if he were trying to convince himself. Then I heard him say, "This hurts me more than it does you!"

When Dad finally emerged from the bedroom, his shoulders were slumped and the cane dangled loosely in one hand. He looked exhausted. But I was waiting for him. I leapt at his chest, attacking him with my fists.

"You cruel, cruel man!" I shouted, surprising myself.

I fled down the stairs, out the veranda door, and down to the lake in the dark, throwing myself into the depths of the lilac bushes that towered over the path.

Dad had looked momentarily confused, startled by my outburst, and only then did I realize it wouldn't have taken much to stop him. I understood in that moment that it wasn't something he wanted to do . . . it was something he felt he had to do, some version of misguided discipline he'd experienced in his own childhood. He must have been beaten hard at boarding school.

I heard Dad calling for me, but I didn't answer. I wanted him to worry.

Upstairs, Mum was at the boys' bedsides, trying to soothe their tears—but we all knew that it was she who'd brought this on. When Dad arrived home from the office, it was Mum who told him of the boys' transgressions; she of the comforting-kisses-after-the-fact knew exactly what punishment she was setting them up for. Why would she do this? Why didn't she know better? I could never understand it. She seemed to have no trouble standing up to Dad on other occasions.

Some nights, after we were tucked in bed, Mum sneaked out to art class, and when she came home Dad would crumple up her drawings and throw them in the fireplace, raging that she should have stayed home and washed the dishes instead. I'd hear her slam a cupboard door and yell, "There's plenty more where those came from!" Then I'd hear her pour herself a drink and shout, "And while you're at it, you should thank me . . . because I'm going to be supplying paper for your fire for the rest of the winter!" I'd hear the metal ice cube tray clatter into the sink as she stormed out of the room.

Almost every other year I skipped a grade at elementary school, so that by the time I graduated to grade nine at the public high school, I was only twelve years old. Many of my classmates were sixteen—including Ernie, who worked after school as a gas jockey at the corner Esso station. Ernie had greasy, slicked-back hair and a comb sticking out of his back pocket. He always wore a leather bomber jacket, pointy shoes, and white socks.

At the end of grade nine Ernie cornered me at the back of art class. He pulled out his switchblade, and as he slowly cleaned his fingernails with the tip of his knife, he explained that he needed my final art project to hand in as his own. Naturally, I gave it to him. When Mum and Dad found out why I'd failed art, they packed me off to a boarding school in Toronto. I didn't understand why I had to live away. Dad drove into Toronto every day—why couldn't I come home every night with him? Mum said it was because it was time for me to "be around girls." Dad said boarding school would "build my character." I knew what that meant—courage in the face of adversity—but I figured Dad already gave us enough of that at home. I pleaded with him not to send me away, but he was unmoved.

"There are some things in life we all have to do, whether we like it or not!" he thundered. "You just have to learn to suck it in." He took his big white hankie out of his pocket and handed it to me.

Dad's rules were far stricter than those imposed by the school. When boarders went home on weekends, Dad insisted I stay in, like the girls from Venezuela and Abu Dhabi. When we lined up on Fridays to receive our allowance issued by the school bursar, Dad instructed them to give me only half, complaining that the recommended amount was far too generous. And he wouldn't allow me to call home. Sometimes the matron took pity and offered her phone, but in those days Oakville was long distance and I had to reverse the charges. Collect calls were intercepted by the operator; I couldn't communicate directly with Dad unless he agreed to accept, so the operator always had a longer conversation with him than I did.

"I have a collect call from your daughter, sir. Will you accept the charges?"

"Why does my daughter wish to speak to me?"

"Your father wants to know why you're calling."

"Tell him I'm sick! I'm in the infirmary! I want to speak to my mother!"

"Your daughter is sick, sir."

"Nonsense! Tell her to pull herself together."

"But she's in the infirmary, sir."

"She's in good hands."

"Sir? Could she speak to her mother?"

"No! I give her quite enough allowance and I will not accept collect calls."

"But . . ."

"Over and out!"

Then I'd hear the operator say, "I'm so sorry, dear . . . I hope you feel better soon."

On stormy days Dad took us sailing in his Snipe. It was a two-person racing dinghy, but he crammed all five of us into it. He stuffed me in the hull—"for ballast," he said. We wore heavy orange life jackets made of kapok, which were so waterlogged they were like lead weights. They would have drowned us for sure, had we ever tipped.

Dad carried the wood centerboard down the street, five blocks to the harbor, and we lagged behind, lugging the heavy canvas bags stuffed with sails. After scrubbing the boat clean, we spent ages preparing the sails—sliding their tiny metal clips one by one into the narrow brass channels on both sides of the mast before finally hoisting them up and casting off.

Dad preferred sailing when seven-force gales churned the water as rough as the ocean. He shouted nautical orders at us *("Hard-a-lee!")* and then sat at the helm with his hand gripping the bucking tiller, forcing the bow into the wind, heeling the boat over, the mast almost parallel to the water. His face mirrored the tension of the sails: jaw set tight, facing the icy spray head-on, daring us to capsize. The boys in their bloated life jackets hunkered down for the ride, but I was stuffed inside, upside down, pressed against the wooden ribs, paralyzed with fear. Occasionally he'd pull me out to wave to Mum. She'd be on the veranda, anxiously peering through her binoculars.

At the end of the day we lowered the sails and all their tiny clips had to be slipped from the mast again. This was my job and I hated it.

One day, as I sat shivering on the dock, my cold hands wrestling with the wet sails and icy clips, I had what I thought was a brilliant idea. "Dad?" I said. "Why can't the sails roll up and down into the boom *automatically*, like our movie screen does?" I'd often watched Dad pull up the screen when he set up the projector in the playroom. It was spring-loaded and would effortlessly wind out of its tube, and when he'd let go, it would roll quickly back in with a satisfying *thu-thu-thunk*.

He swiped at me as if I were a gnat. "Because life isn't meant to be *easy*."

———

"Easy" wasn't in Dad's vocabulary. He liked a challenge. Perhaps this is why Mum and Dad were able to keep their marriage vows, against all odds, until death. Dad once told me that divorce didn't solve anything because you were just trading one set of problems for another. You had to look beyond them, he said.

When my own children were young and I was thinking of divorcing, Dad took me for a walk. He told me the story of when, as a child, he'd gone into the woods and torn down his brothers' tree house in revenge because they wouldn't let him play there.

"I always regretted it," he told me, "because I tore down the one thing I loved."

He left it up to me to decipher this parable, but when I decided to separate anyway, he came into the city to help me move out. I thought he disapproved, but in the kitchen, lifting boxes, I heard him mutter under his breath, "I wish I had your guts."

Mum and Dad's tumultuous battles reached one crisis after another until eventually they simmered down. When they entered old age, their prolonged truce seemed to resemble companion-ship. When Dad got Alzheimer's, it even resembled love. He began to pay Mum compliments that she'd waited sixty years to hear—but we knew by then that he'd lost his mind.

Oakville had now matured into a sprawling, sophisticated commuter town with a population of more than two hundred thousand people—one of the wealthiest in Canada.

Mum hated this change.

"People have more money than sense!" she'd say. "They tear down all these beautiful old houses, build monstrosities with five bathrooms, and then hightail it to Florida for the winter! Who wants to clean *five bathrooms?*"

Mainly she complained that in the old part of town, all the children were gone. "It's like a ghost town! Instead of sagebrush blowing down the streets, *newspapers* are all over the lawns—but nobody's home. All the doors are locked. You walk down the street and you don't see *a single soul!*" Young families, she pointed out, could no longer afford to live here; instead, they came as tourists.

On hot summer weekends, families who live in cookie-cutter housing that was once farmland north of the highway drive down to the lakefront to picnic in front of our house. They peer wistfully over our hedge at a bygone era—at a house that looks frozen in time, the last unrenovated holdout. The veranda, wicker chairs, driftwood doorstops, white porcelain doorknobs, screen doors with hook-and-eye latches, and tall blown-glass windows have all remained much as they were when the house was built in 1902. You can find replicas at expensive home-décor shops uptown, where everything new has been purposely distressed, but here at home every scratch has a bona fide provenance. When Dad finally kicked his dilapidated wooden wheelbarrow to the curb one garbage day, it appeared two weeks later at an antiques shop on the main street with a two-hundred-dollar price tag strung on a pink satin ribbon dangling from its rusted iron wheel.

Tourists now refer to our house as the "Old Slave Driver's House" because of what they think is a historic plaque outside the front door . . . but it's a fake, hung there fifty years ago when we were teenagers determined to spite Dad. Our neighbors have a real one—WILLIAM BOND, MARINER, CIRCA 1874—but ours alleges that the owner was a SLAVE DRIVER, CIRCA 1953. It's signed by THE OAKVILLE *HYSTERICAL* SOCIETY. In our minds, it was a cheeky chance to get back at Dad for perceived injustices—and to let the world know what we thought of his motto: "Spare the rod and you spoil the child." When Dad went away on a business trip we bolted the sign to the outside of the house and giggled behind a tree at our gall.

When he saw it three weeks later, Dad was furious. He unpacked like a madman, ready to come hunting for us. He'd caned us many times for lesser offenses. But before he could do so, Mum handed him his mail. Tearing apart the envelopes, he opened an official-looking letter written on Oakville Historical Society letterhead. It was from the chairman. They had held a meeting. Our sign, they said, made a mockery of their organization and they demanded Dad remove it—immediately!

This intensified Dad's rage but redirected his anger. He stomped through the house shouting, "Who are they to tell me what to do? They have no authority—history be damned!" To our amazement, Dad refused to take the sign down. Not long afterward, a letter to the editor of the local paper cemented Dad's resolve. It said something like:

Dear Sirs, My wife and I recently visited your charming town and one of the highlights of our trip was coming across a sign on a house by the lake signed in fine print by the Oakville Hysterical Society. It gave us such a chuckle. Any town that has a sense of humor like this is one we plan to visit often.

The Oakville Beaver had put a black border around it and centered it on their op-ed page. Dad was so delighted he cut it out and framed it. Mum photocopied it and sent it to all her relatives in Virginia. Not every tourist, however, noticed the fine print. Mum and Dad never locked their doors, and one day Dad found a thank-you note propped up on the kitchen table:

To whom it might concern, Thank you so much for letting us tour your lovely museum! We had no idea it was here.

Another time Mum answered the back doorbell to find an excited middle-aged professor from South Carolina standing there. "Excuse me," he said, "but I couldn't help reading your sign out front . . . I had no idea Canada still had slaves in 1953! Could you tell me a little more about it?"

"You'll have to ask the slaves," Mum told him with a straight face, "and I'm sorry, but they're out sailing."

Dancing Till the End

I was with Mum on her last day in January, but I'd left in the evening before she went to bed. I retrace the minutes of that day in my mind, looking for clues I might have missed, but there were none. Well—maybe there was one: it was one of the few days she hadn't asked to go to Sears. She hadn't even dressed. She'd spent all that Sunday in her dressing gown, sitting in her bedroom, laughing and making phone calls.

The last call she placed was long distance—to Bodrhyddan Hall in Wales—to one of her oldest friends, the 9th Baron, Lord Langford. Geoffrey was born in 1912, four years before Mum, and was the last surviving member of the escape in the *Sederhana Djohanis*—the small boat in which my father and fifteen other British officers eluded the Japanese when Singapore fell in 1942.

Mum had been begging me for weeks to call Geoffrey for her, but I kept refusing. It felt like Mum was always either trying to direct my life or getting me to live hers, and I was desperate to draw the line. It was our perpetual dance.

"Please call Geoffrey for me," she begged.

"You call Geoffrey."

"I don't have the energy!"

"Then wait till you do—he's your friend, not mine!"

"I just want to know how he is," she said quietly.

This time there was something about her tone—a sad vulnerability—that made me suddenly understand her differently. She didn't lack the energy to pick up the phone—she had no problem calling me all the time—instead it sounded like she was feeling insecure, afraid she could no longer muster up her life-of-the-party image and project it long distance, afraid she might disappoint Geoffrey. She wasn't asking me to live her life; she was asking me to cover for her. I felt a surge of compassion and admiration: her spirit was indomitable.

"Okay."

"You will?" Mum looked so surprised. I dialed his number easily, and when Geoffrey answered, Mum didn't want to come to the phone. I acted as a long-distance operator, relaying their messages back and forth to each other.

"Geoffrey? Mum wants to know how you are . . ."

I put my hand over the receiver. "Mum, he says he's turning one hundred soon. He wants to know how Alex is."

"Oh, God," said Mum. "He must know that. Remind him that he's dead."

"Geoffrey?" I said into the phone. "Mum says congratulations!"

Eventually I got the hang of it, digesting huge chunks of information and passing them along in edited bites.

Mum laughed with Geoffrey—"Geoffrey? Mum loved that!

She's laughing really hard!"—and shared war stories. She reminisced about her days in the American Red Cross, stationed in England at the fighter base at Debden, and later at Eynsham Hall and Knightshayes Court. She described the day a pilot had buzzed the base to say good-bye, but he flew too low, clipped the trees, and crashed on the other side. Then she recounted what it was like when she was twenty-one and took her first trip abroad in 1937, aboard the *Queen Mary.*

"Tell him it was so exciting!" she said, "because the Spanish Civil War was in full swing and we heard Germany might attack France—so, naturally, I headed straight for Paris! At the World's Fair, you could pay to jump off a replica of the Eiffel Tower," she continued, waving her arms in the air, "and I just couldn't resist! We took an open elevator up to the top, where a man strapped me into a parachute and told me to walk off this wooden plank . . . but I just couldn't take my eyes off all those beautiful lights in the distance . . . so he gave me a shove and off I flew! I was wearing a yellow dress with a big, full skirt . . . and it went way up over my head. When I landed on my back in the sandpit, here were all these Spanish soldiers standing around, clapping . . . Isn't that the funniest thing you ever heard?"

To Geoffrey I said, "Mum remembers jumping off the Eiffel Tower during the Spanish Civil War!"

Mum just cracked up, laughing so hard that she started to cough and had to grab for the Kleenex box. Her phlegm was mottled with blood.

Alarmed, I covered the phone with my hand. "Are you okay?"

Mum shrugged it off. "It's nothing—just something that's bound to happen at my age," she said.

Geoffrey's voice crackled in my ear. "Tell your mother I turn one hundred soon!" he shouted for the second time.

Mum seemed flushed with happiness after that phone call with Geoffrey. There was no doubt she was still the life of the party. When I left her she was dressed in her pink flowered dressing gown, sitting in the blue velvet armchair opposite her four-poster bed. The TV tray beside her was piled with books. Her dog-eared, black leather Bible lay on top, wedged with paper bookmarks. Her Christian faith had always been unwavering. Dad's, too: it was one of the major things they shared together.

"You need to believe in something," Mum said. "Something greater than yourself. It helps to hand your problems over."

At the end of the afternoon, Pelmo's young niece, Wosel, came into the room to give Mum her pills. Pelmo was about to come back on duty, to prepare a chicken dinner. I blew Mum a kiss from the doorway.

"I'll talk to you tomorrow, Mum!"

I expected her to say, "So soon? Why do you have to go?" But she said nothing. She seemed disoriented, with a faraway look in her eyes—a look I hadn't seen before.

I should have paid more attention, because I hadn't been home more than an hour when Pelmo called.

"Your mum . . . she is dying, I think."

How was this possible?

I thought back to Mum's face in her bedroom, when she seemed to focus on a distant point so far into the future that she was no longer here, with us. It wasn't the normal look of someone in reverie. Had she been concentrating on a journey . . . letting go . . . stepping into infinity?

This was the subtle clue I'd missed.

We called Robin in Virginia. Victor picked me up at my house. Chris was already on his way. As we raced back along the same highway I'd traveled only an hour earlier, Victor's cell phone rang.

It was Pelmo. "Your mum . . ." she said. "She is died."

The moment we thought would never come had come and gone in a blink. I'd worried that Mum's dying would be lengthy and tortured, with a tenacious struggle for breath and the desperate gurgle of drowning, but nothing like that happened. She had simply closed her eyes and was gone.

How did it happen that she—who had bound her children so tightly to her—should choose to die without a single one of us there? How could I have been so hard-hearted as to let her? Why couldn't I have spent the night?

"She complain she is hot," Pelmo told me later. "She told me, 'Hold my hand' . . . not leave her . . . so I call doctor . . . then I told Mum: 'Pray.' I tell her, 'You pray God whole life, so now is time *pray hard*.'" Pelmo looked down at the floor and shrugged. "She just close eyes and go sleep."

Victor, Chris, and I stood around her four-poster bed and looked at her peaceful face, turned slightly in her pillow, the pink flowered sheet pulled up to her neck. She looked alive: her fleshy cheeks still rosy, her eyes closed, her demeanor serene. The shape of her under the sheets was the same mass as always, still taking up the same space as it had when we used to dive in beside her as children, cuddling her cushiony warmth, hearing her breathe, smelling the sweet mix of leather and spice on her breath— tobacco and alcohol—feeling safe.

Dr. Breen was there, signing the death certificate.

We left Mum in bed for the next two days, long enough for grandchildren to come and gather round. Tears spilled silently down cheeks. Arms went around new shoulders in unexpected configurations. People tiptoed and whispered.

Slight bruising began to appear on Mum's turned cheek, where internal blood was pooling, but mostly she remained pink and remarkably unaltered. I found myself unable to cry. I didn't feel sad. I felt numb.

The house took on an echoing quietness, like a vast sacred space. This house, with its broad veranda; its open, expansive, inclusive personality; its tall windows, lake vistas, limitless horizon, fresh breezes, ancient trees, sudden sailboats, surprising wildlife: the fox, birds, ducks, swans, and—Mum's favorite—the geese. Mum loved this house so much she swore she'd never leave. "You'll have to shovel me out of here," she once said.

On Monday morning, Victor and Chris and I drove to the funeral home to make arrangements. We'd been there so many times before that it seemed we could do it with our eyes closed. Mum had asked to be cremated. We chose exactly the same things we'd chosen for Sandy and Dad: the cheapest casket, no open coffin, no embalming, no visitation, and no thank-you cards—everything honest and simple.

We found Mum's many address books and turned the house into a call center. It seemed everyone was in a different room on a separate cell phone, overlapping voices speaking in hushed tones. The first call I made was to Mum's friend Geoffrey, in Wales, with whom she'd talked for hours only the day before. I thought he would be devastated—but he couldn't remember ever having spoken to Mum.

Robin and his family were preparing their long drive north. There was a frantic effort to reach my son, Carter, working in the interior of Turkmenistan, but he couldn't get back in time. He'd been home just a month earlier, for Christmas.

Victor took the frayed Union Jack from its winter storage in the cedar chest and carried it outside to the flagpole. He raised it and then lowered it to half-mast, as a signal to neighbors. It was a worn, moth-eaten bunt made of worsted wool and it hung listlessly. Beyond the flagpole, the lake was heaving up and down in slow motion, slate gray in the growing winter dusk.

"Why are we using the Union Jack?"

"It's all we could find."

"What happened to the Canadian flag?"

"It's in shreds."

"I don't think Mum would like using a British flag."

"She married Dad, didn't she?"

On Tuesday afternoon the undertakers arrived. We watched as they zipped Mum into a dark red velvet bag and carried her on a stretcher from her bedroom, across the upstairs hall, and down the wide staircase, carefully squeezing past the chairlift.

As they started to take her out the front door, Chris shouted, "Wait—stop! Could you please turn her around? She said she never wanted to leave this house unless she went feet first."

It was the same month almost to the day when only three years earlier Dad had gone out the front door the same way. Unlike Dad's January, which had been piled with snow, Mum's January had no snow at all, just ice.

We watched as the hearse drove slowly away, but just as we turned to go back inside, we heard a growing commotion over the lake. In the distance, sounding like a fury of flapping sails, hundreds of Canada geese thundered across the sky toward us, filling the air with their weeping cries. The sound grew louder and louder as they swooped in. The din was deafening.

It was as if all Mum's beloved geese were homing in for a final farewell . . . a fly-past . . . a winged mourning. They skidded and scattered onto the surface of the water in front of the house like torn brown leaves, doing what I couldn't do: crying.

HEEN-HAWK, HEEN-HAWK, HEEN-HAWK.

A year earlier I'd asked Mum what she thought about reincarnation. She was thoughtful for a moment and then she told me this story: "My father was devoted to the Bible and believed in everlasting life. He took that line from John 3:16—'Whosoever believeth in Him shall have everlasting life'—and had it engraved on little gold pennies . . . then he gave one to every conductor he ever met on a train! In those days, conductors had gold watch fobs hanging around their middles . . . and, as you know, Daddy owned the Virginia Central Railway, so he took a lot of trains. I remember as a child seeing all those little gold pennies hanging from the conductors' chains, saying EVERLASTING LIFE . . . EVERLASTING LIFE . . . so it stuck in my head. Who knows what everlasting life is? Nobody knows . . . but it says it in the Bible, so I have no reason to doubt it. Maybe it means you get to come back as something else. I'd like to come back as a tree . . . because a tree gets to see everything that's going on . . . a tree experiences all the seasons . . . and a tree never needs anything! I'm just curious—that's what I am."

And so we already know where we'll sprinkle Mum's ashes—

under the tree we planted in memory of Sandy, at the corner of the garden just outside the fence. Her memorial plaque will be placed there, too, right next to Sandy's and Dad's.

Late that night I drive back to my narrow redbrick house in Toronto to compose the leaflet for Mum's funeral. Boots clutter the front hall and dirty dishes are piled in the sink. Even though my children have officially moved out, you'd never know it; evidence of them is everywhere.

Mum always said my house was too small—she claimed she could stand in the middle and touch both sides—but now I'm noticing the threadbare Persian carpets, the easels with half-finished paintings, the jammed bookcases with paper spilling out. I've lived here for thirty years as a single mother, trying to be an anchor for my children. My children's friends remark that they sense freedom as soon as they walk in; there seems to be no order to anything—creative chaos, they call it. Tonight, for the first time, I realize it looks uncannily like Mum's mess—without the tidying influence of my father.

The next day, up in my second-floor office, I am adrenaline-fueled, relentlessly tapping the keyboard of my computer, trying to write a brief biography of Mum. It needs to be sent to the church to be printed in time for the leaflet. I frantically double-check facts with Robin, who's writing the obituary for the newspapers; Victor is at his house, sifting through photographs, and Chris is conferring with the minister on the order of service. We'd found Mum's handwritten note specifically saying "No eulogies!" but when we read it, we looked at each other and mimicked in unison her own favorite expression: "What? That's ridiculous!" Then we burst out laughing. Children and grandchildren can't wait to step up to the lectern and tell stories about her.

How can I capture my mother's essence in five hundred words or less? I found it so easy to write Dad's—love poured out of my heart—but with Mum I find anger getting in the way and I have to delete and delete. I am conscious of the fact that so many of her younger friends will be at the service, friends who never bore the brunt of her tyranny. I want to hide what I'm feeling.

I stare at my opening sentence: "Mum was an amazing mother to have, as you all might imagine . . ." *Will that do?* Can I live with the word *amazing*?

Good-bye, Mum

The shiny black hearse has pulled up to Point O' View, puffing exhaust into the cold air as it idles outside the front door, the door we use only on special occasions. Mum's casket is visible through the car's open tailgate, and two men in black coats from the funeral home are standing beside it.

I can hear Mum's words: "Never wear black to a funeral—it's too depressing. Wear red! Make it a celebration of life!" We are milling about, beginning to gather for the slow march to St. Jude's church three blocks away. We look colorful enough. Naturally, I have worn red. Pelmo is dressed in her long Tibetan ceremonial coat, and Tashi wears his tall Tibetan fur hat. Twenty-eight of us—children, cousins, grandchildren, and a great-grandchild—dressed in our snow boots and heavy winter parkas have tied brightly colored wool scarves around our necks. Some of us are wearing Mum's white plastic earrings clipped to our lapels. Even my ex-husband takes one. He has come to offer support, and as he hugs me, I feel grateful that our friendship never died; our good divorce has survived far longer than our marriage.

The sky is sunny and cloudless, but the lake has been roaring all morning—foamy green waves rushing onto the beach. The wind from the east has been blowing so hard that the flag in the garden is flying flat-out, stretched half-mast to its pole. Victor suddenly grabs my arm.

He whispers, "We forgot Mum's pins! Get the granddaughters!"

As he runs back in I call after him, "Don't forget the grandsons!"

I hastily call Mum's five granddaughters back inside to the playroom and explain that before she died, Anya had earmarked one of her heirloom brooches for each of them. Victor reads the labels and hands them out so they can wear them to church. Then we call in Mum's three grandsons and give them each one of Bapa's war medals. We'll save Carter's until he can get home from Turkmenistan.

As the hearse begins to move slowly down King Street, we fall in line behind it, taking the identical path we took every Sunday in childhood when Mum and Dad led the way. Conversations are whispered and muted. Some of us hold hands. We beckon to the neighbors we see en route, inviting them to join our cortège, and the hollow crunching of our boots on the icy gravel creates a slow-moving, solemn drum roll. We have already formed this almost-identical funeral procession twice before—once for Sandy, in 1991, and again, only three years ago, for Dad.

Outside St. Jude's, the grandchildren line up—they are the pallbearers this time. I'm amazed to see so many people in the church: it's packed with people of all ages. I count a dozen women in their nineties—most struggling with walkers or canes—friends who first came to Mum's Christmas party in the 1950s when they were young mothers in their thirties.

This is the church where Dad was people's warden and Mum taught Sunday school, where we took up a whole pew near the back, always the same one, as though we had reserved seats. It's where they taught us to sing lustily and to put ten percent of our allowance in the collection plate, even if we had to pluck pennies out in change.

Despite our long tradition here, the service we've designed for Mum is anything but traditional. We have persuaded the minister into a service he wouldn't normally have approved, but since Chris was once his tutor at divinity school, he's gracefully stepped aside. He's also found some dogwood branches, which he's placed on the organ in honor of Mum's Virginia roots.

We start with a short prayer and a hymn, sung by a choir made up of young women in Mum's Bible-study group who have volunteered to "sing her to heaven." Their voices sound just like Mum's—enthusiastic, but completely off-key—and it warms my heart.

I make my way to the lectern next, fumbling with my notes. I survey the congregation and slowly put on Mum's sunglasses—the ones with the red laughing lips that look like something a stoned rock star might wear. "Mum would be horrified to see so many of you here . . ." I say, and the place erupts in laughter. I tell them that a few weeks before Mum died, she said, "I know you're supposed to have a purpose in life, and I've searched for mine and I think it was just to make people laugh."

I describe Mum as a "life force" who valued every second of her life with insatiable curiosity and boundless enthusiasm.

I laud her generous nature. I share memories of her "waifs and strays"—the times she invited whole families who were down on their luck to live with us for months—and I tell the story about the day a vacuum cleaner salesman had the misfortune to ring's Mum's bell, offering to demonstrate his machine, just as the dog was throwing up on her blue shag carpet. I found it impossible to talk about my relationship with Mum. I knew I was using all her funny stories as a smoke screen; maybe that's what Mum used them for, too.

I explain how Mum suffered from claustrophobia and would have sat at the back, close to the exit; how she was terrified of public speaking even though, paradoxically, she was an unstoppable raconteur; how she hated being in the limelight, even though she always stole the show. I tell them it was more like Mum *was* the limelight, that spot onstage, front and center, that was most illuminated. Mum was so intensely interested in other people's lives that her questions shone the spotlight on them; people glowed in her presence. Whenever she met someone new, she'd say, "Now, tell me about you!" The next time they met, Mum would remember everything about them: who they voted for, what they ate for breakfast, where they went to school, when they took their last vacation, the names of their children—everything.

What I don't tell them is that the great *disadvantage* of a limelight at the end of the nineteenth century was that it required the constant attention of an individual operator who had to keep adjusting the block of calcium as it burned, while simultaneously tending to the jets of oxygen and hydrogen that fueled it—exactly like the jobs we held, tending to Mum. She got her oxygen from people, which is perhaps how she lived so long when deprived of the real thing.

After I speak, Chris gives the homily and other family members take their turn, telling more funny stories about life with Mum. These are interspersed with hymns: Mum's southern favorites, like "Swing Low, Sweet Chariot" and "The Battle Hymn of the Republic." Carter has sent his story by e-mail, which Virginia reads in his absence, and Jessica gives a reading from "The King's Christmas Message" of 1939.

By the time we're finished, people are saying they've never heard so much laughter in a church. As we file out through the side door, I pass two elderly women speaking to the minister.

"That's exactly the kind of funeral I want!" says one of the women.

The minister chuckles. "To have that kind of funeral, you have to have lived that kind of life." Then he turns to me, shaking his head at a memory. "The first time I met your mother, I had a headache. And you remember what she did? She made me hold a banana peel on my forehead until it went away!"

"Did your headache go away?"

"I guess it did . . . you don't see any banana peel, do you?"

After the service, friends are gathering back at the house for the reception and Paul, a friend of my ex-husband's, is waiting in the downstairs hall. I pass by and he touches my elbow.

"Was your mother Jewish?" he asks me.

"No—why?"

He waves his arm in front of the bookcase. "Because there are so many Jewish artifacts here."

I explain that my mother was deeply religious. Although she was raised Episcopalian, she valued independent thinkers and liked to be intellectually stimulated, so she went to wherever the good preachers were. She didn't care whether they were in a

Roman Catholic church, a Muslim mosque, a Buddhist temple, a Jewish synagogue, or a Baptist revival tent; as long as a speaker had something interesting to say, Mum would go and listen. She'd made pilgrimages to Jerusalem several times and brought back many souvenirs, including the plate with the Hebrew blessing, SHALOM!, that Paul was looking at now. Mum loved the fact that the word *shalom* meant so many different things—not just peace, but hello and good-bye and harmony and completeness. She said Asian cultures had *namaste*, but North Americans didn't have a word like it.

I show Paul a framed casual snapshot of Bishop Tutu and, on the shelf above it, Mum's photo of the Dalai Lama, but he's fixated on Mum's clay figurine of a Jewish rabbi, looking like Tevye from *Fiddler on the Roof.*

"I hope you don't mind my saying, but if you're getting rid of stuff and nobody wants this, I'd love to have it."

I make a mental note, and several months later it's Bubble Wrapped and delivered to Paul. Mum would be thrilled that her souvenir found a proper Jewish home.

That evening, a few stragglers are still milling about the living room and I'm hearing stories I've never heard before. A middle-aged man whom I haven't seen in decades—one of the young boys who had emigrated with his mother from England and temporarily lived with us in the 1950s—is telling me how he finally met his father for the first time: "After my mother died, your mum said to me, 'Now you can find your father. Here's what I know about him. Look there—don't wait. Do it now!' Because of your mum, I got to know my father just before he died."

When everyone leaves, the dining room table is a sad mess of half-filled glasses, crumpled paper napkins, empty plates, and crumbs. Mum's earrings are littered around the ice cube trays we'd taken from her jewelry drawer to use as the centerpiece. Sambo is comatose under the table. There are dozens of floral bouquets—some on standing easels—sent home from the church. Most of the sympathy cards have become detached from the bouquets, so we don't know who sent them.

The following day, I receive a telephone call of condolence from Elisabeth—my older cousin in England.

"How are you feeling," she asks, "now that you've joined the rest of us with our backs to the wall?"

I don't like this implication that I've moved up a notch—into the line of fire—just because, like Elisabeth, both my parents have died. But I understand her growing feelings of mortality. It happens to all of us as we age. Death, like decline, is inevitable, but to me its timing and circumstances have always seemed random, not exclusively hierarchical, and not necessarily something to be feared.

Life is short, as we learned from the early culling that took our brother Sandy, but it can also be long. Some might say too long. Mum has died in her ninety-third year with her mind still intact, but Dad died at age ninety-two, having been supposedly saved in his late seventies by a triple bypass, only to live the last twelve years in the fog of dementia. Perhaps death isn't the ultimate tragedy.

After Mum died, we received dozens of letters of condolences from women I barely knew—women my age who'd been mentored by Mum, who looked up to her as an "Other Mother." I knew she had these relationships—Mum had always taught me the importance of having friends of all ages—but the *contents* of the letters from her "Other Daughters" filled me with remorse. They didn't describe the forceful mother I had been experiencing for the past twenty years—the one who invaded my privacy, demanded I call her every few hours, who seemed judgmental and disapproving of my choices—they described an Other Mother who was loving and wise, confident and charming, admirable and true. They described a woman I wished I had known.

Or perhaps a mother I had pushed away. A mother I just needed to remember—someone who had been there all along.

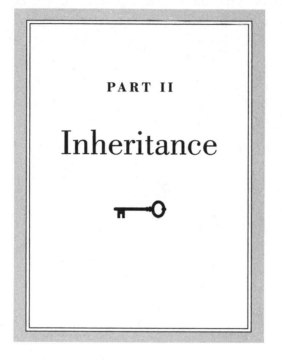

PART II

Inheritance

Other Mothers

In many ways, Mum was the ideal mother for any young woman transitioning from the conservative postwar years to the liberated sixties. She was a feminist at heart. But although I inherited many of her attitudes, I stayed in her shadow, observing. I noticed the close friendships she forged with young and old alike, from all walks of life. I saw how the exchange of new ideas fed her curiosity, kept her youthful and broad-minded, and I understood that we can guide and be guided at the same time, but when she tried to mentor me, our mother–daughter relationship complicated things. It's hard to accept guidance when you're trying to break away. So just as she inherited Other Daughters, I inherited Other Mothers. One thing I learned for sure is that we can all use more than one mother . . . and more than one daughter. It keeps us sane.

One of my Other Mothers is a sculptor named Pat, who lives near me in the city. Over the years she and I have developed a deep relationship. Pat and I frequently have morning coffee together, buying cappuccino and almond croissants at a small café and crossing the streetcar tracks to sit on a bench in the leafy park nearby. Sometimes we meet for a pasta dinner at a restaurant around the corner. Often I simply drop in—the door to Pat's house is always open. It's a restored Victorian workman's cottage, and in summer the oversized French doors in her living room are thrown open to a walled-in courtyard. Wisteria blooms overhang a tiny pergola in the corner; they weave and drip like giant grapes, shading a small tea table. Blowsy pink peonies the size of salad plates mingle along the fence with orange lilies, climbing roses, and purple irises. Pat's sculptures settle into the greenery like silent, meditating goddesses. It reminds me of Findhorn—that Scottish microclimate of positive energy where every plant explodes to double its normal size as if by magic.

Even in the middle of winter, when Pat's French doors are closed, bright sunlight still glances off the high-ceilinged walls and infuses the room. Her indoor furniture is the same as her outdoor furniture—lacy white wrought iron, the tables glass-topped—bringing the effect of her airy garden inside. Vases of fresh-cut flowers are everywhere.

This morning I've made a trip into the city to see her. I holler her name, kicking off my boots, and she emerges from her back-room art studio, her short, steel-gray hair streaked with alabaster dust. She's wearing an old shirt over stylish clothes. Large silver links loop around her neck and a bold copper cuff encircles one wrist. She puts down her chisel.

"What a delightful surprise!" she exclaims. "I'll make us some coffee."

I hear the *tick-tick-tick* as her gas stove ignites and she puts the kettle on. I've brought some pastries in a brown paper bag. She hurries them onto a white paper doily on a pretty scalloped plate, setting cups on a wicker tray. Small paper luncheon napkins are thin as tissue, printed with roses. Nothing escapes her artist's eye.

For years, Pat has been helping me deal with my relationship with Mum. I know she had a similar struggle with her own mother, and I crave her hard-won insights. I feel as if I can tell Pat anything. Even though we're twenty-six years apart, I feel no age difference when I'm with her—I feel completely understood.

"I hate to tell you, dear," Pat says with a laugh, "but we all deal with our mothers until the day we die!"

Pat should know. Even though she recently turned ninety, her own mother lived much longer and her aunt lived to a hundred and one. Longevity is obviously in her genes.

Pat's second career began at the age of seventy-seven when she gave up painting to become a stone carver. When she found this cottage she was a widow in her eighties, an age when most people would have moved into a retirement home, but Pat's only difficulty had been lifting blocks of fifty-pound stone up to a second-floor studio. All she felt she needed was a place with no stairs.

She hates Canadian winters and is leaving soon for a month of carving in Mexico. She's worried about tripping on the cobblestones of San Miguel de Allende, but she's looking forward to the courtyard at the *instituto*, where she can chisel her block of stone outside in the sun. She's taking her new iPad with her so that she can keep in touch via e-mail.

I have four of Pat's sculptures in my living room. Most are mother-child figures, but the largest piece is a two-foot-tall abstract, reminiscent of works by the late British sculptor Barbara Hepworth. It's a flowing, organic form that looks like a pear split open—womblike—evoking the mystery of life's beginning. The alabaster is polished smooth; in some places it's so thin it's translucent. It sits on the ledge of my living room window, where light pours in, illuminating it from behind.

I've noticed that many female artists—as they grow older and find their voices—become more abstract in their work, and Pat and I debate the meaning of this.

"The sculptures I like best haven't really been done by me," Pat says, and tells me that these pieces flow through her, coming from a higher universal place: the sacred place of the divine. These are the shapes that emerge from the stone when she gets out of the way.

I've experienced this energy a few times myself during times of heightened creativity. I've always called it "My Street of Green Lights"—when everything flows and there are no roadblocks. I'm merely a conduit for something that is meant to be. The results are astonishing, even awe-inspiring. Our hands haven't done the work; they've only been borrowed—it's the humility of being a midwife.

The theme of mother and child runs constantly through Pat's sculptures—she has lost two of her four children, and I can ask her questions about grieving that I wouldn't have dared to ask Mum. A lifelong study of Jung has helped Pat transform her tragedies into art, particularly through the interpretation of dreams. Wombs are the provenance of women, to be carried, protected, and celebrated— lamented, and worked out. She tells me that Jung combined spirituality with religion to interpret ancient symbols. I have never studied Jung. Suddenly it seems urgent that I learn more. I want her to help me.

I describe to Pat a recurring dream I've had, concerning Mum's house. I'm conflicted about staying on there, even though

I told the boys I would. In childhood that house was my paradise. As Mum aged, it felt more like a trap. Now that I've moved out there, am I taking a step forward or a step back? I don't want to get stuck there. What will it feel like to be alone for so long?

"When you feel closer to yourself," she says, "you're closer to the divine. Then you can deal with your monsters consciously, without having them destroy you."

Pat urges me to stay with myself. "Some things you can't do in a collective," she says. "We all have a secret life—something we work through creatively, through art—we don't have to share it."

Pat knows that I've been struggling to understand not only my relationship to Mum, but what this ancestral home means to me. I sense that it, too, is womblike, this container—the source of all my happiness and unhappiness, the two inextricably intertwined, to be understood if at all by the untangling of it. But what is my unfinished business there, my purpose? What will I find?

"Don't fight it," Pat tells me. "It's where you're meant to be."

Unpacking the Past

It's been four weeks since Mum died and I'm knee-deep in pocket litter. Each piece is a depth charge exploding a memory.

In a trunk I find an old Langley's Dry Cleaner receipt crumpled into the pocket of Mum's Chinese dressing gown. Suddenly, it's 1953 and I'm seven years old again. Dad's in the shower, late for work. Mum stands in her dressing room, opens her coin purse, hands me thirty cents.

"Quick!" she says. "Run up to Langley's and get your father's shirts!"

I stare in disbelief at the old receipt. How could it still be here after all these years? Did she never wear the dressing gown again after that? Did shirts really cost only ten cents each to wash and iron back then?

From Mum's winter coats hanging in the mudroom I empty the pockets of Baggies, chunks of doggie biscuits, Kleenex, her handwritten grocery lists, a key, chewing gum, a Ping-Pong ball, red lipstick, and more and more Kleenex.

Pocket litter turns out to be ground zero, the debris left behind that no thrift store will take: small mounds of ash, yet mountains to climb, for me. We are the sum of our habits, and this is the proof of my mother—the Mum I once loved but can no longer recall. I start to sob.

Several of my friends in Toronto offer to help me clear out the house, and at first I decline. Many are in the same situation I am. Why should they have to inherit my work on top of their own? But it's exactly this shared experience that motivates their generosity; they understand what I'm facing. And so I change my mind. I accept their help, gratefully. They tell me that the internal, emotional work will be mine alone and it will be onerous enough.

Lesley offers to help with the culling of Mum's clothes. Lesley is a pixie—petite and full of empathy. She's a well-known illustrator, an acute observer of the human condition, and her whimsical drawings vibrate with tart humor. She and I have often helped critique each other's professional work and have taken long walks to critique our parents as well. She recently entered the caretaking mode with her own mother, so she understands the demands, but she shows more compassion than I do.

She drives out from Toronto, and we stuff Mum's sweaters—forty-three nearly identical red ones—into garbage bags and stack them by the front door for the thrift store to pick up. We do the same with dozens of navy blue and black elastic-waist polyester trousers. I grimace at the thought that my children will one day be doing the same for me.

We wade through the sloppy tangle of Mum's handbags and empty them of tortoiseshell combs, theater programs, compacts, and mints. I try not to succumb to the flashbacks—when and where Mum used each one—but when I find her black pigskin change purse from the 1950s, I get mugged by a memory: the tips of my fingers recall the feel of its two metal prongs when I pried them open to steal a nickel. Guilt is seared into my six-year-old brain.

"Aren't mothers interesting?" says Lesley, as she picks up a lime-green clutch bag from the 1960s. "We cling to that last gasp of being loved by them. Giving that up means growing up." She stuffs it into the open garbage bag. "Time to let the old girl go."

When I get to Mum's mahogany dresser, I can't bear to clear it. Her one tube of red lipstick, white rat-tail comb, and small, black-strapped Timex lie scattered on the white linen runner amid emery boards, nail scissors, and the monogrammed silver dresser set inherited from her mother. The fat red tomato pincushion bristles with all her safety pins and brooches. Silver frames, large and small, hold black-and-white family photographs. In 1991, when my brother Sandy died of cancer at age forty-two, Mum had flooded most of the frames with overlapping pictures of him—so there is Sandy in his pram, Sandy on Grandmother's lap, Sandy in his cadet uniform, Sandy riding a camel in Egypt, Sandy skiing with Dad.

Sandy was an elegant, courtly, highly principled young man. He'd spent his life as a banker overseas, first in London, then in Hong Kong (his birthplace), and later in Bahrain and Saudi Arabia. When he developed a rare form of cancer called fibrous histiocytoma, he refused the quarter-section amputation offered at Princess Margaret Hospital—"I'll look like Lord Nelson without his ship," he said—and we brought him home to die.

Sandy's subsequent nine-month period of palliative care rocked our family to its core, even as it stretched out to feel like a well-choreographed ballet with an inevitable ending that we tried to delay. Using June Callwood's book *Twelve Weeks in Spring* as our inspirational guide, we transformed his old bedroom in the back of the house into a hospital room; while he could still walk, we helped him downstairs and laid him on a chaise on the veranda. As winter progressed and his tumor grew, he spent more and more time upstairs in his bed. Robin moved home, promising to stay "for as long as it takes," and Victor and I shared round-the-clock nursing shifts with him. Chris flew in whenever he could.

One evening, I collapsed into a chair at the kitchen table, my head in my hands, hair in my face, sobbing.

"I don't want him to die! How can we not have Sandy? How can there be nothing left?" Then I became irrational, screaming, "I want a little Sandy . . . I want his girlfriend to get pregnant . . . I want to freeze his sperm!"

Mum was sitting across from me, her head down, one fingernail picking at the woven placemat. Dad came up behind my chair and held my heaving shoulders. He let me cry until I had nothing left. But after I stopped, wet tears were still plopping into my lap. I looked up and they were Dad's.

I said, "I'm sorry, so sorry."

"Don't be," said Dad quietly. "You're expressing what all of us feel but haven't been able to say."

By April, Sandy's tumor had burst through his chest and climbed above his left shoulder like a unicorn's horn, a whorl of angry red in a bed of bubbling blisters. It was so heavy Sandy could no longer sit up. The fingers on his left hand had been bandaged in white gauze because gangrene had set in. One morning, as the bandages were being changed, Sandy asked for a mirror. Mum didn't want to give it to him; she wanted to spare him.

"It's his body," I said. "Let him feel in control. If he wants to see it, we shouldn't deny him."

Sandy took the mirror in his right hand and, with great effort, lifted it high above his head. He held it there for a long time, studying the tumor and the gangrene, saying nothing; then he lowered the mirror and closed his eyes. Beads of sweat formed on his forehead.

When the pain came, syringes of morphine lay like soldiers on the table beside his bed. I was squeamish with needles, so whenever I had the midnight shift, I had to wake Robin to help me give the injections.

Sandy often woke with nightmares, describing horrific scenes of carnage on the battlefields of the American Civil War. "The horses are on their backs . . . their legs are in the air . . . their eyes are wild . . . there's smoke everywhere!"

I said, "No, Sandy, you're at home . . . you're just having a bad dream."

"No, no! I'm there! I'm there! Can't you see it?"

Other times, he looked petrified, crying, "I don't want to die . . . I don't want to die!"

I sat in the rocking chair at the foot of his bed, talking of reincarnation. Sandy didn't believe in it.

"I'm going to miss all of you so much," he said.

"No . . . it's us who'll be missing *you*," I said. "You'll be able to be with us whenever you want. You'll be in a wonderful place—full of energy and light."

By early May the needles were gone, replaced by a morphine pump that Sandy could operate himself by pushing a button whenever he felt the pain breaking through. The drug went directly into a butterfly needle implanted by the doctor into his vein. The bandage on his right hand now swelled and wrapped up over his wrist as the gangrene spread upward; when it needed to be changed, shreds of blackened flesh fell away.

Robin sat beside him for hours, gently massaging his arm. Mum and Dad took turns reading to him. The growth of the tumor was now affecting his ability to swallow. We swabbed his mouth with water as he wasted away.

Toward the end of May, the doctor told us it was only a matter of hours. In fact, he had already signed the death certificate, which Robin kept in his bedroom. Sandy lay with his eyes closed in a drug-induced coma, but I felt he could hear me.

"Today is Robin's birthday," I whispered to him, "so please don't die today . . . It would be terrible for Robin if you died on his birthday."

He died the next morning, while Robin was stroking his arm. Dad was outside gardening. Robin opened Sandy's window and quietly called down, "Dad—Sandy's gone." Dad dropped his rake and raced up.

By the end of the afternoon, Sandy's face was gray—waxy-looking and cold. The family had gathered around his bed to say prayers, but after everyone left, I stayed behind and pulled back the sheet. I looked at the tumor. It was red. I placed my hand on it: it was hot . . . angry-looking . . . still growing.

As a mother myself, I don't know how Mum absorbed the loss of Sandy. I wish I could have plumbed the depths of her feelings, but she would never share them with me. When I asked her if she was missing him, she answered sharply, "I don't know what you mean by that question!" But I remember the sound she made the night Sandy died. It was a deep, shattering sonar toll, so loud and echoing it sounded like a submarine sinking to the ocean floor. This unholy noise bounced off the bones of the house behind her bedroom door for hours while Dad paced back and forth in the upstairs hall. He wouldn't let us go in to her, and he didn't, either. He just guarded her door until she stopped.

The loss of Sandy was so devastating that, during his funeral, my brain couldn't grasp the concept that our "sibling team" was no longer five. We were his pallbearers, but we needed three on each side, so I suggested a family friend for the sixth. When Victor reminded me that we needed *two* extra people, I stared at him blankly. He put his arm around my shoulder and said, "Sandy can't carry his own coffin, now, can he?"

I open Mum's middle drawer and pause. Under all her practical flannelette nightgowns I feel something hard. It's an unopened box of the perfume Mum used to wear—Crêpe de Chine by Millot—its glossy black box sparkling with gold dots and art deco fans. Whenever Dad traveled he bought her a bottle. They never used endearments like *dear* or *darling* with each other, but whenever he brought her perfume I got excited—it meant he loved her.

I hesitate before I break the ancient seal. Then I'm intoxicated by the rich, vibrant scent of gardenia, lilac, and leather, transporting me back to a New Year's Eve party when, as a ten-year-old, I was allowed to watch in my nightgown from the second-floor landing above. I've dressed Robin as Old Father Time and Victor as Baby New Year; he sits beside me in a diaper and crown, waiting to be carried down at the stroke of midnight. The rugs have been rolled up and Guy Lombardo's orchestra is playing "I Love Paris" on the gramophone. I can see Dad in his tuxedo dancing in the living room with our neighbor Vera Fenn in her red dress.

Somewhere out of sight, Mum is dancing with Vera's husband, Colin. Someone is calling for more dance wax. An unknown hand shakes a canister of powdered wax onto the hardwood floor to make it more slippery, the little yellow beads skittering across the bottom step. There is talking and laughter and the tinkling of ice cubes in glasses. Mum's perfume drifts up through the stair railing.

I show Lesley Dad's closet. He never bought anything new unless the old one had worn out, so he never accumulated clothes—his closet is sparse; there is the clang of empty hangers. His tuxedo is there, plus two suits, four white shirts, and three pairs of trousers. I save his navy wool blazer with its crest from Tonbridge School—the boarding school in England that was his home for most of his youth—but everything else gets tossed.

His dresser is neat as a pin, just the way he left it three years ago.

In Dad's top drawer there's a collection of items he obviously treasured. In a small cardboard box is a lock of Sandy's blond baby hair along with his hospital baby bracelet. The tiny blue and white beads spell his name. There's an envelope of foreign coins, a booklet of swim tickets for the public pool, and a tiny red pair of Victor's baby mittens with appliquéd monkeys. Dad must have known these would be the last pair of baby mittens he was ever going to see, so he treated them with a special reverence. He treated Victor the same way—or at least that's how the rest of us felt. We had to say "Yes, sir" and "No, sir" to Dad, but when Victor came along he got away with "Okay"—a slang word Dad wouldn't normally let us use. If Victor sometimes said cheekily, "So, how're ya doin', old man?" Dad would just chuckle and shake his head.

In Dad's bottom drawer I find a newspaper. At first I think

he's used it as a drawer liner, so I'm about to toss it out, but it's so carefully folded that I take a closer look. It's the *Hong Kong Sunday Herald* from Sunday, September 9, 1945. Why did he save this? The editorial tells me: this is the first edition after the surrender of the Japanese in Singapore—when Dad was there. The publisher apologizes for crooked lines and bits of missing typeface—they've hastily produced this edition with scrounged supplies. The articles are full of instructions about how to contact loved ones and where to get free cables to wire overseas. There are photos accompanying harrowing first-person accounts from the women and children who survived the Japanese POW camps.

The lead article announces the Stanley Evacuation and shows a photo of the ship *Empress of Australia*, on which 550 women and children internees will be repatriated to their homelands. All 550 unalphabetized names—starting with *Mrs. D. Weir and baby*—begin on page one and continue, column after column, to the end of the paper on page six. Parentheses after their names give their nationalities: Norwegian, Dutch, American, Polish, and British. The very starkness of the list bears witness to the horrors they must have endured. On page six—in tiny, faded script—I notice that Dad has underlined the name *Mrs. M. I. Crabbe* in red pencil, and in the margin he's written *Aunt Poppy*.

What must I do with this artifact that Dad had so carefully made room for in his wartime luggage, carried from country to country, and saved all these years in his dresser drawer? On the Internet, the only reference I can find to the *Hong Kong Herald* is in the national library of Australia. I e-mail and ask if they'd like it. Their offhand response is that they'll take it only if it's in pristine condition, with no rips or tears. I am insulted. What do they expect of a flimsy newspaper that's been through the war?

The next day, I find Dad's old naval uniform and heavy wool greatcoat from the war. We have photos of Dad in this uniform, seated at a table at the Stork Club in New York City, when he reunited with Mum after the war ended. He was always thin, but by the time he'd made his epic escape from the Japanese he must have been gaunt. This uniform was tailor-made and it's small enough to fit me. During the war, an officer's buttons often held secret compartments: you could unscrew the top and unfurl a silk escape map. Dad was with the Special Operations Executive (SOE), a top-secret British organization that conducted espionage, so he might very well have been issued something like this, but I check the brass buttons and they are . . . well, just buttons. If only the greatcoat could talk. Dad would have worn it in the depths of an English winter, going to visit Mum at her American Air Force base.

I pick the best, most expensive dry cleaner in town and drop them both off. When I pick them up three days later, they're twist-tied together in a clear plastic bag, on extra-thick padded hangers, their sleeves stuffed with tissue paper, looking like a body bag. It weighs about the same as Dad did when he died. I pay the seventy-five-dollar bill almost gratefully and lay the bag gently in the backseat of my car.

By Lesley's last day, we're simply heaving filled garbage bags over the banister and hearing them land with a thud inside the front door. The pile looks like a massive landfill and we're exhausted. But just when I think we're finished, I open the door to the double closet in the guest bedroom and gasp at what greets me. A mountain of white plastic grocery bags are jumbled on top of one another, spilling their guts of wooden salad bowls, pink plastic clotheslines, naked Barbie dolls, and out-of-date atlases. I'd forgotten about this—Mum really did leave us Christmas presents for the next one hundred years. I can't even bear to examine them. I can hear Mum's voice: "What? You're throwing away all this perfectly good stuff? What you children need is a good Depression!" But Lesley and I just scoop everything up, wrestle it into three giant garbage bags, and send them off the banister, too.

I wander the house by myself, absorbing the energy from the walls. With Mum and Dad's forceful presence gone, the house seems to spring loose, lean back, and open up for me. Despite all the rules that Dad had imposed on us, this house and its natural surroundings had always soared with possibilities. Now I feel weirdly free—at liberty to inhabit this space the way I'd once longed for all those years ago. I feel the same creative surge I always used to feel as a child here, but now nothing is blocking my way. In the evening I turn to my computer and begin my art project.

I've always wanted to know how many letters Shakespeare used to write his plays, and now I can use the computer to easily find the answer. It feels as though I'm extracting DNA from his work, using synthetic biology to create a new life form: Shakespeare-at-a-glance; Shakespeare as abstract art.

I start with the tragic love story. I assign a color to each letter of the alphabet and throw all the letters from *Romeo and Juliet*, one at a time, onto a digital canvas to see what happens. It is absorbing, solitary work, and the evening passes quickly. I feel the house embracing me.

———

The next morning, the sky is still gray, though brightening almost imperceptibly. The birds are silent—the ones who haven't flown south. Out across the ice-covered pool to the west, the tall, bare walnut trees are silhouetted black against the sky. I can see the blinking red light of the lighthouse at the end of the pier. I go into the living room, open the heavy glass door to the veranda, push open the screen, and pad out in my slipper socks. I wait until the glow of sunrise begins to melt the horizon, blending and fading with a watery brush the nightlights in the distance. On the frozen grass, small gray lake stones lie nestled in a circle like forgotten eggs in an Easter hunt, the remnants of the labyrinth that one of the grandchildren laid out on the lawn after Mum's funeral. Dad's new metal wheelbarrow is dumped over on its side by the bottom of the hill.

This small hill is where we first learned to toboggan. When Dad wasn't looking, we'd start on the veranda and then race down its nine wide steps, execute a sharp right-hand turn, and zoom down to the fence.

Robin and I are having many long-distance telephone conversations. I tell him I found our wooden toboggans yesterday when I pulled into the garage; they're slung up in the rafters. His old Happi Time sled is hanging from a nail on the wall, but he says he doesn't want it. He's preoccupied with Mum and Dad's library.

He's been documenting all the books in the house and doesn't want me to dispose of any before he visits again. Some books are old treasures dating back to the early 1800s, leather-bound with gilt edges, inscribed to and from generations of ancestors with quaint messages in ancient, feathery script. But most are contemporary: history, politics, and biography. There are an ungodly number of religious texts, including more than forty-eight Bibles.

As a self-confessed bibliophile, Robin has a pen-shaped mouse called a "cat" that scans the bar code of a book, automatically entering the title, author, publisher, and date into a database on his computer. With more than two thousand books in the house, the scanner is a godsend for books published after 1980. Unfortunately, most of the books predate the era of bar codes, so Robin has to enter them manually. He started this cataloging project a year ago, before Mum died, but still has a long way to go. He thinks his cataloged list will have more value than the books themselves. He believes future generations will be interested to see what a typical family of the twentieth century had on their bookshelves. I remind Robin of all the books in the kitchen, but it seems he hadn't considered including cookbooks. It's as though he deems them a lesser species. He sounds confused when I ask him. He says, "But I haven't included that . . . that . . . um . . . what is it—a genre?"

He's not sure what to do with the books in the downstairs hall, either. This is where Mum kept material written by or about family members. Stuffed between books are magazine articles and newspaper clippings and binders on family history. There are several books Robin wrote, including a paperback of *Pedaling Northwards*, his travel memoir of bicycling twelve hundred kilometers from Virginia to Canada with his son, Frankie, in 1992. Our whole family had gathered with banners on the outskirts of town to welcome them, watching them pedal their last few kilometers.

There are the Kate Spade etiquette books illustrated by my daughter Virginia, dog-eared copies of my old *Kids Toronto* directories, and a book by Chris, *Something's Wrong Somewhere*, about the moral economy of the farm crisis. Victor is the only one who hasn't written a book.

Last Christmas, when a new book by Chris was coming out, Victor rolled his eyes. "I hope you're not planning to give *me* a copy . . . I've got enough of your doorstops already!"

When I show Victor a new manuscript of mine, he weighs it in his hand and says, "I just want to know what its R-value is . . . How much heat can I get out of it? How fast will it burn?" I know he doesn't mean it—he's full of support for our projects—but he's beginning to remind me of Mum. Mum always gave us mixed messages. First, she'd say, "Don't get too big for your britches!" Then in the next contradictory breath, she'd say, "Never hide your light under a bushel!" But whatever we did, she was always saying, "Why don't you write a book about it?" When I look at this bookshelf now, I realize we were all trying to please her. She was the gifted writer, but there's not a single book written by her.

On the top shelf, there are nine identical copies of *The Negotiator*—Frederick Forsyth's fictionalized account of Sandy's whistle-blowing experience when he uncovered a fraud at his bank in Saudi Arabia. It turned out to be bigger than he thought—an element of the Iran–Contra scandal. Forsyth gave Sandy the fictitious name of Andy Laing. Whenever Mum saw a copy, she couldn't resist buying it. Sandy has annotated one of the copies. Under a snapshot of himself standing next to the author in rural Virginia, he writes, "Frederick Forsyth likes to weave true stories into his novels. Here, the story is mine. The place, Saudi Arabia, the local bank name, and several of the characters are historical, as are the details of my escape from Saudi and the fact of the suppression of my statement to the Chase Manhattan auditors. I have asked, too, 'Is there more in here that's true than even I'm aware?' Perhaps . . ."

I discover that the Centennial Pool at the local library three blocks away has an aqua-fit class. I'm able to swim with the seniors using the set of tickets I found in Dad's top drawer. After his retirement, Dad used to walk down to this pool every day to luxuriate in what he called their "free hot water." They offered free swims for senior citizens, but Dad went for the showers. The tickets are so antiquated they cause the young girls at the check-in desk to giggle. This group of women in aqua fit, roughly my age, gives me an instant community and leavens my days of solitude. I start to feel reconnected to what used to be my hometown. There was a time when I knew everybody. Now I know only the immediate neighbors. Sambo's best friend, Pucci, lives in a house across the garden, and sometimes I take Sambo there to play while Pucci's owners, Phil and Lesley, feed me cappuccinos and keep an eye on me. At night I feel comforted when I can see their lights glowing through the trees.

The following week my friend Jan arrives to help me clean out Mum's kitchen. Jan is a loyal and nurturing friend, a thoughtful artist who used to work as a chef. Her disposition is as sunny as her wavy blond hair, but Jan is meticulously stylish and I worry that she's in for a shock: nothing in her world is ever out of place, while here in Mum's kitchen, the mess is like a creeping mold. I've explained to her how onerous this house-cleaning task might be, but she passes no judgment. She just laughs and says she'll be happy to do it. This is, of course, before she sees what's in the cupboards.

I've warned her that we once heard Chris's teenage daughter scream, "Omigod, this jam's best-before date is before I was born!"

The kitchen is a large square room with the harvest table placed smack in the middle, like a traffic obstacle. The electric stove and fridge sit next to each other on one side of the room, while the sink and cupboards are on the opposite wall. The third wall is a bank of tall windows overlooking the garden. The toaster is plugged in next to the sink, but the electric kettle is plugged in to the stove—as far away from a water source as possible. There are no counters to speak of and the table offers no space for this purpose, since it holds all the clutter of Mum's desk. The dishes and dishwasher are in a separate room altogether—in the pantry. The glasses and cutlery are even farther away—in the dining room.

The simple act of making tea seems to require a meditative hike of a thousand memories—back and forth and around the traffic obstacle, stumbling over chairs, knocking over vases of plastic flowers, circling through three different rooms. I collect my cup from the pantry, spoon from the dining room, tea bag from the kitchen, then back to the pantry for the teapot, and back to the kitchen for the sugar. Then I make three trips around the table to fill the kettle from the stove with water from the sink. It's almost as ritualistic as a geisha ceremony.

The fridge is totally unidentifiable: it's camouflaged as an oversized scrapbook, with dozens of pots and pans stacked precariously on top. On the door, grease-stained magnets—shaped like carrots, orange slices, ice-cream cones, and letters of the alphabet—hold hundreds of overlapping family photos, grandchildren's crayon drawings, and newspaper clippings. There's a printed potholder, stuck there by Dad, that reads A FAT WIFE AND A BIG BARN NEVER DID ANY MAN HARM.

The kitchen cupboards are packed with stale, outdated food. Jan asks why there are so many tins of stewed tomatoes and mushroom soup, and I tell her this is because Mum was a devotee of *The I Hate to Cook Book*, written by Peg Bracken in 1960. Like most good cooks, Jan is unfamiliar with this book, but Mum had a first edition. All Peg's recipes had either mushroom soup or stewed tomatoes as their main ingredient, and Mum learned that to be a good cook all you really needed was a good can opener.

Within a year, Julia Child had published *Mastering the Art of French Cooking*, mirroring the choices and double messages given to young wives in the fifties. Back then, you could don your lacy apron, have martinis waiting when your husband got home, and be proud that your kitchen exuded the aroma of boeuf bourguignon or, like my mother, you could be liberated—wearing a favorite green apron with pockets for tennis balls and emblazoned with I'D RATHER PLAY TENNIS THAN COOK in big black letters. If we needed Mum for anything, all we had to do was walk three blocks down to the Oakville Club. There she'd be, standing on center court, facing opponents half her age, running them ragged and winning every shot by strategically placing balls on the tape with a spin.

Long before fast food became the Holy Grail, Mum was an avid pioneer: the faster the better. In fact, to Mum, food was mostly irrelevant. Good conversation—with lots of laughter— was the essential ingredient. To this end, she delighted in mixing guests who might otherwise never have met. She might introduce her Portuguese cleaning woman to the Portuguese trade commissioner or, at a dinner party, seat a bishop beside a draft dodger.

Her sense of humor had a mischievous quality. I remember the night Dad asked her to prepare a five-star meal for some visiting dignitaries from his head office. You'd think he would have known better. Once the guests were seated, Mum carried in the casserole dish. But before Dad could start serving she ran into the kitchen, giggling, and grabbed me.

"Here," she whispered. "Put this in front of your father!"

I naïvely took the large plate, which was covered by an up-turned silver bowl, and placed it in front of Dad. Mum followed me in, and made a grand speech to the guests about how proud she was that Dad had become such a bigwig that he spent his whole life traveling and ignoring his family. Then she whipped off the cover. Sitting in the middle of the big china plate was a small round tin that said RAT POISON.

"Don't get indigestion," she told him, as the guests roared with laughter at Dad's expense.

Mum learned from *The I Hate to Cook Book* that to make a regal appetizer all you had to do was slop consommé soup straight from the tin into a pretty cloisonné bowl and sprinkle dried celery seeds on top. Her favorite recipe was something called Dr. Martin's Mix—a scrambled mess of ground beef, rice, and cream of mushroom soup. It could sit on the stove forever, and frequently did. Once, when Mum took off for the States to visit an old school friend, she left this casserole for us to eat while she was away. Dad reheated it every night for eight days until we refused to eat it anymore. Then he put it on the floor—and even the dog walked away.

But Mum's worst meal was liver, which she felt compelled to feed us every Thursday night. It was good for our blood, she told us. She'd lift the meat like a slimy, dead rat, throw it in the frying pan, slam on a lid, chunk ice in her scotch, and go off to watch Walter Cronkite deliver the *CBS Evening News*. As soon as we heard Walter say, "And that's the way it is . . . ," we knew what we'd find on our plates.

We weren't allowed to "get down" from the table until our plates were clean, but Robin—who was blessed with a face like a chipmunk—learned to hide whatever food he didn't like deep inside the pockets of his pudgy cheeks. When we later got ready for bed and climbed into our communal bath, Robin would pretend to go deep-sea diving, gradually releasing from his mouth bubbles of gray-speckled scum that would float to the top of our bathwater.

Before Jan chucks out the old tins and packages, I ask her to document them.

"What do you mean?" she asks.

"You know . . . like copy down the name, manufacturer, and best-before dates." I hand her a pencil and pad of paper.

"Why would you want to do that?"

"Robin is documenting all the books in the library," I tell her, "so why shouldn't the food in the kitchen have equal significance? The food tells an even better story of the life lived here—don't you think?"

Jan just laughs and shakes her head, but I describe the documents Robin has found relating to our great-great-grandfather's ships in the early 1800s. The receipts with their prices for items like food, rope, fabric, and wine are fascinating to me—real domestic glimpses of history. If someone hadn't recorded them, how would we ever know?

I show Jan Mum's cookbooks and ask her to document those, too, since I don't trust Robin to do it. They take up a whole shelf above the kitchen sink. They're a slanted, jumbled mess, most of them crammed with clippings and held together with elastic bands. Pages are stuck together with whatever she was slopping around that night, and there are mummified maggots in the bindings. Despite all these books, I don't ever remember Mum baking—except to make us each a birthday cake once a year, and this she did with a Betty Crocker mix. For dessert, she gave us Jell-O. If she was feeling particularly festive, it had bits of canned fruit floating in it. Sometimes, she just gave us the whole box of powder and we licked it off our fingers.

While Jan works away in the kitchen, I start taking inventory of every piece of furniture, china, glassware, silverware, and art-work in the house. I go room by room, making a list and taking digital photographs. The fact that this house has space for every-thing is both its beauty and its curse. In the mudroom I take a photo of the cast-iron woodstove. The last time we used it was in 1954, during Hurricane Hazel.

I remember the fierce roar of the winds and the seemingly endless rain, but what I remember most was the warm, smoky air in the mudroom, the crush of people's legs, and the camaraderie of our neighbors, who, with all the electricity knocked out for three days, had come to cook on our woodstove. Today, though, when I open the stove I find nothing but mismatched woolen mittens.

Next, I take pictures of Dad's workroom. The walls are cov-ered in corkboard, to which are nailed packages of old ski wax, lassos of twine, boxes of putty, and odd metal brackets. Small baby-food jars hold nuts, bolts, screws, and nails. Brackets hold hammers, saws, and various lengths of rope.

Beside every bracket, Dad has traced the outline of the tool that belongs in the spot and thumbtacked a sign: ANNE! PUT BACK! Since Dad's death, the room has accumulated wicker baskets, plastic flowers, broken lamps, old china, and tinfoil plates—something Mum could never bring herself to throw away. Dad would be appalled.

It was in this room that Dad taught us how to build things—everything from water wheels to bookshelves to lamps. And it was here where, as a surprise for my ninth birthday, Dad built me a set of footlights for my theater in the basement. I found them under my bed when I woke up in the morning. Dad had built the set out of old mahogany, shaping it like a window box tilted on an angle and wiring it with four electric lightbulbs. We painted the bulbs different colors with some old house paint, which meant that when they heated up during my plays they gave off the steamy smell of burned turpentine.

The windows overlook what used to be our sandbox, where we played all day with buckets and spades, creating sandcastles and imaginary battlefields. It's a graveyard now, full of decapitated tin soldiers just below the surface. An incinerator stood beside it in the form of an old oil drum, flaky with rust. Every family had one—it was early recycling; garbage was taken to the dump while paper products were burned in the backyard. Dad burned ours each weekend, filling the air with acrid smoke.

But he never burned newspapers—they were too useful. After Mum had read them cover to cover, they became Dad's caulking gun—his answer to everything. He had a special cupboard in the pantry where he saved them, stacked in a neat, precise pile. He told of using newspapers during the war, inside his boots when his soles were worn out and inside his greatcoat for added protection when he was marching against the wind. Newspapers drained our bacon in the kitchen, wrapped good china, insulated the beds between mattress and springs, cleaned spills, lined shelves, trained dogs, formed the base of our evening fires in the old lake-stone fireplace, and kept drafts from seeping in around the edges of the windows. Each spring, when the heavy storm windows were taken down, neatly folded strips of newspaper would tumble out. Dad saved those folded strips and used the same ones year after year. Some strips have been here since we moved in, dating back to the Eisenhower era. One strip documents Queen Elizabeth's coronation.

In the long winter evenings Dad taught us the finer points of folding newspapers into mini–fire logs, almost willing them to return to their original incarnation. It was a precise art, like origami. We wove them into tightly compacted accordions, guaranteed to burn slowly. If our accordions didn't pass muster, we had to unravel them and start again. I could fold those flaming origami accordions in my sleep, but I could never understand putting all that energy into something that went up the chimney in a puff of smoke.

In the evening, Jan and I take a break. She stops counting tins of stewed tomatoes and volunteers to make us a glamorous dinner while I relax with my art project on the computer. When I finish the first few layers of *Romeo and Juliet*, I call her excitedly to come look. I point to the abstract squares of pink and orange on my screen, made up of thousands of tiny letters. "Look at this! I've just compressed some layers . . . and there's a broken heart! See it . . . in the middle?"

"Omigosh!" she says. "It's beautiful! How many letters did you use?"

I check my paper, full of counted letters crossed off like marks on a convict's wall. "Thirty-five thousand two hundred and sixty-two!"

She looks shocked. "You counted every single one . . . like all the *a*'s . . . and all the *b*'s . . . and . . . ?"

"Yep—it's taken a week, but I'm almost a quarter of the way there."

She laughs. "Maybe tomorrow you should come help me count the tins of stewed tomatoes!"

Tonight there are no tomatoes in Jan's recipe. She's made a moist, stuffed pork tenderloin, artfully arranged on the plate. Dessert is baking in the oven—a bread pudding made from croissants slathered in a caramel sauce. The kitchen is filled with a rich, buttery aroma. I tell Jan that we'll serve it on Mum's best dessert dishes.

I go into the pantry and bring out two of the wavy, scalloped glass plates faceted in diamond patterns that sparkle in the light. These were the dishes reserved for special occasions and they could never go in the dishwasher—they had to be hand-washed. I grew up thinking they were the most valuable things in the house, but in the 1970s, after I'd married and moved away, I discovered the truth: that how you're taught to treat something is what gives it value. I'd gone to a hardware store to buy lightbulbs, and moving down the aisle toward the back of the store, I saw a stack of the very same dishes. Stunned and delighted, I bought every one they had and gave my mother a new batch for Christmas.

"I found these at a hardware store!" I told her, thinking she'd be thrilled at my find.

Mum couldn't stop laughing. "What did you pay?"

"Only a dollar twenty-five."

"Well, you got gypped!" she said. "Mine only cost thirty-five cents . . . at Woolworth's!"

In a twist of fate, these pressed-glass dishes are now described as "vintage" on eBay and sell for twenty dollars each—increasing more times in value than Granny's Tiffany clock from 1865.

The next morning, Jan and I are back at work: she's still taking inventory in the kitchen, unearthing more rusted tins from the far reaches of the cupboards, and I'm in the dining room, itemizing kitsch in the cutlery drawer.

Dad believed that in the dining room children should be models of manners and discipline—seen but not heard. He ritualized Sunday lunches into agonizing, drawn-out affairs that tested our patience to the limit. Especially when we were hungry. And if we fidgeted or misbehaved he stood us in the corner. The dining room's square alcove meant that Dad could stand all five of us in corners at the same time, and he frequently did—probably wishing he could stand Mum in the sixth. He and Mum often ended up alone at the ten-foot-long table, carrying on their conversation as if we weren't there.

In the corners, we picked at the dining room wallpaper in silent revenge. The leafy green toile of red-coated fishermen casting their flies over rivers has been here since Mum pasted it up in 1952. I notice now that, halfway up the wall, all the fishing rods have their tips picked off.

I find the "Cuss Bank" that used to sit on the table. It's a ceramic head of a man with a grimaced expression and a money slot in the top of his black hat. We'd never been exposed to swear words at home (I'd never even heard the word *shit* until I went to university, and when my roommate said it as she slipped on a bridge, I almost fainted from shock), but as children there were two really bad things we were never allowed to say: one was "Shut up!" and the other was "I'm bored." If these words slipped out we forfeited five cents into the Cuss Bank.

To Mum, boredom was almost an offense against God. She believed nothing was boring and anybody could be fascinating, so long as you were clever enough to ask the right questions. If you were bored, then this was your failing, your lack of imagination—it made *you* boring. Furthermore, to tell somebody to shut up was unpardonably rude—even though, or maybe especially because, with Mum it was hard to get a word in edgewise.

I also find Mum and Dad's wedding cake topper, made of plaster by an army chef during the war; prophetically, it was a battleship. Now it looks like a shipwreck, its hull encrusted with barnacles of ancient icing, its masts dripping with stalactites of dirty-white tulle. Beside it is a small silver jigger that Mum gave Dad on their first wedding anniversary in Hong Kong. On its rim is inscribed HERE'S TO MANY MORE!—and it's so like Mum, hedging her bets with a sarcastic double entendre. This time, though, the joke was on her: she was the one who got driven to drink by their marriage. Dad tried to embarrass her by stacking her empty gin bottles beside the woodpile in the garage until he had a wall of glass, but it was only Sandy who could get Mum to quit. On his deathbed, he asked Mum for two things: that she'd stop drinking and that she'd stop fighting with Dad—and she granted him both wishes.

I open the cutlery drawers, which used to be so neatly arranged by Dad. Now everything's a jumbled mess, another of Mum's "junk drawers." In among the sterling flatware and engraved napkin rings are plastic bananas, green ceramic frogs, paperweights, candle stubs, rubber bands, pencils, and crocheted doilies. It's all too much for me now. I need a break. Dumping the clothes was easy, but sorting through this miasma is a different thing altogether.

Suddenly, I hear Jan shriek from the kitchen.

She's found a wicker basket of old spice bottles and holds it up to the light to show me. Despite the fact that the rusted lids are screwed on tight and the bottles should be half-empty, the ingredients seem to have multiplied. The rosemary and tarragon jars are alive, hopping like Mexican jumping beans. Who knows if these ever got shaken onto our food? Whenever Dad found a maggot, he'd tell us to eat it. "It's protein! Consider yourselves lucky—in the Japanese POW camps, prisoners would fight each other for these!"

The mold on bread was good for us, too, he told us, because penicillin was made from it. And the charcoal on our burned toast from the wonky toaster was like free Kaopectate—a cure-all medicine Dad bought frequently. He often fed the pink chalky liquid to Sambo.

Mum and Dad always had dogs in our family, starting with Scrappy, the large, dignified Dalmatian who protected us as children. We all loved Scrappy, but after he died of old age, Mum and Dad progressed through various breeds: Buffy, the mutt; Jenny, the beagle; Tanzi, the long-haired dachshund; and Winnie, the Dandie Dinmont—breeds that got smaller and smaller as my parents got older and Dad grew gentler. Winnie died of old age, too—when Mum was eighty and no breeder would sell her a new one. They said she was too old. Insulted, she bought Sambo from an ad tacked up on a bulletin board at the entrance to her favorite grocery store and fell in love. "There's more than one way to skin a cat!" said Mum.

All of Mum's dogs have lived a grand life, sprawled out on the veranda in the sunshine, chasing squirrels in the garden, going for long walks with Dad along the lakefront, barking at the geese, sniffing the fragrant rhododendrons, catching treats from the pocket of Mum's red fringed wool coat. At night, the smaller ones slept beside Mum's bed. In the afternoons she arranged playdates for them, inviting other dogs to come visit in the garden. "Can Sally come play with Sambo today? He's missing her!" Sometimes Sambo even received postcards from his friend Pucci, who spent the winters in Florida.

By late afternoon, Jan and I decide we've done enough cleaning for one day, so we take Sambo for a walk. He seems listless. As we wander along the lakefront, he walks slowly with his head down and seems uninterested in the other dogs we meet, or even in the ducks splashing and kicking. There's steam rising off the lake, like wisps of smoke kiting along with the current. One little bird is cooing loudly in a high-pitched voice, *oo-ee, oo-ee, oo-ee*. We even see two white swans float by, which I've never seen this time of year, but when I call out "Look, Simbo! Swans!" he just keeps his nose to the ground and gives a slow shake of his head as if to say, "Don't bother me with that stuff."

I wonder if he's depressed, missing Mum? At home he lies around all day, and occasionally I find he's gone upstairs to sleep at the foot of Mum's bed. I'm not a dog person, but I have a special place in my heart for Sambo. He's the only dog who's been able to worm his way in there. He did this years ago, when he was only a puppy. I'd come out to look after him while Mum and Dad went on a two-week cruise, and on our first night a terrific thunderstorm shattered the skies. The wind howled, the roof rattled, and suddenly the bedroom lit up with lightning—*bang!* Sambo, who'd been curled on the floor beside my bed, shot into the air like an acrobat in a circus cannon and landed—*thump*—on my pillow. We held each other tight all night, his little heart throbbing wildly against mine.

Mum always said Sambo had special powers. The breed originated in Tibet, she told us, and because of their keen hearing, they were used to guard the Royal Courts—they could hear enemies coming twenty miles away. Sambo looks like a fierce Chinese lion in miniature, with his thick, wooly facial fur splayed back from his nose like petals on a chrysanthemum. He smells like a wet wool sweater. Mum said Sambo was once royal himself—reincarnated. She claimed he was extra-intelligent and understood English perfectly—proven, she said, the day Dad lost his eyeglasses and couldn't find them anywhere.

"Sambo?" Mum called. "Where are Bapa's glasses?" According to Mum, Sambo raced out the screen door down to the bottom of the garden, nosed around in the compost heap where Dad had been gardening, and brought back Dad's glasses in his teeth.

In Mum and Dad's downstairs hall there's a tall, framed portrait scroll of an ancient Chinese nobleman with a white goatee, dressed in a blue jacket embroidered with gold dragons. Mum often carried Sambo over to it. "See, Sambo? That's your ancestor!"

But like everything else in this house, Sambo is way past his due date. I always thought he lived extra-long just to keep Mum company after Dad died. He's arthritic and spends most of every day curled into a ball with his back to us in his warm basket by the kitchen radiator. He seems forlorn. Jan and I try to perk him up, but as the days go by he gets more and more listless. He fights us at night when we try to put the prescribed ointment in his eyes.

On Jan's last day, we decide to take him to the vet. Jan cuddles him in the backseat while I drive. Sambo recognizes the vet in her white lab coat and wags his tail, but when she gently feels his hind legs, he winces.

"Let me take Sambo to the back for a more thorough examination," she says kindly.

I stare at the slick tiled floor and wait with Jan, absently twirling Sambo's red leash in my hands. When the vet calls me in ten minutes later, the news is not good. She tells me Sambo has an infection in his jaw that extends up into his eyes. This must be why his eyes have been weeping.

"Here," she says, stroking Sambo, "let me show you." She lifts up the corner of Sambo's mouth and I almost pass out. The jawbone is exposed in an oozing yellow mass—all the way up inside. She lays out the options: there are antibiotics, there are painkillers, and there's an expensive operation with no guarantees. But when I ask her which one to pick, she hesitates and looks briefly at the ceiling.

"Sambo is very old," she says softly, "and we know he's suffering. If we operate, I'm not sure he'll survive it."

"What do you advise?" I ask her.

"It's really whatever you feel most comfortable with."

I press her. "If Sambo were yours, what would you be doing?"

"I'd probably be doing the kindest thing," she says, and she has tears in her eyes. We both know what the kindest thing is. The awful truth of it drops with finality down a black hole in my heart. I thank her and tell her I'll have to think about this. She nods sadly and I take Sambo out in my arms to the waiting room.

"What did she say?" asks Jan, as she takes Sambo from me and we head to the car.

"Sambo has to be put down." I find myself wanting to turn on the windshield wipers as I pull out of the parking lot, but it's my tears that are blinding my vision.

"Omigod . . . is it that bad?" Jan is stroking Sambo in the backseat, and I'm looking at them both through the rearview mirror.

"His infection has been there a long time."

"Didn't your mother take him for regular checkups?"

"Yes! And the vet showed me the notes. For the past five years she'd been recommending an operation and Mum always refused!"

"What?"

"I know . . . but it was going to cost thousands and Mum said it was too expensive."

I can see Jan kissing the top of Sambo's head. "You poor, poor baby."

I find myself suddenly defending Mum. "I know most people treat pets like people these days, but as much as Mum loved Sambo, she knew he was just a dog." I reach for a Kleenex and wipe my eyes. "I wish we treated people the way we treat dogs."

"You mean, like, the 'kind thing'?" asks Jan.

"Well . . . even the vet called it that. I can't help thinking about Dad . . . and Sandy. How come Sambo can get a painless release from the end of life with a simple catheter in his hind leg for three minutes, but we have to suffer?"

"Nobody wants to play God," says Jan.

"But we already play God all the time! We play God when we use a defibrillator to restart a heart . . . when we hook a comatose patient up to a ventilator . . . when we perform a cesarean to rescue a strangling baby . . . when we give blood transfusions."

"Watch what you're doing!" says Jan as she grabs the seat in front. "You almost went through a red light."

"You watch!" I continue. "By the time we all get Alzheimer's, there'll be so many of us they'll legalize euthanasia."

"Okay by me."

"Me, too," I say. "I used to wish one of my children was an electrician or a plumber . . . but now I wish one of them was a vet."

I discover that I can't easily make this decision about Sambo. Two weeks of debate takes place between my brothers and me. When we finally reach a verdict, we decide we'll do it together. I wish I could let Pelmo know, but she's in Tibet, out of contact. I tell my children, "Sambo will die next Friday . . . we've booked the appointment."

Chris and Victor drive out to Oakville and meet me at the house. At the vet's I'm distraught, so after kissing Sambo and thanking him for all he's brought to our family, I place him in Chris's arms and go to sit in the waiting room. I look at all the other families there with their pets. There's an elderly woman in a pale blue parka holding a black Persian cat, a middle-aged couple with a collie, and a mother and her young son cradling a beige plastic cage. The cage is empty.

When Chris and Victor finally emerge empty-handed from the back corridor, Chris is holding Sambo's small red leather collar with its tinkling tags—a sound I know so well. He tells me he cradled and patted Sambo as the needle went in and that Sambo simply shut his eyes and went to sleep; he didn't even twitch. I can't stop crying. Chris and Victor both put their arms around me and we walk to the car together. We're told to return in a few weeks for the ashes, and we decide we'll sprinkle them with Mum's. Later, when I find tufts of Sambo's hair in his steel-wired brush,

I take it out to the frosted garden and put it in the wiry branches of the leafless forsythia bush for the birds. I hope they can use it in the spring to warm their nests. Maybe the squirrels will use it before then.

When I get home from the vet, I desperately want a bath. But Mum and Dad's bathtub doesn't hold water, the drain mechanism failing like so much else. Even though the lever still works, there's an imperceptible and steady leak. I take the flat rubber stopper from the kitchen sink and for the first time in memory have a bath lasting longer than five minutes.

I stand in my towel in Mum's bedroom and look out her window at the lake. It appears calm on the surface, but underneath I know it's doing some very strange things. There's a phenomenon on the lake called a seiche—a standing wave that sloshes back and forth in a vertical motion, getting slowly and suspensefully bigger, kind of like a mini-tsunami. It doesn't usually cause any damage, unless it gets really big—like the ten-foot one that hit Chicago in 1954 and swept eight fishermen to their deaths. But it's made me remember the recurring nightmare I used to have as a child.

In my dream, I'm standing with Mum and Dad and all the people of the town, silently facing the lake. Our line snakes along the shore, as far as the eye can see, in both directions. We're all holding hands, staring up in horror at a wall of water—a monster wave—that hovers over us at the shore. The whitecap on its lip foams and curls hundreds of feet in the air, threatening to crash down at any moment and drown us . . . but it never does. And nobody says a thing. I used to wake in a cold sweat and run to the window to check that the lake was still flat.

A Fate Worse Than Death

Dad developed forgetfulness fourteen years before he died. His short-term memory wasn't good at the best of times (he could never get our names straight), but the first hint that it might be more serious was when he began insisting on driving on the "British" side of the road and mistaking red lights for stop signs. He kept passing the driver's test, but it was a written test; they never took him out on the road. We children went to great lengths to have his driving license revoked, and it infuriated him. When we sold his car and asked for his power of attorney, he went ballistic.

Victor said to him, "But, Dad—what if you go completely gaga?"

"Then that, sir," roared Dad in his clipped British accent, "is a pleasure we shall have to enjoy when the time comes!"

Those "pleasures" came soon enough. At our next Sibling Supper, we put Dad's banking on our agenda. Dad—who had always run a tight ship and kept meticulous financial records—was going on spending sprees with his debit card.

He was walking two blocks to the bank every day just to have twenty dollars on hand when one of his favorite charities came knocking on the door. They were knocking with alarming frequency, as if his door had become their new ATM. It was also noted that Dad was going to the town hall and paying his annual land taxes—in full—every month. Unusual packages from the Publishers Clearing House started avalanching through the mail slot. Along with magazines, Dad was receiving clock radios and gold lockets—prizes proving he could still paste the right sticker on the right square when ordered to. Eventually his bank account ran dry.

Victor and I went to Dad's bank and asked them to create an "Alzheimer's debit card," something the bank—we found out—had never considered.

"We want an Alzheimer's account," said Victor to the teller. "You know . . . like a fake account . . . with only a little in it . . . maybe two hundred dollars."

"A fake account?" repeated the teller, blanching. "I'm sorry, sir, but the bank doesn't offer such a thing."

"Look," said Victor, "our father can't manage his finances . . . I have his power of attorney."

"Oh, well, then," she said and smiled, "we'll just give him a joint account with you . . . but he can't have a debit card. He'll need your signature whenever he withdraws funds."

"No, no, we don't want that!" I said. "We don't want Dad to feel like he has to come to us for permission every time he wants spending money. A debit card is his favorite thing! We just want to safeguard his money—don't you understand?"

But the teller's eyes had glazed over. "You'll have to speak to head office," she said.

And so it went—for weeks—until we finally found a friendly bank manager who was willing to bend the rules. Victor and I filled out reams of paperwork. We got Dad a lovely new debit card that he put in his wallet. We had all the household bills redirected to Victor's address and told charities that we'd send them Dad's annual contribution, but to please stop knocking on a weekly basis. So then Dad began redirecting his charitable giving to me.

I reported at our next Sibling Supper that Dad had gotten it into his head—about fifty years too late, in my opinion—that I could use some extra cash. Every time he saw me he'd put his arms around me and whisper in my ear, "You look like you could use some extra money, First Daughter—am I right?" Initially I demurred, but he looked so hurt when I turned him down that I realized he still needed to feel like a provider, so I began accepting his generosity.

"Thanks, Dad! That would help a lot!"

He'd smile with pride, immediately walk up to the bank, hand his debit card to the teller, and walk home with a twenty-dollar bill. It gave him such pleasure that I took it gratefully. Then I returned it to Victor, who redeposited it in Dad's account. Our fake Alzheimer's account was working like a dream—until the bank hired a new teller.

When Dad next walked in, she looked at her computer screen and said brightly, "Sir, my records show you have two accounts—this one, which doesn't have much money in it . . . and . . . wait a minute . . . yes—this second account, which has much more! It's costing you extra to maintain the two. Wouldn't you rather con-solidate them?"

"Oh, yes!" said Dad. "Thank you very much indeed!"

About this time, Dad took me aside privately to extract a promise. I was standing by my car, getting ready to drive back to Toronto, when he asked me to come into the garage. After fidgeting a bit, he said quietly, "I'm going gaga, you know."

"Yes, Dad, I know."

He looked down at his feet. "I've been to visit people in those places where they put people like me," he said, shaking his head. "They're horrible places!"

"It's okay, Dad, you don't need to worry."

"Oh, but I think I do, First Daughter . . . I don't want to go into one of those."

"You won't, Dad. I promise you. We won't send you anywhere."

I reminded Dad that we were well practiced in home care because of Sandy. Dad's head jerked up and his nostrils flared—a look I knew so well—and then the subtle sucking in of breath, the sound of his pulling himself together when emotion threatened to overwhelm him.

"I promise you, Dad," I repeated, "I promise you. You're going to stay right here until the day you die."

He grabbed me and hugged me for a long while and then thumped me hard on the back. "Thank you," he whispered into my ear.

I'd always hoped that, if there were any justice in the world, Dad's life would end in a more kindly fashion than it had begun; that instead of deprivation he'd have plenty, instead of grief and loneliness he'd be surrounded by love. I felt he had earned this. In fact, I felt he was still owed some—in God's books—on the plus side of the ledger.

Dad was only fifteen years old when the boarding school headmaster called him into his office. "I regret to inform you that your father has died," the headmaster said offhandedly. "To whom shall we send your bills?"

"I don't know, sir."

"What about your mother?"

"My mother is dead, sir."

"Blast!" said the headmaster.

Dad had been born into the British expat community of Oporto, Portugal, where his father was a partner in a shipping firm that exported wine to Canada. They lived in a grand villa overlooking the port on the River Douro, but when Dad was an infant his mother died and his father remarried. According to Dad, the new wife rejected the role of stepmother and issued an ultimatum—"It's me or the children"—so Grandfather sent Dad and his older siblings to England to live in a rented house with a hired governess, Miss Penfold. Dad saw his father only twice after that, and never saw his stepmother again. Ten years later, a tsunami off the coast of Newfoundland wiped out the uninsured shipping fleet and the family was plunged into bankruptcy. The stepmother had run off with the manager and Dad's father died of a heart attack.

Miss Penfold was the one who picked Dad up from boarding school. Creditors arrived at their rented house in England and stripped it of any furnishings worth selling. But Miss Penfold continued to make a home for Dad and his orphaned siblings, finding odd jobs to earn income. She remained a spinster and spent the rest of her life treating the children as her own. Dad carried her photograph with him everywhere.

Forced to leave school, Dad found work as an office boy in London. He bicycled to and from his rented room at a boarding-house, reading discarded newspapers from trash bins and studying for insurance exams at night. His one social activity—because it was free—was joining a rowing club on the Thames, although he denied himself the drink with his mates later at the pub: he couldn't afford it. When he was twenty he won the top prize from the Institute of London Underwriters, leading to a job with the New Zealand Insurance Company. They sent him overseas, to their Singapore office. But he wasn't there long before World War II broke out.

In 1939, at the age of twenty-four, Dad was mobilized into the Malayan Royal Naval Volunteer Reserve. In 1942, when Singapore fell to the Japanese, he made a daring escape with fellow officers in a small native sailing vessel. From Malaya they crossed the Indian Ocean and were rescued off the coast of Ceylon. After eluding Japanese dive-bombers, Dad would soon be introduced to Mum. They both believed their meeting was preordained; there were just too many coincidences.

They liked to tell the story of how, when Dad was rescued, the ship was prophetically called the *Anglo-Canadian*, piloted by a Captain Williams—no relation, but with the same last name as Mum's. Dad was then transferred to another ship called the *Duchess of Richmond*—the city where Mum was born. It was bound for New York City—where Mum was living. Dad was to have only a three-day layover before continuing to Europe, but his ship was unaccountably delayed. In a chance encounter, he met a fellow officer in an elevator who was on his way to Mum's apartment for a date with her roommate. He invited Dad to come along. Mum didn't want a date—she was in pajamas and hair curlers—but when she learned that Dad had been born on her father's birthday, she changed her mind.

Before Dad was diagnosed with Alzheimer's, he could remember all these events in great detail. Several books had been written about his famous escape across the Indian Ocean, and he took pride in correcting the authors' accounts by making notes in the margins of his editions. But in his final years, he wasn't sure who any of us were.

At the kitchen table, he would lean toward Mum, tap her on the elbow, and point across to Victor.

"Who is that young man?"

Irritated, she would say, "He's my son!"

"Really? How fascinating!"

Then he'd turn to me and say, "Did you know your mother had given birth to a son? She never ceases to amaze me!"

Other times, Dad would make Mum blush. He'd lean back in his chair, point to Mum, and say to me, "Look at that woman over there . . . the way the light catches her hair . . . Isn't she beautiful?"

Then two seconds later, he'd turn to Mum and ask, "Have you seen my wife?"

As time passed, our Sibling Suppers grew more urgent. We still shared our personal concerns about Dad and commiserated with each other about all the demanding, early-morning phone calls from Mum, but now we were entering a new phase. There were staffing requirements to consider and medical matters to understand. It wasn't just the latest information on Alzheimer's we had to learn and assess; now we had to worry about its effect on Mum. Living with Dad tested her patience to the limit. She craved intelligent conversation, but he was no longer capable of providing any. She worried about him all the time.

One weekend when I was staying with them, we were awakened after midnight by a commotion on the lakefront. We could hear loud voices and beer bottles being smashed on the rocks. Dad got out of bed and marched out the front door, wearing nothing but his sarong and slippers.

"For God's sake, stop him!" Mum said to me. "It's not like the old days—those kids could have weapons!"

I ran to the window on the second-floor landing and peered out. The loud voices had died down and I could see shadowy figures in the moonlight. Dad was quietly talking to the teenagers and I heard him say things like "clean up" and "noise" and "respect for other people." Then I heard him raise his voice.

"It's not 'Whatever'—it's 'Yes, sir!'"

"Yes, sir!" all the teenage voices repeated.

I turned to Mum and smiled. "We don't need to worry about Dad!"

I frequently spent weekends with Dad so Mum could have a break, but by Sunday night I felt like I was losing my mind. Mum was living with this on a daily basis, so I was surprised she was still sane. Of course, this was in question.

Dad's memory seemed to have completely lost its foothold. It slid all over the place. While he couldn't recall an event of five minutes earlier, he could recall an event of seventy years ago, in great detail. At Sibling Suppers, I described for the boys the drives Dad and I took together. Dad told me tales of his youth as if it were yesterday, simultaneously sprinkling those memories with the slogans he was reading off billboards and storefronts as we drove by. Sometimes he'd just recite license-plate numbers. It was a curious habit. Was it his way of anchoring himself in the here and now? I didn't know.

Once Saturday, in early summer, I thought if I could engage him in gardening it might help. He used to love it so much—especially his pumpkin patch. So I put him in the car and we drove to the gardening center.

"So, you want to plant persimmons, I understand?" asked Dad.

"No, we're going to plant pumpkins, Dad."

"Ah," he said, "I remember when I was eighteen . . . in digs in London. You know what 'digs' are?"

"Your old boardinghouse in 1932?"

"Exactly. There were ten of us. I was the only one who had a room to myself. Mrs. Goldsmith ran it. She had a daughter named Puck. It was in Streatham . . . and I had to walk about three miles to the tube to take me into the city."

This was the longest-running sentence I'd heard Dad make in weeks, so I tried to probe for more. With a bit of luck, he'd be on a roll.

"What was Puck like?" I asked.

"She had dark hair and I had a bit of a crush on her. Do you know Plum?"

"Who?"

"Plum . . . Do you know Plum?"

"*I am* Plum."

"You are?" He looked at me, surprised. "Oh, of course you are! *Black's Is Photography!* . . . Then who was that girl who was here this morning?"

"That was me."

"No, no . . . that other girl who looks like you."

"That was *me*!"

"Really? Does Plum have dark hair, too?"

"Yes." I sighed. "She does."

"Ford Econoline."

"So . . ." I said, trying to get Dad back on track. "What happened to Puck?"

"Puck Goldsmith?"

"Yep."

"She was killed . . . during the war . . . driving a truck. *Shoes for Less!* Did you ever marry?"

"Yes, I did."

"And who did you marry?"

"Don."

"Construction Ahead! . . . Any children?"

"Three."

"Three . . . really? Good for you! And where were you born?"

"In Virginia."

"I see . . . that was your mother's idea, was it?"

We finally arrived at the gardening center and I pulled into the parking lot.

"Can we buy persimmon seeds here?" asked Dad.

"Pumpkin seeds, Dad, pumpkins." I unhooked Dad's seat belt and helped him out of the car. He stood, unsteadily.

"Now," he said, "your mother gets back today?"

"Tomorrow." I closed the car door and took Dad's arm.

"Tomorrow's Friday, right?"

"Today is Saturday."

"And your mother comes back today?"

"Tomorrow." I looked up at the signs, looking for seeds.

"Now, let me get this straight." Dad was scratching his head. "You say today is Sunday?"

"No, no," I said. "Today is Saturday. Mum comes home tomorrow."

"She comes back Saturday?"

"Sunday, Dad! *Tomorrow.*" I was distracted, trying to find a shopping cart for Dad to hold on to, and I was no longer sure what day it was or even what my own name was.

"And she's been gone, what, about two weeks?" asked Dad.

"Two days, Dad."

Dad took me by the shoulders and looked me in the eyes. "Now," he said calmly, "I heard what you said, but it's been about ten days—right?"

"1 know it feels like that, Dad . . . it feels like that to me, too . . . but it's only been two days."

Dad looked up into the sky. "And she comes back when?"

"Shall we buy persimmons, Dad?"

"*Cadillac Seville!*" he said happily. "*Discover Ontario!*"

Watching over Dad always brought surprises. One day Robin and I had some important paperwork to attend to in the playroom, so we put Dad on the piano stool behind us, where he seemed content to stack and unstack the music books. Suddenly, we heard Liszt's "Liebesträume"—Dad's favorite, "Dreams of Love"—filling the air. We turned, startled, thinking someone had turned on the radio. But it was Dad's fingers racing along the keyboard, Dad's hands crossing back and forth, Dad's runs soaring and dipping flawlessly as if he were giving a recital—by memory. The music books were upside down on the stand. We hadn't heard him play like that in years.

As a child, I had the bedroom directly above the playroom and would fall asleep to the sounds of this piece filtering up through the floorboards as Dad played in private with the door closed. When I was too young to understand what he meant, Dad told me that playing the piano was like making love: one should stroke the keys gently.

I raced for the tape recorder. "Play it again, Dad!" I begged. "Play it again!"

But Dad only blinked. Whatever circuit briefly sparked a reconnection in his brain had flamed out. He went back to shuffling the music books.

Dad loved long walks, and despite the extra locks we put on the doors, his wandering became a chronic worry. For Dad, the local landscape was deeply ingrained. Like his piano playing, once he started on a familiar route, he rarely got lost. It helped if he had the dog on a leash: Sambo knew the way home. But despite Mum's vigilance, Dad began to elude her. Often he managed to take a train—we have no idea how—and find his way to my house in Toronto. This became an untenable situation for me because I ran a publishing business from home. Dad would show up in the middle of a deadline and I'd be forced to cancel meetings, drop everything, and drive him back home—a two-hour round trip. This was when we hired Pelmo to help with Dad during the day; she and her husband, Tashi, moved into the back of the house and Tashi commuted to his day job from there.

Occasionally, Dad got angry and lashed out, but we learned to exploit his long-term memory, resurrecting his Navy days during the war when discipline was key. Any time he'd try to raise his arm in anger, we'd say, "Sir! Do you have written permission from headquarters to do this?"

"No, sir!" he'd say.

"Then lower your arm, sir, if you don't have permission!" And like a dutiful officer, he'd obey.

As we passed the twelve-year mark, Dad became more and more depressed. With arthritic hips he could no longer take his lengthy walks, and without his fitness regime his spirits sagged: he described seeing heavy storm clouds where there were none. Even on sunny days the fog of what we now know to be Alzheimer's came rolling in relentlessly. Sometimes, Dad thought he saw crowds of people whispering in the bushes. "Who are they?" he'd ask.

It was clear that Mum was at her wits' end. Frankly, I don't know how she stood it for so long. I reported to the boys that at a recent church rummage sale Dad had plunked himself down in an antique rocker and gone to sleep. Mum couldn't rouse him, so in the end she just bought the chair for five dollars and left him there.

Unable to engage Dad in the arguments and lively political discussions that had been a staple of their marriage, Mum was now living with his repetitive, wistful bleats to go somewhere warm. Every day, Dad kept asking, "Bluebells, where are the bluebells?"—remembering, I suppose, the spring flowering of his English youth. We investigated respite facilities to give Mum a break, but they were expensive, so at one of our Sibling Suppers we cooked up a more creative plan. Instead of the twelve hundred dollars per week the respite facility was charging for a locked ward, we could send Dad on a weeklong Caribbean cruise— flight to Miami included! We reasoned that, on a ship, Dad could wander in a circle all day and never get completely lost. Of course, one of us would need to accompany him, so we drew straws: Victor got the short one.

I went shopping and bought Dad new clothes for the trip—a new swimsuit, two new shirts, a lightweight navy blazer, and pale linen trousers. We packed his silk cravats and gold cuff links, and one of his long cotton sarongs that he'd worn to bed every night since his days in the Orient. I wanted to pack his traditional English straw boater, but Victor nixed that idea and packed a cotton baseball cap—something Dad would have never knowingly put on his head.

Midway through the cruise, Victor called Mum from a pay phone in the Virgin Islands.

"How's your father?" she asked anxiously.

"I'll let him tell you himself," Victor said. "He's right here." Dad got on the phone. Mum asked if he was having a good time.

"Oh, indeed!" he said happily. "We've seen Hong Kong, Singapore, and all of South America. Right now we're flying over Brazil . . . we should be landing in London any minute!"

When he got back, Dad's eyes were dancing. "I guess you heard about the trip I had to Europe?"

"Yes!" I said. "Did you have a good time?"

"Marvelous! We saw all of Austria . . . went right the way round the Mediterranean . . . then shot through Gibraltar . . . and arrived back in Florida!"

"Really?"

"Oh, yes!" He paused. "Of course, I was left alone for a bit in Israel."

"You were?"

"It seems your brother wanted to see Greece . . . but we

managed to find each other again, so it worked out just fine." The following week, we held a Sibling Supper at a large Italian restaurant on the outskirts of town. We'd booked a quiet private table in the corner, but by the time Victor finished regaling us with stories about his trip we'd become so raucous that the maître d' had moved the four of us outside to a table in the courtyard. I asked Victor how he dealt with Dad in the cabin at night, to stop his wandering.

"I just locked the door and put a chair in front of it."

"And that worked?"

"Sure! Dad would reach for the door . . . find the chair . . . and just sit down."

"Was Dad this confused the whole time?" I asked.

"Yep," Victor said, "but he was happy! At the pool he spent all day going from one deck chair to another, folding and refolding everybody's beach towels!"

"Didn't anyone complain?"

"They tried to . . . but if a passenger came up to him, Dad would ask them how far we were from Borneo. So then they'd just blink and back slowly away. I heard one guy actually mutter, 'Oh, about eight thousand miles.'"

Victor couldn't stop laughing and by then neither could we. Our plates were bouncing, our wineglasses sloshing, and everyone in the restaurant was peering out at our table. All four of us were doubled over.

"But you know what I was thinking?" said Victor.

"What?"

"The rest of us only saw the Caribbean, but Dad saw the whole world—he had the cruise of a lifetime!"

It was the last holiday Dad would take.

———

Over the next five years, Dad became less and less mobile and eventually stayed upstairs, bedridden. I had relinquished his personal care to Pelmo; I told the boys I couldn't do it anymore—it was affecting Dad's dignity.

The last time I showered Dad, he had crud halfway up his backside. As I was hosing him down, he clung to the safety bar and said quietly, "I'm sorry, First Daughter . . . you shouldn't have to do this."

"It's okay, Dad, it's only a body—it's not you. I'm sure you did this for me when I was a baby, and I'm happy to do it for you."

But the truth was I wasn't happy to do it; it needed to be done and nobody else was there. I thought Dad was too far gone to notice, but it was clear he was having as hard a time as I was.

During his last few months a hospital bed was erected in my old bedroom, where Pelmo spoon-fed him and gently massaged his thin limbs with lotion. I made him a hospital gown in black flannelette with a white bib and bow tie to resemble his tuxedo, and he wore it whenever friends came upstairs to visit.

One night he was having difficulty swallowing, so the doctor sent a nurse to teach us how to hold Dad's head. She'd never been there before and I could tell from her expression that she was shocked by Dad's condition. His decline had been so gradual over so many years that we didn't see what she saw. He was almost a cadaver: he'd been so lovingly cared for, especially by Pelmo, that he'd reached an end point most people never reach while they're still breathing.

Chris was planning to spend the night, but he'd forgotten his toothbrush and so I volunteered to take his place. For the past decade I'd regularly kept a toothbrush in my glove compartment. Unable to get comfortable on any of the guest room mattresses, I had dragged a pillow and quilt to the living room sofa; then I changed my mind and went back upstairs.

"Dad?" I whispered into the dark. "I'm getting into bed with you, okay?"

He was lying on his side. I spooned in behind him, crinkling the plastic sheet and pressing my back against the metal rails, careful not to put any weight on his fragile bones. It was like being in bed with a tissue-paper bird.

I reached across his hip and searched for his fingers.

"I'm here, Dad," I said softly, "and I'm not leaving."

His eyes fluttered open, but he could no longer speak. His hand patted mine.

Outside the window, over the lake, the moon was a waning crescent. The only sound was the steady breathing of Mum's oxygen machine in the hall, its clear plastic tentacle snaking its way across the carpet and into her bedroom next door. It seemed to me incongruous that, after sixty-five years of married life, Mum and Dad were now separated by this thin blue wall—Dad ending up here and not there with her. How many times as a child had I lain in this room, listening to them making love on the other side?

Sometime after midnight, Sambo stumbled in from Mum's bedroom. I could hear the tags on his collar jingling.

"No, Sambo!" I whispered angrily, as I put him out and closed the door.

When I awoke, early-morning light bathed Dad's face with a translucent shimmer; his neck yearned upward and his cloudy eyes were wide open, but his body was stiff and cold. I hadn't even heard him take his last breath. I ran into Mum's bedroom.

"Mum?" I said softly. "I think Dad has died."

She lifted her head from the pillow and looked at me as though she was trying to get her bearings, but with no surprise. After fourteen years, Alzheimer's had finally stripped Dad of everything; she had said her good-byes long ago.

Sambo cocked his head up at me, and I wondered, Had he been the first to know? Had he come in at the exact moment of Dad's death, trying to say good-bye?

"Would you call Dr. Breen?" Mum asked.

When Chris and Victor arrived, they went into the snowy garden together and lowered Dad's flag to half-mast.

Just as I'd promised him in the garage all those years ago, Dad hadn't gone into "one of those horrible places." He hadn't died in a sterile environment with a background noise of bleeping machines, having his veins pricked every few hours by a nurse needing to check his vital signs. Dad had a different definition of a vital sign: he died peacefully in his own bed, with the gentle sound of the waves rolling across the lake.

Just as his firstborn son had done, sixteen years earlier.

After Dad died, so many people came up to me at his funeral to speak of his many kindnesses to them—events that didn't surprise me, but of which I had known nothing. I discovered that he'd inherited some Other Daughters and Other Sons, too. Dad's early deprivations might have hardened or destroyed most men, but they had served only to humble Dad. At his core he was firm and fair, always elegant and dignified, but he never took anything for granted.

He knew life was a crapshoot.

Appraisals

In April, the first appraiser I call is Mary McQueen from Whim Antiques. She's a specialist in silverware and I've dealt with her for years. Mary drives out from Toronto and sets up her little brass weights and scale on a long table in Mum's bedroom, where there's lots of natural light. A slim, elegant woman with silver-gray hair, delicate features, high cheekbones, and dancing eyes, she speaks with a lilting Irish brogue. Her specialty is eighteenth- and nineteenth-century English, Scottish, and Irish silverware, but she's brought extra reference books just in case. It takes her several days.

Throughout the first day, I bring Mary batches of silverware from the locked closet and lay it out on Mum's bed. Mary is able to distinguish sterling silver from silver plate just by lifting an item and noting its luster and patina. She shows me the difference: sterling has a delicacy and lightness to it. Some of the things I thought were sterling are only plated and vice versa. Mary examines each piece with her jeweler's loupe, looking for hallmarks.

Then she weighs it and documents it in her notebook. At the end of each day, I lock it all back up again. There are some surprises: we always knew that most of the pieces were old, having been handed down for generations on both sides of the family, but there are rare pieces from the seventeenth century, and many hallmarked by Tiffany. When we come to a fitted leather box holding a pair of serving spoons, intricately carved with raised flowers and fruit on their bowls, it still has the identifying tag from when Mum inherited them during the dispersal at Rokeby. Mum felt they were too valuable to use, but Mary just shakes her head.

"They would have been valuable," she says sadly, "if someone hadn't embellished them with all these flowers. People did this in the Victorian era and immediately devalued an otherwise fine pair of plain seventeenth-century spoons by a well-known maker."

It turns out Mum's diamond, emerald, and sapphire rings aren't worth very much, either—under the magnifying glass their stones are chipped and worn. Mum got good use out of them. I have a pang of regret when I see them. Why did I so callously reject them when Mum offered them to me? It's true that I have more rings than I can wear, but I don't have rings that remind me of Mum. I decide that I'll try to bid on one of them at the dispersal.

By the time Mary is finished, she's tired. She's gone full-tilt, without taking breaks, for three days. She tells me that most of the value is in the meltdown—the gram weight of the silver or gold, with nothing added for its beauty. I can tell this grieves her.

"These days, nobody wants something they have to polish," she says wistfully. "'Tis a pity."

The furniture is a similar story. I hire a furniture appraiser to come out for the day. He's a retired auctioneer from one of the well-known auction houses in the city, and we walk from room to room while I write down his estimates on my clipboard. He calls all of our mahogany and walnut antiques "brown furniture" and basically dismisses it with a wave of his hand as having no value at all.

"Nobody wants this stuff," he says. "They all want IKEA."

I can't believe it. I follow him around like a bleating lamb. "But this piece came from Mum's family in Virginia . . . it might have belonged to Martha Dandridge—George Washington's wife!"

"Doesn't matter," he says. "It's all the same—it's brown." He seems to have a favorite price in his head. "You might get five hundred dollars, if you're lucky."

When he gets to Dad's desk, I'm insulted. It's a handsome, early-nineteenth-century mahogany Sheraton secretary with hand-blown glass in its upper bookcase; we have the original documented provenance from when it was shipped here from Dad's family home in Portugal. It's museum-quality and in mint condition. When he gives it a value of five hundred dollars, I know something's not right—designer shoes cost more. He hasn't looked at anything closely or even picked an object up and turned it over to look at its joints. I decide he's nothing but a tired, disillusioned auctioneer who wants to go home to bed. Disappointed, I send him away and start a search for a new appraiser. This is taking longer than I thought. I consult Mary and she tells me about John Sewell, who writes a weekly column on antiques for the newspaper.

In mid-April, John Sewell arrives to give us a second opinion. Unlike the first appraiser, John is careful as he moves from room to room with me. He lifts up the pieces and examines their dovetailed joints. He dates each piece and points out details I'd never noticed before—like the handsome flared feet on Mum's Edwardian dresser. His values aren't high, since condition is everything and our pieces are well used, but they're significantly higher than the previous estimates. John acknowledges that old furniture, like silver, isn't fully appreciated by younger consumers; they'd rather own cheap modular pieces that fit into tiny condos. He figures it will take another generation before antique furniture is once again appreciated. "It needs a generation that hasn't seen it before," he says.

I can't believe people would rather have pressed sawdust and glue made with noxious chemicals instead of solid wood and square-headed nails, but without perceived value, it's no wonder all this stuff ends up in the thrift stores. I mark down the values John gives me for the purposes of the sibling dispersal, upload the photos to my computer, and label each one. I figure this task will take several weeks to complete, but I'm doing a little each day. We're planning to hold the dispersal right after Virginia's wedding in early June, when the whole family is here.

All of Mum and Dad's possessions—a lifetime of collecting and inheriting antiques—add up to one hundred thousand dollars. I spend another whole day at my computer, typing up the inventory. I add and double-check the numbers. It looks like we'll each get twenty-five thousand dollars to bid with.

We know what Dad spent because he kept meticulous records; the poverty of his youth had forced on him a lifelong habit of careful budgeting. We've found his ledgers—one for every year here—in which he recorded every purchase, down to the penny, and balanced his books each month. Moreover, the ledgers are written in his elegant, distinctive, cursive handwriting, which makes them works of art in themselves.

TOP: Mum and Dad's wedding in England, 1944.

CENTER: En route to the Far East by ship after the war to meet Dad for the first time, and with my amah, Ah Kan.

BOTTOM: Reunited in Hong Kong, 1947.

In 1952, Mum and Dad found a barn of a place overlooking the lake.

Dad began to shore up the exterior.

Mum named it Point O' View.

On Saturday evenings Dad rolled up the carpets and sprinkled wax so dinner guests could dance more gracefully across the hardwood floors.

Mum got all dressed up and Dad often wore his tux—even for my thirteenth birthday party in the dining room (*below*).

In winter, when the ice shelf formed on the lake and icicles hung from the windows, Dad taught us how to make newspaper fire logs as he carefully stoked the fire.

We frequently lined up after church for photos.

After Mum sacrificed Dad's vegetable patch for her pool, guests were invited to use bathing suits from the big wicker basket.

If we needed Mum, we could usually find her playing tennis.

In the summers we often drove south to visit Mum's family in Virginia.

Mum wearing her favorite red sunglasses, which were shaped like a pair of laughing lips.

Pelmo in her Tibetan ceremonial robes.

Mum always said she thought her purpose in life was to make people laugh . . . and here she surprises Dad with her Rudolph nose.

We held two weddings at the house after Mum died, and she ordered perfect weather for both.

In 1971, I wore Granny's wedding dress, which had been worn by many brides before me.

By 2010 the dress had disintegrated, so my daughter Virginia *(above, with her father)* started a new tradition.

We find an old lesson book from his school days, with instructions for practicing circular wrist movements. I remember watching him move his wrist rapidly with a flourish at the start of each sentence, before he even put pen to paper. And then we find Dad's record of our weekly allowances—the homemade "Wowance Book." There are fewer than twenty words to a page, nothing but a record of our childish signatures—nickled and dimed to death—but it's so laden with memories that it's worth its weight in gold.

Robin has been trying to interest secondhand dealers in the books but finds no serious bidders. Some of the ancient editions we possess are going for as much as two thousand dollars each on AbeBooks, but the only bid we get is from a dealer who offers to take our whole collection for two hundred dollars. When I Google "how to get rid of used books," I find all kinds of chat rooms full of people with the same problem. Helpful suggestions include taking a band saw and turning them into flower vases or bolting them together to make into chairs. An artist in the U.K. is turning books into stylish jewelry, and an international architect has even built an entire staircase out of used books that seems to spiral upward into infinity. Realistic suggestions include putting them out on the lawn with a FREE sign (just before garbage day), but another tells the bitter truth: "Forget it," the blogger writes, "the best thing is to burn them—it's cheaper than buying those fire logs."

We look sadly at Mum's prized leather-bound, twenty-three-volume set of Sir Walter Scott's Waverley novels, published in 1834; her six-volume set of Boswell's *Life of Johnson*, published in

1896; and the six-volume set of J. M. Barrie, circa 1900. The larger heavy volumes of *Century Dictionary & Cyclopedia*—that as children we were never allowed to touch—have now turned to sawdust, their gold-embossed, leather-tooled covers disintegrating in our hands. Books, it seems, are like our "brown furniture": nobody wants them. However, given the fifteen hundred percent rise in sales in e-books from last year to this, perhaps it won't be long before a generation comes along who's never seen a book before. Robin decides to take the best ones back to Virginia and stuff them into his scriptorium. Chris and Victor drive out one day and help cart the rest to the church rummage sale.

I ask Victor to look at the dining room ceiling—strange brown stains are appearing, and I worry that the overhead pipes might be leaking. But he dismisses this with an irritated wave of his hand.

"Those stains have been there for years!" he says. "Mum always thought they were coming from her bathroom, but the plumber says no."

"Are you sure?"

"Positive."

"Can we get a second opinion? I don't want the ceiling to cave in."

"Look," he says, exasperated, "I'm not about to investigate. If it's lasted a hundred years, it'll last another hundred—we're selling the place, remember?"

I don't need to be reminded. The longer I stay here, the more attached I'm becoming and the more I'm grieving the sale. Years from now we're going to wish we'd kept this house.

I have no sooner locked away our silver and china than I realize I can't continue to live in this house if it's denuded of knives and forks and cereal bowls. I need a second set of everything. So I hightail it over to the local thrift store to buy someone else's cast-off flatware to put in the empty drawers. I make the thrift store a weekly pit stop, to "fluff" the house for the real estate agents. Gradually, things in the house relinquish their hold on me. The new thrift-store pieces don't hold any memories—or, at least, the memories they hold aren't mine.

Pelmo and Tashi have returned from Tibet, bearing gifts from their homeland and moved back into their apartment at the back of the house. But they've been home less than a month when the world gets news of a devastating 7.1-magnitude earthquake in Tibet. It's the first such earthquake in the region in more than two thousand years, and the epicenter is where Tashi was born. It has devastated his village; he fears that more than ten thousand people have been killed. They hear that the orphanage Tashi's brother operates in the village was flattened, but luckily the children were outside and escaped unharmed.

Tashi wants to take donations back to Tibet for the children, so he and Pelmo spend every day driving back and forth to the Chinese consulate in Toronto, standing in line, trying to get a visa to go back, to take supplies of clothes and medicines— anything Tashi can scrounge from the community here. Finally, after several weeks, he's successful, but Pelmo's application has been rejected.

"They give only the visa if you born in village," says Pelmo.

"Dalai Lama, he not permitted also. Tashi go. I stay here and pray."

The devastating rubble on the other side of the world, with so many lives lost, makes me realize how insignificant our own rubble is here.

When the mail arrives, there's a letter from a cousin in Virginia. She's heard about my eulogy at Mum's funeral when I quoted Mum's story about the little gold pennies Grandfather handed out to train conductors, and she's found one in the pile of stuff she inherited. She encloses it for me in the envelope.

I remember the lake stone Pelmo found. *I am reaching for your hand. Please reach back.*

I take the penny out, thread it onto a gold chain, and wear it around my neck.

Buried Treasure

It is late April, almost three months since Mum died. The forsythia bushes are marking the transition from winter to spring. Naked, wiry branches surprise us with tight yellow buds and bright green leaves as they poke through the white wooden railings of the veranda.

The boys and I are sitting on the steps overlooking the lake, taking a break at the end of a long and exhausting morning. Robin has driven up from Virginia again to join Chris and Victor and me for a mini-reunion. This will be our first year alone, without parents.

Adult orphans.

Who were our parents? They are in everything we see around us, everything we touch, but did we really know them? Can we get to know them better by sifting through what they left behind, like forensic archaeologists? What does it all mean? It feels like we're wading through a pile of puzzle pieces, with no finished picture-guide on the lid of the box. I still want to know more—to turn the clock back to before our lives began, to who our parents were before. I've just found a home movie taken when they were in Curaçao, on a holiday without us . . . and they're holding hands!

We're about to tackle the one room upstairs I've been dreading: the trunk room. The cedar rafters of the steeply pitched ceiling give it the dry aroma of a sauna, and a small window at the back, shrouded in a spidery embrace, lets in a sliver of light. We have to crawl on our hands and knees to reach the corners. It's going to be a lengthy archaeological dig.

The room is stacked with yet more steamer trunks and wooden crates dating back generations. Scattered around them is the usual debris of a family—layered in circles, like the growth rings of a tree. The top layer reveals our most recent chapter: Dad's old metal walker and rubber-tipped walking canes, bags of Mum's oxygen tubing, a metal bedpan.

But underneath there are boxes of Halloween masks, bags of broken Christmas lights, old paintings, bunches of plastic flowers, chairs with missing rungs, shoeboxes of unsorted toys, sets of hard luggage, and—deep in the farthest corner—dozens of white plastic grocery bags, bulging and knotted.

I've been too afraid of spiders to reach into the deepest corners, so Chris drags everything out into the light and piles it in the upstairs hall. He finds a shoebox of assorted papers and brings it down onto the veranda. He sits on the top step in the sun, scans through the pile, and then hands the whole box back to me.

"Here," he says. "You can trash all this."

Irritated that he seems to be motoring through tasks in such a casual manner while I'm drowning in detail, I shake one of the envelopes. Out falls a letter on Buckingham Palace stationery written by Princess Elizabeth to Grandmother in 1947. She's writing to thank her for a contribution to one of her charities.

I wave it victoriously. "See?"

"Omigod."

"You almost threw it away!" Then I listen to myself—it doesn't take much for me to revert to childhood, the bossy older sister. Later in the afternoon, Chris brings down an old black-and-white photograph in an easel frame.

"Ever seen this?"

It is the figure of a young girl wearing a checkered shirt and bib-front overalls with white ankle socks and tennis shoes. Her dark, wavy hair is held back from her face with a hair band. She's sitting on a chintz-covered sofa, head tilted, with an impudent smile on her face. One elbow is on her knee, her hand cupping her chin; the other hand is clutching a stuffed canvas sailor's bag between her legs. She seems to be saying, "You're not leaving *me* behind!" She looks about ten years old.

"She looks so . . . familiar," I say. "Is it Mum?"

"No, I think it's you!" says Chris.

I study the photo. Wouldn't I know? The sofa looks like the same one we still have here, but there are shuttered windows in the background and it's the wrong era; the clothes are from the twenties. I place the photo on the table in the downstairs hall, and every time I walk by I think, *I know you . . . but who are you?* I send a copy to every relative I can think of: "Do you know who this is? Is this your mother, your roommate, your cousin?" Nobody knows.

Chris brings down more stuff, including a small wooden jewelry box with a painting of Rokeby on the lid.

"Remember this?" he says.

"Aunt Mickey painted those for everybody!" I open it and find an old postcard from the motel we used to stop at in Trout Run, Pennsylvania—the halfway point.

During the summer holidays, when school got out, we didn't explore Canada the way our friends did. We didn't have a cottage in Muskoka or Georgian Bay. The landscapes of the Group of Seven—droopy pines; choppy lakes; barren, windswept rocks— were unfamiliar to us. In the summer we always drove south.

We packed up the station wagon and drove to Virginia—to my mother's clan, a place of cattle farms and racehorses, stately white-columned mansions, rolling green hills, and the scent of box bushes and honeysuckle. It took two days to drive down Route 15 in ninety-degree heat, with no air-conditioning. Our luggage was strapped to the roof rack and we took turns sitting shotgun in the rear. I listened to the boys playing I Spy or reading the alternate Burma Shave signs erected every few miles alongside the highway (SHE PUT A BULLET . . . THRU HIS HAT . . . BUT HE'S HAD CLOSER . . . SHAVES THAN THAT . . . BURMA SHAVE) and crying that they had to pee. Dad would never stop.

When we passed the roadside shop that sold confederate flags and GUNS! GUNS! GUNS! ("Stop, Daddy! Stop . . . Awww- www"), I knew we were nearly there. As the smells of pungent cow manure and freshly cut hay began to drift through the open windows and the high-pitched whine of cicadas sounded like electrical wires humming in the heat, I knew we had arrived.

Rokeby was the 350-acre estate outside Fredericksburg, where Mum and her seven siblings had spent their own childhood sum- mers. Mum's brother George and his artistic wife, Mickey, ran the farm after Granny died, and despite having four little chil- dren of their own, they generously opened their arms to us. The grand, Federal-style antebellum house, with its white-columned portico and wide screened-in veranda, sat high on a hill, commanding views of the surrounding Rappahannock Valley. Nestled in among the magnolia and dogwood trees were acres of daffodils and narcissus, a boxwood maze, and a two-room children's playhouse. Wild asparagus grew around the tennis court and plump figs could be plucked from the tree outside the kitchen door near the swimming pool.

A self-contained oasis, Rokeby had its own gas pump and water tower, and a whole dusty barnyard to investigate—with chickens and cows and tractors and hay wagons—and a tool shed that smelled of sawdust and oil, filled with every imaginable spare part. There were horses to ride and a pony named Stonewall that we hitched to the wagon to trot down the half-mile back entrance to the Comorn Post Office. On any given day there could be a slew of aunts and uncles sitting in wicker rockers and a dozen children to play with, most of us first cousins, more or less the same age.

The high-ceilinged kitchen was always hot and steamy, with the aroma of juicy tomatoes baking in brown sugar or sizzling with cornbread and bacon. Each morning the cook left breakfast in silver chafing dishes on the mahogany sideboard in the dining room and cousins would drift in from farm work or tennis or swimming, dragging dust across the wide-plank floors.

On hot summer nights, while the adults sat on the veranda discussing world events, tinkling the ice of their mint juleps in frosted silver cups, the children moved onto the sleeping porch. In this screened-in dormitory above the portico, older cousins, in a row of metal beds, told ghost stories until we all fell asleep. We clutched Mason jars full of lightning bugs and listened to the mantel clock snoring at the top of the back staircase.

Each Sunday the whole family piled into the wood-paneled station wagon and bounced down rutted dirt roads to the small country church, where mothers in straw hats and flowered dresses cooled themselves with cardboard fans that had Bible verses printed on the front and ads for funeral parlors on the back.

The South was a culture steeped in history. I learned what it meant to be American—the "can-do" spirit of inventiveness and ingenuity—and tried to crack the particular code of diplomacy spoken by our Virginia cousins. Mum was a renegade, and before she was twenty she'd escaped north to Bennington College in Vermont—a hotbed of feminism and liberalism. I was used to my mother speaking her mind, but in Virginia few women were forthright: they were unfailingly polite and well mannered, so I never knew what they were thinking.

I look more closely at the painting of Rokeby on the lid of the box. Wouldn't Aunt Mickey love to know we still treasured this?

"There's more!" says Chris, and he unwraps a framed watercolor, painted by Dad. We'd forgotten he had this artistic talent, since his was always overshadowed by Mum's. It's a lake scene with loons, painted at his cottage on Lake Kashwakamak in eastern Ontario. When the youngest boys were teenagers and we'd stopped driving to Virginia every summer, they helped Dad erect a small cottage on the property, later adding a spider-infested bunkie. The cottage was Dad's getaway, where he learned to truly relax, but Mum never liked to go. She called it "a godforsaken place."

In another one of the trunks, we find that Mum has carefully saved a number of magazines. I knew she hadn't saved the 1952 issue of *McCall's* because of its article on new kitchen color schemes; it was more likely the article titled "How Much Does

Your Husband Annoy You?" There's also a 1948 issue of *Business Week* with her brother Langbourne on the cover.

Dad, meanwhile, has saved the *Illustrated London News*, complete editions of *The Globe and Mail* with headlines like BRITONS CONQUER EVEREST and CHURCHILL DEAD, and forty years' worth of *National Geographic*—enough to insulate the greatcoats of the entire Royal Navy.

What do we do with all these historical primary sources? Not even the library wants them. I decide to stack them throughout the house, on bedside tables and coffee tables, for visiting guests to peruse over the summer, but I know I'm only postponing the inevitable. The next afternoon I hear Robin yell from the playroom—"*Yahoo!*"—and I run in to see what new treasure he's unearthed.

For decades, sitting on top of Dad's gray metal filing cabinet in his library, there's been what we've always referred to as "the old tin trunk." A watertight black metal sailor's box, about twenty inches square with a hinged lid, it has our great-grandfather's name stenciled in gold paint on the front.

Robin holds out a flimsy brown notebook. Scrawled on the front are the words KOLEK TOMDJOENG SEDERHANA SASAK 50.82 KM. 17.93T.

"What is it?" I don't even recognize the language. Dutch? Javanese?

"The original logbook of the *Sederhana Djohanis* . . . the fishing boat Dad commandeered in Padang, when he escaped from the Japanese!"

We flip through the pages in amazement. The first few pages are recorded in an unknown hand of her original native crew, documenting routine trips up and down the coast of Sumatra, picking up cargo. It's all in Dutch, each page signed by a port master and officially stamped. But ten pages in, I recognize Dad's handwriting.

On March 5, 1942, he's commandeered the boat and begins to meticulously record their escape voyage, day by day. He lists the names of all the men on board with him, and we see that one of the officers is Major Geoffrey Rowley-Conwy—Lord Langford from Wales—the man Mum telephoned just before she died. Dad has recorded each man's duties and what his intentions are ("to avoid capture by Japanese; to proceed up coast using land breezes until latitude of N.E. Monsoon, with which we could cross Indian Ocean to Ceylon"). When Dad wrote all these words in pencil, he was only twenty-six years old and had no way of knowing what a harrowing thirty-seven days at sea he was about to endure—surviving Japanese strafing, high seas, limited rations, and little water—nor that fate was guiding him across the Atlantic Ocean to New York City, where he would, by chance, meet Mum. Even more miraculously, photos exist of Dad and other officers on board the *Sederhana*. Dad has a beard and looks half starved, more like Errol Flynn than Cary Grant—but who thought to bring a camera . . . plus film . . . in the rush to escape?

I scan the pages and send the whole file off to an online site called Treasure-Book, in Vancouver. Two weeks later, four replicas of the *Sederhana* logbook are returned in the mail—we all want a copy.

While Chris continues to excavate the trunk room, Robin, Victor, and I dig into the old tin trunk—the careful repository of Dad's family history.

We'd heard stories about Dad's great-great-grandfather George, born in 1792 in England. He was captured at sea by the

French during the Napoleonic Wars when he was only thirteen. For the next eight years—until he was twenty-one—he remained in various French prisons, carving the ship out of wood and bone that Mum bequeathed to Robin in her will. During our lifetime this ship always sat on the tall dresser in the upstairs hall. George kept a diary, and that's here, too, tucked into his original leather wallet.

Written on hand-stitched paper, it details his many escapes and recaptures, and the distances he walked between prisons. We turn it over in our hands—amazed to think we're touching something that George once touched in 1805. He was condemned to death but pardoned by Napoleon in 1813, and we find his handwritten safe-conduct passport, signed and stamped by Napoleon's minister of war.

But even more intriguing are the documents we find relating to George's son, William—about whom I had known nothing. William eventually became a sea captain, like his father. On a voyage from Liverpool to Cape Town in 1842, he disappeared off the coast of South Africa when he was only twenty-two years old. Official accounts claim he was "lost at sea," but it's a mysterious tale, and we find scores of original documents that cast doubt. We take a batch out to the veranda and read through them. There are copies of records from Lloyd's Shipping Register, insurance claims, cargo lists, and, more importantly, family letters and eyewitness accounts.

On a foggy morning in March 1843, a local eyewitness, walking along the beach on Saldanha Bay near Cape Town, spots the 242-ton ship *The Conservative* foundering offshore with all its sails set. Two of its three rowboats—in good condition and "with not a drop of water in them"—have washed ashore. Suspiciously, however, the ropes on one of the boats appear to have been intentionally cut and . . . the third boat is missing. The eyewitness organizes a search party, but once aboard ship, they find it curiously empty. There is no sign of a struggle, no dead bodies, no baggage, and no provisions except for "a piece of cold meat in the pantry and the men's hammocks hanging forw'd." They also find a woman's petticoat.

A woman's petticoat?

William is unmarried . . . I love this part!

Over the next three months a search party hunts for any bodies washed ashore along the coast, but none is ever found and eventually the whole crew is presumed lost at sea.

It seems odd to us now, in our age of fast travel and instant communication, that a family wouldn't investigate further, but it appears from his letters that George accepted the disappearance of his son with resignation and despair. My imagination goes into overdrive and I find myself wondering, What if William was kidnapped? What if he was sold into slavery? What if we have Arabian cousins in Timbuktu? This is a slice of family history the grandchildren will love, and I put the letters aside to scan. I have a special file for these stories—anything that smacks of romance or mystery is going to be turned into another treasure book.

Chris shoulders through the screen door, his arms full of white plastic grocery bags.

"Where'd you find those?" asks Victor.

"In the back of the trunk room!"

As he dumps them on the wicker chair, fat beige envelopes and small blue airmail letters sift out onto the yellow cushion in the fading afternoon light.

"What are they?"

"Letters Mum and Dad wrote to each other . . . hundreds of them!"

The plastic bags are in the final stages of decomposition; they fragment into filmy confetti as we grab for their contents. The tiny white polka dots stick to our fingertips and cling with static to our clothes.

Robin flaps open a letter postmarked NEW YORK CITY, 1942.

"Here's one that Mother wrote to Grandmother, telling how she met Father when the war started."

Dearest Mum, I know you probably think I've lost my mind, but it's only my heart!

"She writes that she's been out dancing every night and is already in her nightclothes, but this British officer needs a blind date, so she and her roommate flip a coin and Mother has to go."

Alec came to the door in his Navy Lieutenant's uniform and you know what he did? He handed me his cap! Can you beat that? So I threw it on the floor and said, What do you think I am—a hat rack?

We all burst out laughing—it sounded so like Mum.

Robin points to the page in his hand. "Yes, and then she writes that Father 'looked so surprised'!"

"Wait a minute," I say. "Go back . . . she actually writes 'Alec' and not 'Alex'?"

"Uh-huh."

"That's so funny. She got his name wrong from the beginning!"

"May I continue? This is a twenty-six-year-old American working girl falling for a British naval officer."

"Confiding to her mother," I point out, with a twinge of envy.

*We spent the weekend together and on Wednesday he asked
me to marry him!*

"Whoa . . . wait a minute . . ." Victor says. "Mum and Dad only knew each other for one week before they decided to get married?"

Chris laughs. "That explains a lot!"

"Like why she hoped the American Red Cross would send her to England," I say.

Robin continues reading: *These last 10 days have been worth
anything that may happen in the future . . .*

"That's a good thing," I say, wondering if all war brides felt that way.

From 1942 to 1946, Mum and Dad wrote to each other almost every day, and Mum wrote to her mother every week. Miraculously, hundreds of these letters got saved. Some are ten pages long. We've each got our laps full of airmail paper, trying to read and listen at the same time, interrupting each other—so typical.

Chris says, "Here's one when Mum was stationed in Devon at Knightshayes Court, in the converted manor house of Lord and Lady Amory. She's writing to Dad in Sumatra."

I picture Mum in a grand hall with a marble fireplace and

gilt-edged mirrors, now converted into a Rest Home for convalescing American Air Force pilots. Mum was in charge of entertainment.

"It's typed on American Red Cross letterhead."

"She took her typewriter to war?" I say.

"Yes!" says Robin. "Along with her fur coat, high heels, and hot water bottle. I remember she told me that."

"I thought they were supposed to pack light . . . and take only what they could carry!"

"Uh-huh, those were the rules, but since when did Mother follow rules? She figured a troop ship would be full of men tripping over themselves to carry her luggage, and she was right—that's exactly what happened. Especially since she was the only one wearing high heels!"

My darling Lackee: Ambo Sayo Baye Beenee! . . . Lord &
Lady Amory were over last nite & I asked them WHY the
British have such a custom of segregating the males &
females at dinner parties? Women leave, while the men
drink Port till they're wheeled off unconscious to bed by their
butlers. They're known as "1-2, or 3-bottle men" depending
on their capacity . . .

"Hold that sentence!" says Robin. "I need more bourbon." He heads indoors, tinkling ice cubes in his empty glass.

"I'll be the two-bottle man!" I say, and follow him into the pantry for a new bottle of pinot grigio. When we return, Chris has flipped his page over.

"Mum's back to the Battle of Britain now—she's describing Germany's invasion."

Sir John said he went grouse shooting in Scotland &
complained about the German strafing because they had to
quit hunting for half an hour. He glanced at the newspaper
headlines: "129 Shot Down!" & calmly remarked,
"Hmmm—a bit more than we got grouse!"

"I reckon Mother was having a bit more fun than Father," says
Robin. "This one says Knightshayes Court even had its own golf
course on the front lawn."

"Here's a nice, loving ending," says Chris.

It is now late evening—peaceful & still—with only the
singing of the birds & bleating of sheep to break the
silence—and of course my longing for you which seems to
reverberate from every distant hilltop.

"They were married by then—right?" asks Victor.

"Yep, but they didn't really know each other."

"Go back a page," says Victor, "and reread that bit for Plum
about Mum writing a book."

"Mum wrote a book?"

"Not exactly . . ." Chris looks at me with a raised eyebrow.
"She was delegating again—she gave Dad the title and told him
to write it!"

Now that we've found all these letters, not to mention the
bins and boxes of loose photographs, the task of clearing out the
house feels much more daunting. There's much more at stake—
our whole family's history. There's no time to read them all.
We've got to put them into some kind of order.

Robin and I buy hundreds of acid-free plastic sleeves, and over the next ten days he sleeves Dad's historic documents in the playroom while I sleeve Mum's letters in the dining room, sorting them into piles chronologically. We don't separate the pages of letters; we slip the whole letter, plus the envelope if there is one (to preserve the postmark), into one sleeve. We're focused and committed, working methodically in our separate rooms. Occasionally I hear Robin grunt, or slam a file drawer, but it feels like we're working on an assembly line in a factory.

Each afternoon we take a break for a glass of wine on the veranda. I have a cigarette and Robin has a thin cigarillo. The smoke hangs in the hot humid air like a halo over my head and fights to escape the tangle of Robin's gray beard. Then it drifts out over the railings into the garden as we reminisce about our childhood.

We both dress for dinner, as Mum and Dad would have done on special occasions. Well, not exactly . . . It's more like we're putting on plays in the basement fifty years ago. Instead of Dad's tuxedo, Robin wears his short Scottish argyle jacket in Lovat blue that matches his eyes, his plaid kilt with its sporran, and his ivory-colored hose, cuffed at the knee, with a fountain pen stuck in it. "The pen is mightier than the sword!" says Robin, when I ask him what his pen is doing there.

Instead of Mum's pale green satin evening dress, I wear Dad's freshly cleaned British naval officer's uniform—black, with gold braided stripes on the sleeves of the double-breasted jacket. It fits me perfectly. Dad was only twenty-eight years old when he last wore this.

We lay the table with care. Even though I'm using the thrift-store silverware, I remember Dad's attention to detail: the proper number of forks and knives, depending on what we're serving; dessert spoons at the top facing left, forks underneath facing right unless our guest is left-handed (in which case they're reversed); condiments in small glass bowls, each with a proper curved-handled spoon. The only things missing are the crested silver napkin rings—they've been locked away.

After dinner, Robin takes one of Dad's gnarled wooden walking sticks, puts on his Scottish Glengarry cap with its ribbons hanging down the back, and we go for our evening hike. We walk with a bounce in our step—the "Family Stride"—as we march west along the lakefront, north on Navy Street, and back along the main street, inspecting Oakville as we used to do all those years ago with Dad. I can't help looking for litter; the only difference now is that I don't pick it up. But I still hear Dad's voice: "Pick that up! Treat this town like your living room!"

One evening, as we're walking onto the pier, three teenage girls in black puffy jackets, black tights, and UGGs on their feet pass us, stop, turn around, and run back.

"Excuse me," they say to Robin, "but aren't you somebody famous?"

"I might be!" he says, as he bows courteously and tips his cap to them.

We walk on as they giggle and run away. I overhear words like "Gandalf!" and "the actor in *Harry Potter*!"

Robin shrugs. "I get this all the time, but in Canada it's usually Farley Mowat."

The next day, back in the dining room, I've finally finished sorting Mum's letters. They fill twenty-three binders, bulging with airmail paper. Her life is literally laid out in front of me—

the most valuable things in the house to me now—but I can't start reading yet. There's too much else to do.

Robin has found, among Dad's letters, a collection of small pocket diaries. They're bound in golden brown calfskin and each has a tiny pencil slotted into the spine. In one diary, 1946—the year I was born—I see Dad has scrawled across my birth date, "Received cable—eldest daughter born!" I always thought he wanted only sons, but here is my first hint that he expected more daughters. When he recorded my birth in this diary he was on a ship in the South Pacific. Mum was in Virginia, preparing to join him in Hong Kong. I turned out to be his only daughter, but he called me First Daughter the rest of his life. In the Far East, this is a sign of respect.

From the postwar years in the Far East, I find a pocket dictionary published by *The China Mail* in Hong Kong titled *Useful Cantonese Words and Phrases for the Visitor and the Resident.* Thumbing through its pages, I'm shocked by phrases like "This bathroom is not clean!" and "Who broke this plate?" and "You always tell lies to cheat me!" Given the context, even innocuous phrases like "What are you looking at?" take on a more sinister interpretation. Mum couldn't have used it with our amahs—could she?

And then suddenly, as if fate has guided my hand, I find evidence of my first amah, Ah Kan. Tucked inside Mum's 1952 passport is a letter and a photo. All my life I've been searching for details of her, and here she is.

My full name is Leung Kan Hoi, aged 32, native of Nan Hoi, Kwangtung. I first came to H.K. in 1938. I am very glad to hear that you, Master and the children . . .

It seems Ah Kan was missing me, too, and wanted my parents to sponsor her to Canada. She must have been twenty-nine years old when I was wrenched from her arms at dockside, and by now would be almost ninety, probably dead. But I'm thrilled to find this. I think again about the writing on the lake stones. Can we reach that far back?

Thank goodness people wrote letters. When I recently taught a university English course, I discovered that none of my students under the age of twenty-five had ever received one; two remembered receiving a postcard; and one thought he'd seen his father's handwriting—on a check. They could hardly recognize a full sentence; all my students text-message. What's going to happen to all our histories if computers crash? What happens when software formats change? Storing things is one thing, retrieving them a whole other matter—a lesson we learned with Dad's Alzheimer's. These days I take more photos than ever before . . . but they're stored on my hard drive, so who sees them? I'm certain my great-grandchildren won't. All the so-called letters my son and I have exchanged from abroad have been e-mails—which I can no longer access now that I've upgraded to new hardware. With computers, the more we think we've preserved, the more we may have lost.

I decide to make a photo album of the interior of the house. I want to record every detail before we lose it all. With my camera, I take a close-up of the dining room wallpaper, the hole in the upstairs window screen, the white porcelain doorknob on the door to the basement, the latch on the back door, the wicker mail basket, the crack in the chimney plaster, the drawer pulls in the pantry. When I interrupt Robin in the playroom and get down on my hands and knees to photograph the scratchy paw marks at the base of the double doors, left there when Dad locked the dogs inside for barking too much, he looks at me quizzically.

"Don't mind me," I say. "I'm just recording Sambo's paw prints for posterity."

"And Scrappy's and Buffy's and Jenny's and Winnie's . . . ," Robin reminds me. "And if you look a little higher up, you might even find mine!"

Later in the day, even though it's wintertime, I take all of Mum's identical skirted bathing suits from the basket in the basement and hang them on the laundry line outside so that I can take a picture of them, too.

I get the feeling my brothers are worried about me. I sense they've been having telephone conversations behind my back, because Victor's been making pointed remarks about my state of mind a little too often. He's all puffed up with confidence when he delivers them, as if he has the authority of a crowd behind him. Maybe I *am* going off the deep end, but how would I know? What I'm doing just feels right. I feel responsible for our memories. I don't want them to disappear into thin air.

Tonight I lie awake, listening to all the familiar sounds of the wildlife settling down in the walls—the scrabbling of tiny feet above and below me—and the sound of the waves and the wind predicting what the weather will bring tomorrow. It sounds like it's going to be a clear day for Robin's drive south. He's sound asleep in his old bedroom next to mine.

The next morning I come downstairs in the semidarkness and pull back the curtains in the same manner as Dad once did— first the curtains on the long row of windows facing the lake in the living room, then the street side, then the dining room. I love the sound of the tiny wheels scraping along on their metal tracks.

The sky is slate gray, with fingers of apricot clawing across the horizon. Even in the time it takes me to open the curtains, the apricot is winning and the gray is brightening to white. The lake is dead calm, with shimmering patches of robin's-egg blue striped with bands of navy.

A lone bird is chirping. As the sun lifts its head other birds start chattering, and when it pops fully formed over the horizon there's a cacophony of birdsong, pitching higher and louder, rising in a crescendo as if in concert, applauding the sun. Now the horizon turns silver—so bright the reflected light hurts my eyes—and the sky is breaking into high clouds shaped like fish scales, picking up speed, swimming eastward. It's a scene I have all to myself, much the way Dad must have had it before we all stumbled noisily downstairs.

I go to unlatch the veranda door and pass by the framed picture of the impudent girl. She's like a phantom limb—something connected to me, but missing. I keep whispering, "Who are you?"

To my surprise, the door's already unlatched and Robin is coming up the veranda steps, swinging Dad's old walking stick. He looks windswept and his cheeks are flushed pink.

"Where have you been so early?"

"Up the high street," he says. "Nobody's awake."

As he passes the picture beside me, he takes his hands and forms a frame around the girl's face, blocking out her hair.

"This looks so much like Carter that it has to be you!" We both laugh—the resemblance is uncanny—but it's not me.

We share a fast cappuccino and toast in the kitchen before Robin gets in his car for his twelve-hour drive home. As he lugs his suitcase out the boathouse door, he tells me not to give away the garden bench—he's made arrangements to donate it to the

Oakville Museum. Then he spies Dad's fire-escape ladder—the fat coil of sisal rope I've put aside for the garbage—and he's so viscerally affected that he heaves it into the backseat of his Volvo.

"I think I'll rescue this," he says.

"Just a sec," I say. "Let me take a picture of it first."

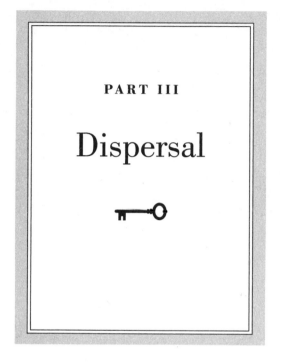

PART III

Dispersal

Two Weddings and a Funeral

Virginia calls me in early May. She's started to plan her wedding—four weeks hence.

"Is it really as simple as you say it is?" she asks.

I tell her I think so, but then I had Mum as my wedding planner, who brought her relaxed nature to bear. My reception was at home and the whole affair was potluck. When I asked Mum how many people I could invite, she was generous.

"Invite as many people as you want!"

"No, no, I mean how many people will fit in the house?"

"Don't be so silly," she said. "There's no limit . . . if guests arrive and it's too crowded, they'll walk home and come back later!"

"What if it rains?"

"They'll bring umbrellas!" she said. "For goodness' sake—trust people's intelligence!" And sure enough, my photo album shows the lawn covered by a rent-free canopy of multicolored umbrellas. Neighbors brought casseroles, a friend made my wedding cake, my bridesmaids and I picked flowers from a neighbor's garden, and everyone but the bride walked to the church . . . so no limousines were required. Dad proudly drove me in his newly waxed Volvo.

I remind Virginia that there's another precedent she could consider. Her brother, Carter, and his bride, Diana, married a year ago using the postmodern idea of a "public elopement." They flew from Turkmenistan to Las Vegas, where they married in the Chapel of the Flowers. The whitewashed ceiling was studded with video cameras and we were all given a website to attend via a live-stream video link. There was no limit to the number of guests they could invite—the whole world could attend, uninvited.

Pelmo had trundled Mum and her oxygen tank to the back of the house to watch on her computer, and I'd stayed home in Toronto and watched in my pajamas.

Diana wore a purple dress and Carter carried the bouquet. After their vows, Carter kissed his bride, waved at the camera, and said, "Hi, Mom!" I was transfixed . . . sucked through the screen. It was better than watching *The Bachelor*.

Later that night when I phoned Mum and asked how she liked it, she said, "Oh, it was wonderful! Especially the bride's white dress . . . but who was that chubby man standing next to her?" It turns out Pelmo had clicked the wrong link and Mum had watched the wrong wedding, but that hadn't dampened her enthusiasm. Las Vegas offered digital photographs of Carter and Diana, so we downloaded one for Mum. It slid out of the printer with the word PROOF smacked across their foreheads.

Virginia decides to use Mum's relaxed model for her wedding to Louis, except I remind her that the guests who brought casseroles to mine in 1971 are probably not on her guest list. Jessica steps in like a good sister and volunteers to bake the wedding cake. In Mum's desk drawer we unearth a pile of leftover engraved invitations from my wedding and discover that the date is the same, so for a moment Virginia even considers crossing out her father's name and mine and recycling them. Later in the week, she chooses a caterer in Oakville purely because of its name: Plum Catering. Luckily, it turns out to be an inspired choice. A week later, she calls me again.

"Hi, Mum," she says. "Are you able to meet Jessica and me at a store next Tuesday night?"

"Sure . . . what for?"

"I think I should buy a wedding dress."

Of course! How could I have forgotten this small item? I'd worn Granny's, an antique silk-and-satin relic from the post–Civil War era. It had so many hooks and straps inside it that it took three of my brothers, with their combined high-school-cadet-uniform experience, to buckle me in. The puffed-sleeve bodice was delicately ruched in silk chiffon. The heavy satin skirt was the color of candlelight, splashed down the front with the faint stain of hot chocolate accidentally spilled there on a beautiful spring day in 1898. None of the subsequent brides had had the heart to remove it; instead, they'd embroidered their names around the inside of the hem. Most of the females in the family had worn this dress except Mum, who couldn't risk shipping it to England on a troop ship during wartime. She'd worn a white Confirmation dress. Virginia would have happily worn either of these dresses, but they'd both disintegrated long ago.

I drive into the city and find the bridal store in downtown Toronto. Jessica is waiting inside the doors, but Virginia arrives late. When she finally dashes in, the bridal consultant smiles broadly.

"When is your big day?" she asks Virginia.

"June fifth."

"Next year?"

"No," says Virginia, "this year."

The consultant takes a step back and gasps. "In four weeks? Most people plan a year in advance!" She waves toward a small rack near the door. "Those are last year's samples," she says. "If you can find something there, we can help you; otherwise, I'm afraid . . ." Her voice trails off and she wanders away, as if she's got better things to do.

Virginia rifles quickly through the rack, chooses three, and we head upstairs to the dressing room. She dashes behind the curtain and comes out in the first one, ruffled top to bottom in white feathers that make her look like the lead ballerina in *Swan Lake*. When she sees herself in the mirror, she giggles and does a perfect death dive onto the floor, head down and arms outstretched. The second one is a one-shoulder pleated affair that looks like a Roman toga, and we all roll our eyes. But the third one is perfect. It's a strapless, form-fitting sheath of heavily encrusted handmade lace that could easily last into future generations. The moment she steps out we all yell, "Yes!" We slap down several credit cards and run next door for a cosmopolitan. Saying yes to the dress has taken less than half an hour.

The house will be gussied up in time, too. Chris has been diligent about getting the painting quotes, and now a team of six energetic Ecuadorians swarm all over the exterior, laughing and singing and slapping their brushes against the clapboard. They're careful to cover Dad's bushes with plastic sheeting before they begin painting the veranda, and they tidy away everything before they leave each evening. I'm so impressed I spend many days tagging along with my video camera.

The south face of the house is a good forty feet high, and sometimes, when they're up at the peak on the tall extension ladder, they jump it like a pogo stick to move it sideways a notch. It's death-defying, but I can't wait to show the video to grandchildren. I feel like a war correspondent—not wanting the men to fall or come to harm, but knowing that if they did it would make really good footage. When the men finish, I buy a dozen hanging pots of red geraniums to hang from the hooks on the veranda columns.

We hire our friend Heather to weed and prepare Dad's long perennial flowerbeds, but it's hard to know what's there so early in the season. When we were growing up, Dad lavished his plants with tenderness. As soon as he got home from the office, he'd change out of his business suit, put on what he called his "rough clothes"—brown corduroy trousers, long-sleeved green plaid shirt, heavy leather boots—and go outside to garden. Since he died, though, the plants have basically gone to wrack and ruin. Mum always said she could never understand the "urge to dig," and for the past several summers she'd stuck plastic flowers into the drought-ravaged beds to give them splotches of color.

The garden was one of Mum and Dad's many battlefields. Cutting Dad's flowers was like beheading his gods, so if they'd had a fight, Mum immediately turned her attention to flower arranging. Dad would arrive home from work and find the house ablaze with blooms. Vases of every description, on every table and countertop, were stuffed to overflowing with tulips, daffodils, irises, and buttercups. Dad would stand rigidly still and blink, as though he'd just seen the living dead. Then, bursting through the door onto the veranda, he'd survey his denuded flowerbeds and roar, *"Aaaaaannnnee!"* But Mum wouldn't be home. She'd be down at the club . . . playing tennis.

Today I walk the length of the flowerbeds with Heather, peering through a lattice of dead stalks and examining woody brown tubers.

"What do you think?" Heather asks. "Weeds?"

"Dad called them his Canadian buttercups."

"They look like weeds to me," she says, poking them with a stick.

Heather spends three days hauling away dead brush and dragging the debris down to Dad's compost heap. She's dressed in baggy tan pants and a loose plaid shirt, and even though it's chilly, her face is damp with sweat and her brown bangs cling to her forehead like limp sea grass. What used to be a long line of tangled wilderness is beginning to look tamed. The gray stalks are gone, revealing a rich contrast between the freshly dug black earth and the bright spring clumps of pointed green shoots. Mum would say the whole garden looks like it's been to the beauty parlor. We've asked Heather to plant red impatiens in between the spring bulbs as a quick summer fix. With enough rain, we hope they'll spread, providing color through the fall for Victor and Peni's wedding as well.

Our landscaper comes with his men to prune the hedge and give the lawn its first haircut. They also bring a trailer to haul away Dad's compost heap. We're amazed to see the bottom of the garden without it. The empty space seems large enough to build a second house.

Gem Pools comes to empty, clean, and refill the swimming pool, just as they've done every year since they built it more than forty years ago. Huge plastic hoses snake from the pool, across the garden, and out the garden gate to the sewer grate in the road. The bilge pump makes a deafening *rat-tat-tat* sound that goes on for hours as it dredges up the slimy winter muck from the depths of the pool. Men with long-handled scrub brushes are wearing orange boots and yellow overalls. From a distance, they look like minia-ture rubber duckies in a concrete cavern. They'll repaint the tur-quoise border and fill the pool with clean water from Dad's green garden hose, attached to the outside tap by the laundry room door. Water will trickle in over several days, making the pipes rattle in the basement, and the kitchen walls will vibrate like a reproach from Dad that we're wasting water.

The weatherman is predicting violent thunderstorms for Vir-ginia's wedding day, so we watch the sky nervously. Chairs have been delivered for the garden, but there's no tent and the service itself is to be conducted outdoors, under the walnut trees. A hun-dred guests have been invited. Unlike Mum, I don't trust people's intelligence, so we buy three dozen clear plastic umbrellas and rehearse plan B. The orchestra they've hired to play big-band swing music can still play on the veranda, but the service will have to be moved indoors to the living room if it rains. I can hear Mum's voice: "Accept what you cannot change."

On the morning of the wedding we awake to find that the storm has blown over and brought clear blue skies and a warm breeze. Mum always said the lake tells you the weather better than any weatherman, if you learn to read the signs. I look out at the lake and it's smooth as glass. By noon it's cloudless and hot—like midsummer.

Jessica arrives with eight round layers of freshly baked cake in tinfoil and six pounds of butter, and proceeds to spread out all her paraphernalia on the dining room table. She's working against the clock to ice the cake because the caterers will arrive soon and need the room. As the clock ticks on, I notice that Virginia is in the swimming pool with her one-year-old son, Ben. Every time I look at Ben, I see my mother—he has the same infectious smile that crinkles his nose; I just hope he hasn't inherited her teeth. I open the kitchen window and holler down to Virginia.

"Sweetie, don't you think it's time to put on your wedding dress?"

"In a minute!"

The catering truck pulls into the driveway, and women in stiff white jackets swarm the kitchen with silver trays of canapés. Jessica has managed to spread smooth white icing on the cake, but not to decorate it. She still has four pounds of butter left in her car. Virginia runs in with a towel tucked around her bathing suit, holding a fat, pale pink peony in full bloom.

"Here," she says, plucking off some petals and tossing them onto the cake, "just decorate with these. It looks beautiful—I love its simplicity! And then can you come upstairs? I need you to braid my hair."

Upstairs, the rooms are humming with activity. Virginia's dress is hanging from the canopy of Mum's four-poster bed and Louis's suit is hanging on the door of Dad's closet. I'm in my old bedroom, changing into my favorite pink dress—it's heavily encrusted with cotton lace, too, and perfect for today. Virginia's out-of-town friends have arrived. They're milling around, laughing, playing with Ben, pouring champagne, offering advice on which white flowers to stick in her hair. A red peony gets stuck into mine.

At last, we're ready. The orchestra on the veranda begins playing Pachelbel's Canon, the bride takes her father's arm, and the wedding party wends its way down the grassy lawn, past the seated guests to the lace-covered table under the walnut trees. Baby Ben is the ring bearer, with the wedding ring of Louis's late mother hanging from a red ribbon around his neck.

Over the hedge, strangers ambling along the lakefront stop in their tracks when they realize they're witnessing a wedding. There's a hush as the bride and groom repeat their vows. I wish Mum had waited one more year to see this; she would have loved it. I find myself wondering if she would have hollered over the hedge and invited the strangers to come have a piece of cake. I miss her.

The sun is shining and there's not a cloud in the sky. Just like my wedding thirty-eight years ago, there's a canopy of umbrellas, except that today they're not for rain: guests are holding colorful paper umbrellas to protect themselves from the sun. After the food and speeches and champagne, people wander over to the pool. They find Mum's swimsuits in the big wicker basket in the basement and start selecting ones for a swim. Some just hitch up their dresses, kick off their shoes, and dangle their feet in the water. Just before the bride and groom make their departure, speeding off in an old sports car, Virginia throws her bouquet and I catch it. (Actually, I duke it out with an eight-year-old and embarrass myself.)

Later that night we clean up the debris and nibble on leftovers, celebrating the fact that everything has gone off without a hitch—especially the wedding cake. Suddenly, Jess comes running in from the garage, her face ashen.

"The backseat of my car!" she says. "It's soaked in slime—everything's ruined. It stinks!"

"Why?" I say. "What happened?"

"Remember all that extra butter?" She grimaces. "I forgot to bring it in . . . and it melted in the heat."

The day after the wedding, we hold another service for Mum. We've already sprinkled one plastic Baggie of her ashes at St. Jude's with Dad and one at St. Mary's with Sandy. Now we sprinkle the third around the maple tree at the corner of the garden. We commingle Sambo's ashes with Mum's. The bronze memorial plaque that Victor ordered has arrived, and he's sunk it into concrete beside Dad's and Sandy's. We gather as a family, stand in a circle, and say good-bye one more time. Mum is well and truly put to rest now, I hope.

When everyone leaves, Victor stays behind to help me clean up. We pick up stray champagne corks in the garden, put chairs back where they belong, and carry in vases of wilted flowers from the veranda. Upstairs, we tidy Mum's bedroom, which had been the bride's room only yesterday, pinching up hydrangea petals that had fallen from her hair onto the carpet.

I find some stray bobby pins and open Mum's top dresser drawer to throw them in. As I do this, something catches my eye—a small piece of folded paper wedged into the right-hand corner, now protruding from the piles of earrings, hankies, and nighties that I'd crammed into this drawer for grandchildren to look at. I unfold it and recognize Mum's familiar handwriting.

It's a letter to me, dated on my fiftieth birthday. She tells me how much I mean to her and how much she loves me.

I gasp and start to tremble.

"What's wrong?" asks Victor. He's standing by Dad's dresser, brushing away cake crumbs.

"This." I hand him the letter as tears spill down my face.

He starts to read it . . . *Darling, you've always been and always will be God's blessing to me . . .* Then he stops and looks at me tenderly.

"Why didn't she ever give this to me?" I ask, sniffling. "She wrote it fourteen years ago."

Victor hands me a Kleenex. He wraps his arms around me and squeezes me in a long bear hug as I cry into his shoulder.

"She wanted you to have it now, I guess," he says. "She knew you'd find it."

Dividing What Remains

Two days after the wedding my brothers return and we hold the dispersal. We start at ten in the morning, set up the old square table in the playroom, and draw numbers out of a hat to establish the order of bidding. I've drawn number one. Rokeby Rules are that the order of bidding rotates with each round, so the person who goes first goes last the next time: 1-2-3-4 becomes 2-3-4-1, then 3-4-1-2, and so on. Our mathematician, Louis, tells us that statistically it doesn't matter—everyone gets the same fair chance no matter what the order—but we do it this way for tradition's sake.

I've given everyone an annotated inventory list complete with photographs: there are 422 items, running eighty-one pages long. There are two categories: one for all the furnishings that have been appraised and priced, and one for historical items that we consider priceless—things like family portraits, a pair of epaulets from World War II, the plastic sign of the gun from the mudroom window, the antique ship's gongs that used to hang on the wall in the pantry (Dad banged them with the little rubber mallet to call us to dinner, or played reveille if he wanted to rouse us out of bed early in the mornings).

There are only two things I desperately want from the first category—Mum's four-poster bed and the dining room chairs—but I decide to use my first bid on one of the three carved Chinese chests because I think there'll be more competition for these.

To my surprise, nobody else bids on one. Robin chooses Dad's desk, Victor chooses the mantel clock, and Chris chooses Dad's favorite beer mug. Then Chris—who went last in the first round—goes first this time, and he takes Mum's four-poster bed. Victor gets the flatware and Robin takes the dining room chairs. I let out an audible gasp—I'm last and both my favorite things are gone. Louis was wrong—statistically I've been skunked. But it serves me right for bidding competitively, instead of with my heart. I lament the loss of the chairs, so Robin whispers in my ear, "If you bid on the silver basket in the next round, I'll trade you for the chairs," so that's exactly what I do. Meanwhile, Robin scoops the eighteenth-century candlesticks engraved with the tower of Udny Castle—the only remnant of Dad's Scottish ancestry during the Jacobite Rebellion. As soon as anyone bids on anything I feel a pang of regret. I swear to God, it lasts only a nanosecond, but for the first time in my life I fantasize about being an only child. I don't want to share—I want to hoard. I feel as if the past is slipping through my fingers. It's getting complicated.

We motor through the eighty-one-page list at quite a clip, but by three o'clock we're still nowhere near the end and we need to take a break. Chris has just bid on Mum's mah-jongg set and we're down to the dregs: bronze bookends and carved gewgaws. It's emotionally exhausting for everybody, and I've noticed that

Victor, now that he has his flatware, clock, and opium-bed coffee table, seems not to be bidding on anything else. It's as though he's taking a backseat, conditioned as the youngest to taking the leftovers after the rest of us are done. Or maybe, with his impending marriage to Peni in September and the combining of their households, he just doesn't have room for more stuff.

I speak to him during the break. I remind him that there are certain things his children wanted. In particular, I know that his daughter, Hannah, would like Mum's engagement ring. I've been holding off bidding on it because I know Mum would love Hannah to have it.

When we get to the priceless historical items, the first things to go are the family portraits: Robin takes Great-Grandfather and I take Grandmother. Nobody wants Great-Grandmother: she languishes loudly on the staircase in her black dress, sitting on a black chair against a black background with a black lace shawl draped over her head. She haunted me as a child. I still nip by her haughty, disapproving glare as fast as I can without looking.

"She's a copy," Robin reminds us. "The original is in New York."

"Why would anyone in their right mind want a copy of her? She's deadly-looking."

"Ah-hah!" he says. "That's what you think. Our copy was probably made from a soot-stained original. It's been cleaned since then—I've seen it. And guess what? Her lace shawl is white and the chair is red!"

"That doesn't change her expression!" I say.

We wade through a list of old Masonic medals, nineteenth-century English-school prizes for Latin, the house guest book, Dad's naval uniform, two large family Bibles documenting the change of our surname to an "alias" when our ancestors fled the Jacobite Rebellion of 1745, and even a purported chunk of the wall from Pompeii that some ancestor must have purloined on their grand tour.

As much as I'd love to have some of the ancient Napoleonic documents, I know the boys want them more, so I avoid bidding. Victor finally comes alive and asks for the dinner gongs.

Robin is amassing a museumlike collection of maritime items owned by our seafaring ancestors. Since Mum already bequeathed him the prison ship, he's bid on most of the related documents. He would have grabbed Lord Nelson's sideboard, which Grandfather used to own, except that an uncle has already donated it to the naval museum in Portsmouth, so he has to make do with a photograph showing the sideboard in Grandfather's office.

Chris has smartly bid on small items, mostly silver. He's in the process of moving to the West Coast and doesn't have much room, but the one major piece of furniture he does win is the dining room table—a vast Victorian oak piece that, when extended with its eight leaves, could comfortably seat twenty people or more. The rest of us had expressed no interest in it, but now, realizing it's going to B.C. when Chris moves in the fall, I experience a deep sense of loss. It has no historic family provenance—it came with the house—but for the past half-century it's where we've eaten our meals, played board games, held family meetings, and watched Mum type her letters. I did my sewing there, too. When Sandy was dying, I made his hospital-style gowns in brightly printed flannelette, spreading the fabric on the table and cutting out six at a time. I console myself with the knowledge that Chris is a wonderful chef, so no doubt this table has many more adventures in store.

There are some items none of us want, so these will be sold at auction later. But what of Mum and Dad's cake topper, shaped like a battleship? Who's going to sink that?

I start to think about the antique music box that Mum left me in her will. I'm conflicted as to what to do with it. It's so rare that we've never been able to locate another like it. I feel it should go to a museum, where the whole world can see it, but within the family there's a debate on this subject. I feel that important objects or documents shouldn't be hidden away or hoarded by one family when the wider public might appreciate them. Even though Robin plans to build a special room to display his Napoleonic artifacts, what happens to it all when Robin dies? Will his infant grandsons grow up to protect them and to pass along their stories? I worry about these things.

Robin feels that all historic items should remain in the family, although he's willing to turn over some historical papers to professional archivists. He's already given many of Sandy's papers to the Virginia Historical Society, which has a large collection of Williams family papers going back to our great-great-grandfather, John Williams, The Immigrant. We all agree that Mum and Dad have left us a great treasure, but it comes with a daunting responsibility.

Chris suggests that Mum's old alma mater, Bennington College in Vermont, might like her college scrapbook and letters, and Victor thinks a naval museum in England might like Dad's wartime letters. Several books have already been written about Dad's exploits, including *Escape from the Rising Sun* by Ian Skidmore and *Alarm Starboard!* by Geoffrey Brooke. Dad's annotated, dog-eared copies were in his desk.

Some of Mum's exploits have been published, too, in a book

called *"Flak" Houses Then and Now* by Keith Thomas, but men got the lion's share of a nation's gratitude after the war. Contributions by female veterans, especially American Red Cross workers, were largely ignored. On Remembrance Day, each November 11, Dad marched to the Cenotaph with his war medals, but Mum wouldn't even stand up in church when they asked veterans to stand. "They don't mean *women*," she said. We've found a Certificate of Merit awarded to her by the U.S. Army, "in recognition of conspicuously meritorious and outstanding performance of military duty" when she was an Assistant Red Cross Director. On her U.S. government ID card, she was designated "2nd Lieutenant" in the event of capture by enemy forces, but after the war, Mum wasn't even given a pension.

I argue with my brothers that the era of large families, anchored by one ancestral home where everyone gathers on special occasions, is long gone. The majority of modern, nuclear families are coping with divorce, blended offspring, downsizing, and far-flung relatives, so who has the time and space to properly display these things anymore? My children certainly don't. Carter, for example, is living and working with his wife in Turkmenistan. He's a seeker, a globetrotter, drawn to exotic locales. He hates being tied down by possessions and always travels light. Virginia expresses no interest in anything except the portrait of Grandmother and Mum's ancient flowering geranium tree, which is staked together with old oxygen tubing. She and Louis have recently built a sleek modernist town house, with no room for brown furniture. Jessica has no room for anything in her one-bedroom apartment, and all of my brothers' children are in similar situations.

I'm shocked that none of the boys wants the framed watercolor painting of Dad's cottage on Lake Kashwakamak. It's a good painting, evoking the solitary, rustic nature of the place, surrounded by birch and pine. It always hung in a place of honor beside Dad's bed.

"I can't believe you don't want this!" I say to Victor. "Are you sure?"

He looks at me as though I'm as thick as one of its planks. "If you had survived a concentration camp, would you want a painting of it?" he says.

"But you helped Dad build the cottage . . . I thought you loved going there!"

"What do you know? You'd bailed by then—you were away at university. It was a mosquito-infested swamp! All I remember are the blackfly bites and the calluses on my hands. Thanks, but I don't need any souvenirs."

I try to superimpose this new piece of information over the old tape in my head. I thought we all criticized Mum for not going with Dad to his cottage, but it sounds like the boys would have rather stayed home with her if they could. Did I judge Mum too harshly? Did I listen only to Dad's side of the story? Sometimes our remembered experiences make it seem as if we each came from a different family. I keep forgetting that Victor spent time as an only child. He and I—the bookends—were the only two children who did, but the parents I experienced had just turned thirty, in the bloom of early romance; his were in their forties and fifties, getting ready to kill each other. Not only were Victor's and my vantage points different, our backdrops were different as well.

When the boys and I finally finish, we go out on the veranda, drinks in hand, and do some horse trading. There are private trades going on all over the place. Robin has something Chris wants and I have two things Robin wants, so with a bit of circuitous swapping, we all end up happy: I get the dining room chairs plus Mum's bed.

Robin smiles. "You know, I think Mother would be quite pleased with how we've worked things out. She told me once that she was amazed by how well we got along, given how different we are."

"She said that?"

"Yes! She thought maybe it was because we all share the same sense of humor." He takes a sip of his bourbon. "But I corrected her . . . I told her it was because we all share the same crooked teeth."

We're all laughing by the time the boys' wives have returned from their day trip, and we celebrate with a homemade feast.

We sound Dad's dinner gongs for the last time.

Robin plays reveille.

Earthquake

$\longmapsto$O

At the end of June, Victor's children come to spend the day by the pool. I've been sitting at my computer all morning, working on my Shakespeare project. Suddenly, all the letters on my screen begin to dance in slow motion. Then I feel unsteady, as though the floor is shifting under my feet. Even the pictures hanging on the wall look like they're sliding back and forth. I run outside to the veranda, where Nick is strumming his guitar.

"Nick? Did you just feel that?"

"Feel what?"

"An earthquake!"

"Nope," he says and keeps on strumming.

I call over the railing to Hannah, who's lying in the sun down by the pool, eyes shut, earbuds plugged in.

"Hannah!" I shout. "Did you just feel an earthquake?"

She lazily takes out an earbud and looks up at me quizzically. "An earthquake? No, I didn't feel anything."

Did I just have a stroke? Seeing shaky letters is one of the warning signs. Maybe my prayer to outlive Mum by a few months wasn't so far off. Maybe I should lie down. I head upstairs and take a two-hour nap. When I turn on the radio at suppertime, however, the announcer is talking about the earthquake in southern Ontario—5.0 on the Richter scale. I'm so relieved I want to celebrate. But how was I able to feel it in the downstairs hall—the part of the house that rests on solid ground—while Nick, at the end of the veranda, raised on stilts, and Hannah, down below him by the pool, never felt a thing?

Does a fault line run straight through this property? If so, the rectangular slab of concrete that we call our pool may very well be our Maginot Line. It was, after all, the site of an epic battle between Mum and Dad back in the 1960s.

In those days, Dad spent much of every winter in Argentina, insuring cattle. Mum wouldn't go with him, but she resented his time away. While he was gone, she said, the boys lacked a father figure. She also complained that Dad never left her enough money. He would return spilling words in Spanish, describing lavish dinner parties in Buenos Aires, lyrical rides in the moonlight across the Pampas on grand *estancias* . . . and the many beautiful stewardesses he'd met en route.

So finally Mum eyed the unused maid's room next door to Sandy's bedroom at the back of the house and came up with a plan to teach Dad a lesson. At the local high school, she posted an ad for a room for rent during the fall term, when she knew Dad would be away. Only males need apply.

One Friday afternoon a shy, thin, bespectacled math teacher arrived for an interview. Mum was giving him a tour of the kitchen to show him where she kept her pots and pans.

"Don't expect me to cook for you . . ." she said. "And if you want clean sheets, the laundry's in the basement."

At that precise moment Dad walked into the kitchen carrying his briefcase. He'd come home early from the office.

Dad looked the man up and down and said, "May I ask who you are, sir?"

"Mind your own business," said Mum. "This has nothing to do with you!"

Mum started shouting that since Dad had decided to abandon his family every winter, she had decided to take matters into her own hands. Dad was furious. How dare Mum turn his home into a common boardinghouse! Mum wanted to know who the hell Dad thought he was, speaking to her like that. Dad accused Mum of being a spendthrift! Extravagant! Lazy! Mum accused Dad of being a killjoy! Insensitive! Obstinate! Voices rose and doors slammed as the math teacher fled out the back door.

Eventually, Mum took off to Virginia to cool down and spend a few weeks with her brother. While Mum was away, Dad called in the contractors. They demolished the wall between Sandy's bedroom and the maid's room, thus eliminating the room Mum had planned to rent out. Sandy was happy—he now had a huge bedroom with twice as many windows as before—but Mum returned in fighting form.

The day after Dad left on the plane for Argentina, Mum was on the phone to the contractors herself. A maiden aunt had died and left her some money, and now she planned to sink it into a hole in the ground. In came the bulldozers and backhoes. They rolled through the garden gate, trundled down the manicured lawn, and hunkered down beside Dad's beloved vegetable patch.

In giant mouthfuls, they scooped out the earth that had harbored Dad's pumpkins, carrots, and lettuce plants, and regurgitated it onto the lawn. A truck, with its big vat of churning concrete, parked itself by the edge of the fence, and by the time they were finished we had a sparkling blue thirty-foot swimming pool where Dad's vegetables once grew. A truce was declared when Dad got home. You couldn't see the pool—it was blanketed by snow and ice—and Dad was glad to be back. He had missed us.

Basically the pool was a concrete pit, just like the one Mum had known as a child at Rokeby. It had no heating apparatus and was best used in the winter—as a skating rink. But Dad grew to love it. He was hardy. More or less as soon as the ice melted, Dad would dive in. Naked. He had it all to himself.

An inspector comes for the day to comb through the house with his flashlight and tools. We want to know if there are any structural problems so that we can be upfront with potential buyers. He crawls into the knee walls, goes up the trapdoor into the attic, and takes his flashlight under the house. He's surprised by how sturdy the house is. "Rock solid," he calls it. There's a little dampness under one of the windows in Mum's bedroom, but this is no surprise. The plaster is falling away in clumps and has been for years. Mum's favorite bird, a brown speckled swallow, always builds his nest outside that window, plugging the eavestrough. The only way to stop the moisture was to evict the bird, which Mum refused to do.

We decide to contact the three individuals who have expressed interest in the house and hold a private auction. Victor designs an official bidding form, sends it out in early August, and we sit back and wait. But as the days tick toward the deadline, we receive disappointing news: one by one the bids evaporate.

On the last day, I get an urgent call from a man who wasn't on our list. He says our house has always been his favorite, but he's only just heard it's for sale. Can he come see it? When he arrives, I give him "The Cook's Tour."

In the nineteenth century, Thomas Cook & Sons was a British travel company famous for organizing guided sightseeing tours that crammed as much as possible into the shortest period of time. It spawned expressions like "Around the world in eighty days" and "If it's Tuesday, this must be Belgium." I lead this man in and out of the house in less than half an hour, but I can tell he's smitten. He asks for the bidding form; one day later we receive his offer. It's close to our asking price and Victor's pleased—now we can celebrate his wedding to Peni in September without any house-sale negotiations hanging over our heads. The papers aren't signed, since the buyer still has to confer with his bank, but we agree on a handshake. The details will be ironed out when Victor returns from his honeymoon.

The night after we accept his offer, though, a strange thing happens. I'm alone downstairs, cleaning up my dinner dishes, when I hear a loud bang upstairs. I run to investigate and find that Mum's bedroom door has slammed shut. When I try to pull it open it's locked . . . from the inside. Dread slithers through me—because her lock is a small hook and eye. It's entirely possible that a gust of strong wind sucked her door closed, but what are the chances that the tiny hook at the top of her door could fly up and land precisely in the tiny metal eyelet on the door frame? My heart starts pounding wildly. I race downstairs, out the back door in the dark, and over to Pucci's house. Even though it's late,

I can see across the garden that their lights are still on. Phil helps me search room to room, but there's no evidence of intruders or ghosts.

What am I to make of this? Does this mean Mum is giving her blessing to the sale, telling me I can leave her bedroom now and move on? Or is she telling us this is the wrong buyer and she wants him out of her bedroom?

In a frenzy of confusion, I ask if I can paint the buyer's portrait. I'm having difficulty visualizing him in this house, so I think that if I can paint him in context, it might help me. He agrees to sit for me on the veranda when I offer to give him the finished portrait as a housewarming present.

Victor thinks I'm crazy.

"Why would you paint a portrait for free?" he says. "And why this guy? You don't even know him!"

But I can't explain it. I just need to work things out through my art.

The next day I open the broom closet looking for paint rags and find a plastic bag holding what looks like a matted gray wig. *Eew . . .* what is it? It looks strangely familiar and yet at the same time repugnant. I take it out in the sunlight and feel it with my hands: animal, mineral, or vegetable? Its strange coarseness resonates deep within me—a living, breathing memory—and suddenly I drop the bag. It's animal! I find myself battling nausea. I run to the phone to call Pelmo.

"There's a bag on a hook in the broom closet that has something . . . that's, uh . . . gray and . . ."

"Sambo, is it?"

I'm bent over double, afraid I will faint.

She giggles. "Your mum, about the knitting she is reading in her news. From the dogs they take the wool. She save when I give brushing to Sambo. Your mum, she thinks this can be good."

When I get over my shock, I shake the whole bag into the forsythia bush so that Mum's favorite bird can pad his nest. Maybe he'll take the hint and leave the eavestrough.

It's August 12 again—Mum's birthday—and I decide to make her a homemade birthday card and place it with flowers on her memorial plaque. I take my mug of morning coffee and go out through the garden gate, lifting the fox ears on the latch and hearing their *chink* behind me. I associate the garden gate with so many memories. When the ears on the cast-iron fox flop down, their muted *chinking* sound reminds me of playing hide-and-seek with Dad. I can hear laughter, feel my heartbeat as I run, see fireflies in the dusky sky. I also associate it with afternoon tea—a neighbor's head appearing through the bushes, a wicker chair scraping across the veranda, Mum standing up: "Hello there!" Opening the gate. *Chink-chink.*

There's a bench by the fence, but I don't sit down; I just stand by the tree and let its energy surge through me. We have such deep roots here.

I read Mum's plaque: ANNE ARMISTEAD WILLIAMS . . . BORN AUGUST 16, 1916. Wait a minute . . . *the sixteenth?*

Shit! That's not her birthday—that's the date of her wedding! I race back up to the house, spilling my coffee. I call Victor.

"There's a typo on Mum's memorial plaque! Her birth date is wrong!"

"Don't get your knickers in a knot," he says. "It's no big deal."

"How could we have done this to her?"

"Didn't you proofread it?" he asks. "You were in charge of the wording."

"No, I wasn't!"

"Yes, you were!"

"We have to change it!"

"It's cast in bronze! You can't just take an eraser and rub out bronze."

"We have to order a new one, then."

"Are you crazy? It's concreted in!"

"I don't care," I say. "This is important to me."

I have memories of Dad, tromping through all the family graveyards in England and Portugal, making copious notes of names and dates on ancestral headstones so that he could leave us with a genealogical trail back to the early 1700s. Mum's family did the same thing: her brother built a separate cottage on his property to house the family papers.

"How many people are going to know—or care—when Mum's birthday is?" says Victor. "At least we got the month right!"

When I tell Robin, he seems not surprised. "I hate to tell you, but last time I was home I noticed there's an error on Dad's as well."

"There is?"

"Yep . . . the dates of Dad's years with his company are wrong. Instead of 1931 to 1977, it should say 1933 to 1978."

"What should we do?"

"We could order a fourth plaque," he says, chuckling, "and title it 'Errata.' We could issue it from the Oakville *Hysterical* Society's Department of Corrections!"

I will never trust information on gravestones again.

The tree that shades Mum's plaque is a sapling that we planted after Sandy died. My parents outlived the 120-year-old maple that used to stand in the same spot. It was a grand beauty with a ninety-inch girth and sweeping arms that branched out over the lake. It seemed almost human to me. I used to wonder what it had seen—who had paddled by in a canoe or stroked its bark in the 1800s? As children, we used to pitch our tent under its leafy canopy in summer and swing on one of its long, sinewy arms, propelling ourselves out over the beach like Tarzan. Sadly, despite being fitted with steel cables over the years, it hollowed out, and one day the town sprayed a bright orange *X* on its side. Then men came with a two-story crane and buzz saws and cut it down, amputating its limbs one by one. My brothers saved a large chunk of its belly in the hopes of reincarnating it as a tabletop, but over time it rotted under a tarpaulin in the bushes and eventually got hauled away to the dump.

For years, the town has permitted memorial trees to be planted along the lakefront. It irked Mum that these saplings were congregating like a forest in front of her house, memorializing people she'd never met, threatening to block her view. "They make us pay huge taxes for a lakefront view, and then they plant all these trees so we can't see a damn thing!" She wanted to sneak out at night and hack all the saplings off at the knees, but her oxygen tubing wouldn't reach that far.

It's September now, close to Victor and Peni's wedding, and the weather's turning chilly. The lake still sparkles with dancing light, but the maple leaves are turning color, adding syrupy golden hues to the fiery red of autumn. In the garden, Dad's perennials have died down and folded inward, but the red impatiens—though taller and spindly and not quite so lush—are holding their own, just as we'd hoped.

The squirrels have started collecting their nuts. They've set up their bowling alley in the ceiling above the dining room as they do every fall, and I can hear their tiny feet scrabbling back and forth overhead. I also hear a strange vibration, like a faint humming, coming from the stains in the dining room ceiling. I'm worried about the pipes again.

"Oh, jeez," says Victor. "Now you're hearing the walls hum? What have you been smoking?"

"Aren't you worried about the plumbing?" I ask. "Your wedding is next week! What happens if the pipes burst just as all your guests are arriving?"

"So? I'll invite a plumber to the wedding." He laughs. "Get a grip!"

But the pipes don't burst and nothing mars his wedding day.

While Victor and Peni are away on their honeymoon, our house buyer stops by frequently. I often find him early in the morning, Starbucks in hand, sitting on the public bench at the bottom of the road, watching the sunrise over the lake. Sometimes I invite him to sit on the veranda. I relate to his sensitivity, but I want to know more about him—this man who will inhabit our space and inherit the layers of energy soaked into the walls. He answers my questions in vague, noncommittal ways and remains private and enigmatic. He seems irresistibly drawn to the house, yet this seems implausible to me. He's single, without children, so why would he want so many rooms?

I've set up a painting studio in the dining room, with light flooding in from all sides. His portrait is taking shape. I paint his youthful figure in a pensive mood, sitting on the steps in his leather bomber jacket and polished boots, staring out at the lake. He has handsome, chiseled features, his blond hair neatly combed to the side, and I get the feeling he's meticulous: his shirts are always pressed, with button-down collars, and when I walk him to his polished car, it looks as if it just came from the BMW showroom; inside, there's not a scrap of paper anywhere.

I stay up late every night, painting. I feel as if I have my own private observatory. The unobstructed view of the sky over the lake is pulsating with twinkling stars. Sometimes the Big Dipper is suspended right outside my bedroom window, and when the moon is full it's like a huge searchlight, bathing the garden in an unearthly glow. Sometimes I paint all night and in the morning watch the black sky slowly separate from the lake as pale light creeps up over the horizon.

I feel supercharged by the creative energy in this house. The walls literally sing to me. I put Dad's old Vera Lynn LPs on the record player in the living room and move my easel into the center of the downstairs hall, surrounded by space and memories.

From time to time I e-mail the buyer photos of his portrait as it moves through various stages so that he can see how it's progressing, but he seems strangely aloof. When Victor gets home from his honeymoon he sees it on my easel and jumps.

"Yikes!" he exclaims. "For a minute, I thought he was in the room!"

I feel jumpy, too. Now there's a stray black cat on the veranda every morning. "Shoo! Scat!" But he remains poised on the top step, switching his tail, his eerie yellow eyes staring up at me. He claws at the screen door and scratches at the wicker chairs. Sometimes he slides in unnoticed and I'm startled by a streak of black in the upstairs hall.

Mum and Dad hated cats because they stalked the birds, but this one seems to know something . . . I wonder what.

The buyer keeps postponing the closing date and Victor's gut is telling him this deal is evaporating, too. He thinks we should start interviewing real estate agents to get the show on the road. We take all the disguised sympathy notes out of Mum's gold-wire Slinky and reread them.

We pick the top agents and invite them to come and give us their dog-and-pony show. They all come with slick, overblown proposals and inflated ideas of what the house is worth. One has even gone to the trouble of printing up a mock brochure with our house on the cover. Another brings his laptop to give us a PowerPoint presentation, but his battery's dead and when he wants to plug it in he can't believe we have only one three-pronged outlet in the house. Victor tells him to be grateful we have electricity. If Dad had his druthers, we'd still be operating by candlelight.

I go back to Mum's Slinky letter holder and pull out a handwritten note. It's the only one from an agent that's not disguised with sympathy; it's refreshingly direct. It just says that when we're ready, please call her.

The agent arrives with no presentation except her own voice, and I feel immediately drawn to her. Alex is nurturing and sisterly, with an enthusiastic, down-to-earth nature, a wide smile, and a ready laugh. At a subliminal level, it doesn't hurt that she has the same name as Dad. We give her the inspection report, the appraiser's assessment, and our new survey.

The only thing Victor wants excluded from the sale is the SLAVE DRIVER sign on the outside of the house. Although most people these days read it and laugh, there's more awareness that Oakville was once a stop on the Underground Railroad, and I've seen some young African Canadians stop to take photos. I worry they're researching a university paper and mistaking our sign for the real thing. I think it's time to take it down, and I'm glad Victor wants it.

"Wait a minute!" I say to Victor. "Let's exclude the garden gate, too."

"What do you want that old thing for?"

"I'm going to hang it on my bedroom wall!"

"The whole rotten gate?"

"Sure—the fox latch has meaning for me."

"You can't take the whole garden gate—that's ridiculous!"

"You know who you sound like?"

Victor grins. "Okay, okay." Then he turns to Alex. "Exclude the garden gate."

Alex quickly arranges an agents' open house and puts ads in magazines, and over the following weeks there are numerous showings. This means disassembling my painting studio, carrying my easel back to the playroom, cleaning my palette, storing the wet canvas, and removing the floor cloth. I have to shut down my computer and hide all my papers. It also means vacuuming all the rooms and mopping the kitchen and bathroom floors—no small feat in a house this size. It takes me a good six hours. But the repetitive quality of mopping gives way to meditation, the way school classes did in childhood when I had to listen to lessons in Latin.

After each showing, Alex debriefs me. She says, "Everyone loves it—they call it their lottery house!"

Me, too, even though I've been buying tickets all year and haven't won a thing.

Throughout October no bids come in. It seems the market is in the doldrums. Either that or buyers know this is an estate sale and think the price will come down if they wait. Some feel it's overpriced; some wish they could tear it down; some say the property would be worth more if the house weren't here. I am appalled when I hear what some clients plan to do with the house.

"I wouldn't keep anything on the inside," says one.

Why would she buy it, then?

Another considers building a double garage down by the pool that would block the lake view of our neighbor to the north. This is unthinkable to us. Why shouldn't they have a view of the lake, too?

We confer many times with Alex about the house. We're not going to lower the price and I'm happy to continue living here, even if it's for another two years. Especially if it's another two years. I am acutely aware that I'm living in paradise. I can't save it. I'm living here on borrowed time. Everybody else is moving on: Victor and Peni are moving east; Robin and Kitty will no longer drive up from Virginia for family holidays; Chris has been offered a new job as director of an Anglican retreat and conference center in western Canada, and so he and his wife, Anne, have decided to relocate to British Columbia. Even Pelmo and Tashi have moved out for good. They've taken a job down the street: it seems their kind services will always be in demand.

A huge white moving truck arrives to pick up the items Chris bid on during the family dispersal. I can hear its air brakes wheezing and hissing as it pulls up to the front door. It takes up the whole block and looks like a black-headed dragon. Four burly men in black T-shirts and jeans hop down from the cab, carrying protective canvas, padded blankets, and tools. They stop at the door and pull white paper slippers over their boots. When they walk in, they survey the space and whistle. "You call this a cottage?" says one.

Chris has left me a list of his items, and I direct the men to various upstairs bedrooms, where they lift out a dresser, some small side tables, mirrors, and two beds. Ironically, the brand-new mattress I had insisted on buying, so that guests wouldn't have to spend the summer at the chiropractor, is now heading out the door. Why did I ever put it on the dispersal list? The men are taking all the furniture apart. Drawers are removed, legs are unscrewed, and knobs are taken off—each piece to be separately wrapped and labeled.

"Careful! Careful," I say, "that hasn't been taken apart in over one hundred years!" But they just ignore me.

There's a wrapping station in the living room, where a man wearing wide bracelets of masking tape on each wrist spreads brown padded blankets on the floor. He lays each item on the diagonal and then deftly wraps the corners up and over as if he's diapering a baby's bottom. Then he encircles the whole thing with a tight cinch of tape.

I've spent the morning saying good-bye to the mammoth dining room table. It's been in the house since 1917. I've run my hand over the grain and taken photos of it from every angle. When it goes, this house will feel a whole lot emptier. The men remove the leaves and then heave the table over onto its back. It looks like a dead dinosaur with its feet sticking straight up in the air, exposing its ribs. They have to eviscerate it section by section and amputate its legs bolt by bolt. It takes them a long time. Bits of bread crumbs flake to the floor. I wonder how old they are—from which last supper?

The following week, Chris calls from B.C. to tell me the table has safely arrived and now has a brand-new life in his kitchen. He's left out the extra leaves, so it's now square—a shape it's never inhabited before in its lifetime.

It's November 5, and we've turned the clocks back. The light has changed. By early afternoon, long fingers of blue shadows are slanting across the lawn as the sun descends behind the house. Most of the tree leaves have fallen, pale gold, dry, and crunchy. At the far end of the veranda the leggy vines of the Dutchman's pipe stand out in their nakedness, a few straggly leaves, shaped like huge brown lily pads, dangling from the vertical wires Dad strung from railing to roof. Walnuts fall from the three ancient black trees at the bottom of the garden. I hear them land with a sudden thud, unsure whether they've fallen of their own accord or been thrown by a squirrel. The pile of dried leaves blown along the base of the fence is so deep that when the squirrels land it sounds like an army of men booting through; I look up to see who's there. Then I watch them jump from a branch onto the eaves and duck inside our house.

There was a time in the 1950s when Mum and Dad hired a man to sit in the garden with a shotgun to shoot the squirrels, but the older Mum got, the more she believed in sharing this house with wildlife. She wouldn't have evicted the squirrels any more than she would have evicted that bird outside her bedroom or the spiders that laid claim to the high-ceilinged corners of the veranda. The birds are still singing this late in the season, but their melody has changed to a cacophony of urgent chirping, and smart flocks of geese are flapping their wings and heading south.

As I walk from the hall to the living room, I catch a glimpse of something out the playroom window: Is someone riding a bicycle through the heaps of leaves? I run to the veranda to look out, but it's only a golden retriever running with his owner. I realize how much this house aided and abetted Mum's insatiable curiosity. Now I have it, too.

I've finished my five abstract Shakespeare prints and Robin suggests a title for them: "Shakespeare Unlettered."

Jessica says, "You need to send them to a gallery in Stratford!"

"Uh-huh. For a *Shakesperience?*" We both laugh.

Then I wonder, *Is that what this is all about? Have I been obsessively counting letters all year just to please Mum?*

I remember grade six, when she insisted I could imitate Shakespeare just because I had the same twenty-six letters of the alphabet that he did. Have I finally completed the task she asked me to do when I was ten?

I tell Jessica there's no point in contacting a gallery—I have no reputation as a printmaker.

"That's ridiculous . . . it's as good as anything they have at the Tate! You're an artist," she says.

"I'd probably have more confidence if I'd gone to art school."

"Why didn't you?"

"Mum wanted me to have a proper profession . . . just in case."

Mum lumped "having a profession" into the same category as "knowing how to drive a car with a stick shift"—you never knew when you might need it in an emergency—but in her mind, motherhood was still the most important job. Dad sat me down at the kitchen table after I'd graduated from high school. He had such a low opinion of art as a subject worth studying that when I won the art prize that year I'd been too embarrassed to tell him. He thought theater and art were nothing but frivolous hobbies, so he gave me two choices: I could be a nurse or a teacher. After considering my fear of needles, he crossed out ~~nurse~~.

"So you just went along with it?" Jessica says.

"In those days, that's what we did." I laugh. "I wasn't a rebel like you are."

"I'm not a rebel—you didn't give us anything to rebel against!"

"You rebel against everything!" I can't believe she doesn't see herself the way I do.

At university I began to appreciate Mum, to admire her rebelliousness, her radical ways of thinking. Now when she didn't give a damn, I was as titillated as everyone else. But still I didn't rebel. Like a dutiful daughter, I got my degree, returned home, taught high school briefly, and then became an advertising copywriter—just as Mum had done thirty years before. When I married, gave up my career, and took on the role of housewife and mother, it seemed I was finally pleasing everybody.

I became the young mother in the park with a baby on my back—and during those years Mum was my role model and advocate. She was always there for me, calling every day, inviting me to bring the children out so she could help look after them. She taught me not to sweat the small stuff, to encourage their creativity, to let them make a mess.

I ask Jessica, "Do you remember the summers in Oakville when you were little?"

"Of course! Camp Anya!" Jessica says, recalling the T-shirts we had specially printed. Mum always had Popsicles for children in her freezer, and she kept a drawer in the pantry full of crayons and toys. She'd even pile her nightgowns on the veranda for dress-ups.

"She was younger than I am now," I say wistfully.

Once Dad retired, Mum began traveling and going on cruises with him. But then things changed. Life as we knew it began to fall apart. Most of us started divorcing. Sandy died. Dad got Alzheimer's. Mum's feisty, rebellious nature began battling for breath. Those are the years that have clouded my memory. They seemed to go on forever.

Ten years ago, when Jessica was studying at the Florence Academy of Art, I was still trying to juggle the duties of being both a mother and a daughter at the same time. Mum was eighty-three, recovering from a stroke, and Dad was well into his Alzheimer's.

Jessica called me from Italy one night. "I have a crazy idea . . ." Her voice crackled through the phone line. "My roommate is leaving for August. Instead of me coming home for the holiday, why don't you come here to Florence?" In the background I could hear the crashing of dishes, the clatter of cutlery, and shrieks of laughter.

"Where are you?" I asked, noting that it must be four o'clock in the morning on her side of the Atlantic.

"Pay phone . . . Restaurant!" She giggled. "Think about it. We could paint together!"

I'd just seen the movie *Tea with Mussolini*, so I lay back on my pillow and imagined myself as Judi Dench, floating through the streets of Florence in a billowing kimono with Sambo in my arms. I didn't know if I could leave Mum and Dad for two weeks, but Jessica's plea gave me courage. I called Mum the next day.

"Florence?" she shrieked. "But it's so hot there this time of year!"

"No hotter than here," I said.

"But it's expensive!"

"It'll never be cheaper!"

"But it's so far away . . ."

"I know . . ." In my mind, that was the best part about it.

I went shopping . . . in search of a 1930s kimono. I found one in a vintage shop on Queen Street and twirled around in front of my bedroom mirror. Mum called back.

"I've been thinking," she said. "Why can't Jessica come home . . . and the two of you go to an art school in Rochester instead?"

"Rochester?" I felt the umbilical cord snap.

"There's a wonderful art school in Rochester!"

"Mum, somehow Rochester doesn't sound as *romantic* as Florence."

"If you lived in *Florence* you would think Rochester was romantic!"

I braced myself for her arguments. Mum was so powerful in the art of persuasion that I always acquiesced. This time I wanted to be the mother. I wanted to be with my daughter. I needed to find the courage to disappoint Mum—to put my needs and my daughter's needs before hers.

I drove out to Oakville and took the kimono out of the bag. Mum looked wistful and stopped talking about Rochester; she knew my mind was made up. She fingered the cream-colored silk with its embroidered green leaves.

"This is the trip I always wish I'd taken with you," she said quietly. Then she rummaged in her desk and brought out a small cloth-bound book. "Did I ever show you this?" The title *Scribble Book* was gold-embossed on its blue cover. Inside its yellowing pages were the pencil sketches she'd made of her own trip to Italy in 1937.

"Oh, Mum," I said, "I didn't know you'd gone to Florence when you were the same age as Jessica!"

What happens to a woman's dreams? Why hadn't Mum and I ever gone painting together? I thought about all of Mum's artwork that went up in the flames of Dad's fireplace. It made me more determined than ever to grab this opportunity with Jessica. I didn't want to be eighty-three, looking back with regrets.

"Promise you'll call me every day!" said Mum. "Promise me!"

A month later I'd packed my paints and brushes and was high in the sky with Alitalia, endlessly rehearsing the only two words in my Italian vocabulary: *Ca-poo-chee no, pear-fuh-vor-eh!*"

I turn now to Jessica.

"Do you remember that summer I stayed with you in Florence?"

"Of course!"

"How come you don't paint anymore?" After studying languages and then learning to paint in the classical style, Jessica returned home and got a degree in psychology. Now she works in the hospitality industry.

She shrugs. "Because it doesn't make me happy anymore. I've found something else that I enjoy doing."

"Wait a minute . . . you flew there by yourself . . . you chose the school . . . you stayed three years. You painted all those beautiful masterpieces."

"Maybe you should go to art school. Maybe *you* have an unfulfilled dream!"

I'm stunned. Are all our unfulfilled dreams unconsciously

passed down from mother to daughter for generations? Does it never end?

A week later, my Other Mother Pat drives out to spend the day with me. I tell her I've been having dreams about Mum. Last night I dreamed my bedroom was missing its furniture. In its place was a miniature child, about the size of a paper clip. I picked her up and went looking for her family. I met Mum in the hallway and placed the child in the palm of her hand. I hurried to lock all the doors, but I was too late: in rushed a group of gypsy archaeologists. They were clutching valuable artifacts that they were excited to tell me they'd found in the basement, but when I looked closely, I could see they were holding only the old props I'd handmade as a child for my theater. "How dare you trespass into our house!" I yelled. "This is not a museum! This is our HOME!" They wanted their daughter back, but I wouldn't give her up until they returned our old furniture.

"What a marvelous dream," she says. "A real *epic*! You must be exhausted."

She tells me that in a dream, when someone is breaking into your house, it is to force you to confront something. She thinks the tiny child is me—representing the start of something, perhaps the new life I'm being given.

"The problem is, dear, you're still prepared to give her up for old furniture, for goodness' sake!" she says. "You're still trying to lock the door. Don't you see? The furniture belongs in the past. The child is now." Then she laughs. "Basements always represent the unconscious, our creative side, our deeper self. And you have a very deep unconscious!"

Pat and I wander through the rooms. She's astonished at how big the house is, how empty it feels, how much clutter is gone. I tell her it's turned out to be harder than I ever imagined. I've felt like Alice through the looking-glass, going down so many rabbit holes.

"I know how you feel, dear," she says. "It's why I decided to do the final edit myself."

"What do you mean?"

"After Geoff died, when I moved to the house where I am now, I was ruthless. I was eighty-one, you know. I gave away or threw away everything. I didn't want to burden my children." She giggles. "I even burned all my diaries!"

"You burned your *diaries*?" I am aghast. "Why?"

"They were private . . . full of personal feelings."

"But didn't you think your children would want to know you in that intimate way after you're gone?"

"I didn't think it was fair for others to read them."

"Don't you wish you'd been able to read your own mother's diary?"

"Actually, I would . . ." says Pat, looking into the distance. "I regret it now."

Earlier I'd resolved to clear out my own mess, too, so my children wouldn't have to face it, but since then I've had a change of heart. Now I believe this clearing out is a valuable process—best left to our children. It's the only way they'll ever truly come to know us, discovering things we never wanted them to find. I'm still hoping to find a diary of Mum's. The only thing she ever showed me was her sketchbook.

At least my dreams are changing. In my childhood dreams I always feared I was about to drown, overwhelmed by a threatening wave; now they're about discovering how deep my creative powers are. I can see that Pat's right: my dreams are about letting go. They're telling me that the most valuable things come from within myself.

But—if dreams are to be believed—I'm still trying to give myself back to my mother.

Careful What You Wish For

In late November I dial home, into my archived phone messages, clicking through until I find the one Mum left me a year ago, two months before she died. In a happy, heartfelt, enthusiastic tone, with her lilting southern accent, I hear her sing *"Hap-py birth-day, m'dah'lin'!"* I listen to it over and over again. Then I burst into tears. I had wanted her to leave me alone, and two months later she did. Now I find myself looking up at the sky, searching for her.

"Are you there, Mum?"

Yes, darling, I'm right here.

"What do you want me to do with all this stuff?"

Whatever you want—they're only things. Nothing lasts forever.

I'm recognizing that this house is only the shell my mother and father left behind, but it represents their marriage, the life they built together, their frugality, and their generosity. It represents their personalities, too—the pairing of two opposites. When I look out at the lake—sometimes smooth as glass, sometimes gently waving, sometimes roiling with stormy whitecaps—the vista reflects their life together. Like the rocks and pebbles under the surface, their edges eventually fit together, rubbed smooth over time, because beneath it all there was a commitment to stay together. This house still dances with that powerful energy, even though Mum and Dad have died. Its bones are soaked with the DNA of all who went before, in this wide-open setting, so attuned to nature. The house hums and rattles and whispers to me. I want to burrow back into it, reconsider my past, find the mother I once knew, reconnect our broken link. I want the house to help me. I want to bathe in the memories.

Why can't we keep it?

On the other hand, why can't I let go?

Every time I drive in and out of the driveway, past the FOR SALE sign staked on the lawn, I'm reminded that we're about to lose another member of our family—this house that we took for granted would forever be here as a backdrop to our lives. I worry that we're saying good-bye to more than just a house. What will hold the family together after it's gone?

Victor was right about our first potential buyer: unable to secure financing, he has reluctantly withdrawn. I gave him his portrait. I didn't feel right about accepting any fee, so he made a donation in honor of Mum to Oomama, the charity that sponsors African grandmothers. Mum would have liked that. He tells me that our family and this house have had a profound effect on him, and that although he's sad to have lost out, he believes everything happens for a reason. I still have coffee with him from time to time, whenever I find him sitting by the lake in the early mornings. We share a common bond now: both mourning the loss of this house. I'm glad I painted him sitting on the veranda steps, evidence of one last guest—a stranger—invited in. Mum would have liked that most of all.

In December, the *Globe and Mail* runs a half-page feature of our house in their Homes section and we get a surprising hit. Alex has just called to say that a Mr. Baines has booked an appointment to see the house tomorrow. He saw the write-up and couldn't believe it—this house once belonged to his grandfather! It was their summer cottage, affectionately named Summerholme.

Only three families have lived in this house since it was built in the nineteenth century. The Baineses bought it in 1917 and sold it to Mum and Dad in 1952. I usually don't hang around when Alex shows the house, but the next day I'm so excited that I'm cutting short my scheduled lunch to be here. I want to meet Mr. Baines. What are the chances that, while Mum and Dad's descendants can't find a way to hang on to this house, grandchildren of the previous owners might save it? My hopes are soaring. I race back to meet them as they arrive.

Two generations spill out of their car: two middle-aged grandsons of the original owner with their wives, and a great-grandson in his thirties, Robert, who's never been inside the house before. In their arms they carry ancient oversized albums with black pages stuffed with photos held in by gummed corners. They run through the house, pointing things out to Robert, matching pictures to rooms. They can't believe everything looks the same.

I am mesmerized. The photos in their albums could have been taken of us. Black-and-white snapshots show their similar-sized family assembled on the veranda, sitting in identical wicker armchairs, and gathered beside the beach-stone fireplace in the living room, just as we have done. In the corner of one photo, an old CCM bicycle like mine is thrown haphazardly on the lawn, lying on its side, looking like its wheels are still spinning. The garden bench is the same one Robin donated to the museum—I recognize its decorative iron base even though the wood slats have been replaced. A teepee is pitched in the garden—almost identical to the one we used to play in. It feels as if we've found a whole new branch of the family we never knew we had.

Robert tells me his ancestors brought their furniture out from Toronto each spring and then packed it up in the fall, leaving the house empty all winter.

"I always heard about a huge chest of drawers," he says. "My grandfather said it was blue and had a magical secret drawer!"

"Would you like to see it?" I ask him.

"What do you mean?"

"It's still here!"

His eyes widen. "You've got to be kidding!"

I take him to the upstairs hall where the monster wardrobe sits. It's got a gleaming mahogany veneer now. Dad removed the blue milk paint years ago, a "restoration" that, as it turned out, dramatically reduced its value. I slide out the middle bonnet drawer and show Robert the secret button inside that releases what appears to be a decorative rim above. He is agog.

Downstairs, I show him a few Victorian pressback chairs with their worn leather seats that also came with the house. Sadly, the others have broken and the matching table has gone with Chris to B.C., but there are so many other things to see. His father tells me that the room we always called our playroom was originally designed for a pool table, and now the low-hanging brass light fixtures we found in a cupboard make sense. We pore over the photos and talk for hours, promising to keep in touch. It's obvious they didn't come to buy, merely to take a trip down memory lane, but the house is speaking again and Mum would have loved this encounter.

Early the next morning I awake to find my body aligned to the Earth's magnetic pole, as if my head has been pulled due north. I'm not a practitioner of feng shui, but just for fun I check my Ming Gua number and find that it's six: metal. This tells me that if I sleep facing north, the influence is separation. Could my body be telling me something—that separation is what I need right now?

I see another beautiful sunrise accumulating across the horizon. It is so dramatic. In the west, a horizontal wedge of deep indigo is sandwiched between a deep splotch of apricot, which is feathering into the opaque, milky white of the lake below. The tiny pinholes of electric light along Burlington Bay cut through the ink. I run to my paints, but even as I open the lid I know I might be too late to capture the changing light. I plunge my brush into a mixture of aquamarine and raw umber and let it flow onto the only blank card I can find: the backside of one of my *Romeo and Juliet* prints. I've just had them printed for Christmas cards, but I don't care. I have to sacrifice one to this scene. I scrumble and scratch and lay orange on thick and then wipe it with a dishcloth. Within minutes the inky blackness is dissolving into puffs of smoke, the water is changing to slate gray, and the apricot is fading to shell pink.

Will I ever get used to the beauty of early mornings here?

The optimism of the rising sun shoots through my veins like adrenaline. A lone duck has appeared on the surface, serenely bobbing on the waves near shore. Another joins in, washing its feathers nearby. Our Canadian flag has woken up, flapping sleepily. It was a formless black line half an hour ago; now it looks russet and its maple leaf becomes clear.

I have unlocked the veranda door. Even though the thermometer outside the kitchen window reads only forty degrees Fahrenheit—just above freezing—it doesn't feel cold; it feels fresh. The sun has popped up over the horizon, directly across from the door, and shines a searchlight onto my face. All the living room furniture is backlit, outlined by a halo of orange, as if I'm at Stonehenge during the winter solstice, on a pilgrimage of healing, worshipping the recently deceased.

Joggers run by, laughing, their running shoes crunching on the gravel path. The geese honk, but no birds are singing. They should have all flown south by now, but I've learned that the swallows stay here. A woman walks by briskly in a long coat, hurried along by her golden Labrador.

Now the clouds have parted, as if the sun has swept them aside. They fan out in brilliant white plumes, leaving behind streaks of lavender and robin's-egg blue. It looks like one of those holy paintings on the ceiling frescoes in Florence.

I need a last hurrah. Maybe I should make Mum's famous eggnog this December?

Once we moved to Canada, Mum could never attend her own family's massive annual Christmas Eve party in Virginia, so she attempted to replicate it at Point O' View. Instead of hordes of cousins, Mum invited everyone she met to our Christmas parties, and sometimes more than two hundred people crammed into the downstairs rooms. One year, a guest even rode in on his horse. Carols were sung around the piano in the playroom, food was laid out in the dining room, and halfway through the evening Dad turned off all the lights and marched through the rooms like the Pied Piper, carrying aloft a platter of flaming raisins that he'd soaked in brandy and lit with a match. He lowered it for the children so they could see the flickering gas-blue flames up close. He urged them to put their hands in to grab a few. It was the only kind of flame that didn't burn you, he said.

Mum would bring down Granny's music box—the antique automaton that she kept wrapped in a sheet and stored throughout the year in a special cupboard upstairs. She set it on a low table so that visiting children could turn the crank and watch the figures come to life to the tune of the old German carol "O du fröhliche." I suspect the music box has lasted because it was only ever cranked each Christmas—a total of about 133 days since 1878—and also because the old linen sheet Mum wrapped it in was probably as organic and acid-free as the Shroud of Turin.

But the pièce de résistance was Mum's eggnog. Using her family's bourbon-laced recipe, she served it up in Granny's silver punch bowl. It predated Peg Bracken's recipes by about a hundred years, but it followed her ideology: as long as it got stirred once a day, you could continue serving it until the dog walked away. The recipe required staggering quantities of rum, bourbon, scotch, and sherry, and Mum delegated the making of it to me. We began fermenting it in late October. By Christmas, it was lethal. Mum served it to adults in tiny juice glasses; more than two and they'd have to spend the night.

I carry the old five-gallon stone crock into Dad's workroom and start cracking the three dozen eggs. I mix in the sugar and skim milk and dribble the quarts of mixed liquors in a slow, steady stream, stirring all the while with the long-handled wooden spoon until my arm aches, just as it did in childhood. I cover the crock with a heavy board and make a note to stir it once a day until

Christmas. Dad's workroom is cold, so the eggnog will safely do its lethal fermenting, just as it always has.

M y plan of spending six weeks here has stretched into a year. For the first time in my life I'm free to have Christmas in my own house in Toronto, but I'm still feeling tugged in two different directions, wanting to be there with my children but unable to let go of the tradition of being here. Nobody else in the family feels this way, it seems. My brothers have long since raised anchor.

Victor is excited to tell me that he's found a friend who'll house-sit Point O' View for a few days so that I can have Christmas at my own house, as I've always claimed I wanted. In his mind, he's giving me the ultimate Christmas present. As I drive into the city with a bottle of eggnog tucked in the backseat, I think how strange it feels, leaving Mum's house just before Christmas, still having to hit the road, only this time driving in the opposite direction.

This time last year, I was helping Mum wrap her presents and decorating her house. In previous years she had always directed me—"Why don't you put the angels up there"—but last year she'd just dismissed them with a wave of her hand: "I don't care where you put the damn things." I watched her sit on the guest bed, picking through her bags of junk, trying to decide who would get what. She handed me pieces of old gift wrap—folded and reused so many times they felt like soft suede—and strips of ribbon that were wrinkled and frayed. When Dad was alive, he used to iron them.

The turkey was a disaster. I usually cooked one ahead of time and brought it out on Christmas morning, but last year, to give me a break, my brothers suggested we pick one up from a hotel.

Dry slabs of tasteless, pre-cut turkey, square potatoes, and bland stuffing arrived in huge tinfoil pans. We didn't even pretend to disguise it: we served it up assembly line–style, as if we were in an institutional soup kitchen, and sat helter-skelter. I didn't eat with Mum—she was in the other room. We forgot to say grace. There was no warm aroma of gravy simmering, no anticipatory scent of cinnamon in the air. The kitchen smelled cold and tinny—conversation drifted up to the ceiling; nobody was listening and sentences trailed off.

When we opened Mum's presents, my son received a pad of writing paper with the name "Mary" printed on each sheet. He looked surprised and reminded Mum, plaintively, "But my name isn't Mary."

"So what?" she snapped. "It's perfectly good writing paper, isn't it?"

We took pictures of each other wearing shirts with NORTEL emblazoned on the sleeves and clutching books with titles like *All the President's Men* and *Terry Waite: Man with a Mission*. Then everyone quickly departed.

Mum's house was the originating maypole, but divorces and remarriages and grown grandchildren and their new in-laws had added a million extra ribbons to the dance tangle. Most of the younger generation spent Christmas Day on the road, rushing from one turkey dinner to the next, and church was forfeited altogether—there was no time.

What had started out as a lovely tradition on holidays—after all, her house was the only one large enough to accommodate all of us—had, over the years, tied me inexorably to Mum. I'd never established a Christmas tradition in my own home with my own children, and now they'd all moved out.

Mum had looked despondent as one by one the grandchildren bundled into their coats and hustled out the boathouse door—on to the next set of in-laws.

When I tried to blend in with the departing crowds, Mum said, "You, too? Can't you stay?" And I felt trapped. I was the only one with no prior commitment; my children were off to their father's house. As I watched the other rats leaving the sinking ship, I felt abandoned, too. I took off my coat and agreed to stay a little longer.

"It's so lonesome here," Mum had said as she trailed her oxygen tubing into the TV room. "Let's watch *Lawrence Welk*!"

This Christmas feels ironic: my own house feels alien after a year away. The air smells musty: the radiators *ping* and *clang* as I turn up the heat. There are dust bunnies everywhere. The refrigerator is empty.

When I bought this house thirty years ago, all three of my children were under the age of seven. I had enrolled at York University in its MFA theater program, giddy with the freedom of divorce, deluded into thinking I might finally achieve one of my childhood dreams of becoming an actress. After walking the children to school I took classes all day, then rushed home, fed them dinner, and lugged them back to rehearsals, where they sat in the back of the darkened stage and watched me perform. Mum was appalled.

"Acting is no career for a mother!" she said. "You can't abandon those precious children of yours. At the end of your life, which do you want: a bunch of old movies you've acted in . . . or memories of watching your children growing up?"

I wanted it all, but fate agreed with Mum. Six months later I was in a serious car accident, bedridden for weeks, unable to dress myself, unable even to hold up my spine for longer than ten minutes. Mum came in each day to help, happy I was forced to withdraw from the program. She thought I had come to my senses. She hoped I would buckle down, remarry, and become a stay-at-home mother again. But I wanted more. I loved my children—yes—but I didn't want to spend my days on the tennis courts like she had. Mum had never resumed her career as a copywriter and a columnist after she had children. I wanted to use my talents. Besides, now that I was divorced I needed to support myself. How could I have a career and be there for my children, too? I plunged into a depression.

Dad came to see me. "First Daughter," he said, "there is something I learned in the Navy: you only have to turn your ship a few degrees to end up on a completely different shore." I did end up on a completely different shore, but then so did Mum—and she didn't sacrifice her marriage to do it; she chose to sacrifice other things. I remember Dad telling me that "the grass is never greener on the other side"—it just looks that way. Did Mum have any regrets? Did her life turn out the way she'd expected? Did she ever think back to her choices and wish she'd made different ones? I wish I'd asked her.

I spend the first day grocery shopping and the next day cleaning. On Christmas Eve I put up a small tree, throw an old wreath on the front door, and fill a pot of boiling water with cinnamon sticks and cloves to give the house a festive scent. My table should be laid with fancy garlands and Christmas crackers, the aroma of roast turkey and shortbread wafting in from the kitchen, but the big convivial dinner I always envisioned doesn't happen. People have other plans: my children alight only briefly on Christmas morning to exchange presents and then rush off for turkey at their father's house; Robin has no reason to drive up anymore; Chris has moved away; and Victor has flown south on a holiday with Peni.

I remind myself that I'm the grandmother now.

I'm alone on Christmas afternoon, surveying the wreckage of crumpled wrapping paper, idly wondering if I should iron the ribbons. Is this how Mum used to feel after we left? I can hear her saying, "Careful what you wish for, you just might get it."

From every window of my city house, I see nothing but brick walls outside. Mum was right: I can stretch out my arms in the front hall and almost touch both sides. She was right about so many things.

The house feels small now. I feel hemmed in, missing the sky and the lake. I've no sooner put up my tree than it's Boxing Day and time to take it down again.

The very next day I speed back—west along the highway, back to Point O' View.

Separation

In the mail on the boathouse step there's a touching letter from Chris in B.C. He writes, *So much has happened . . . I feel like events have overwhelmed our ability to process them together.* He remembers Dad's and Mum's deaths as being so closely linked that they seemed like two sides of the same page. He reminds me how I and my toothbrush "won the toss" the night Dad died . . . how Victor had to hold me back from running after Dad's coffin as the hearse pulled away from the church . . . and how we all went to the vet together to say our last good-byes to Sambo.

Then he writes, *One of the things I'm not sure I ever told you was how concerned Mum was about her relationship with you. She loved you deeply and wanted to be close to you, but I honestly think she didn't know how.* Chris says he kept urging Mum to share her own self-doubts with me. *Did she ever do that?* he asks. He tells me that Mum's struggle with me was a constant theme in their conversations together.

As he reminisces about our childhood, he says,

I know how much you would have rather played with your friends than look after your baby brothers, and I wish you hadn't had to do that, for your sake . . . but I want to give thanks for the role you played as my big sister. When you went off to Boston (to university) I felt a mixture of fascination and desolation. One of my rocks was disappearing. I came to visit you there, do you remember? You took me to Tufts University so I could explore some alternative possibilities. When I was at boarding school in Tonbridge, you sent me a towel with a heart sewn in the corner . . . I held on to that towel for the longest time. When my first child was born, where did I go when I left the hospital? To your house—that's where. When my marriage broke up, you sent me a television and a set of kitchen pots. What an extraordinary gesture! Mum couldn't do that—not even close. She was too conflicted about divorce. No, that gesture of love came from my other mother—you! I still have the pots!

Now I'm on the other side of the country and you're in Oakville once more. I know it's complicated, but I want you to know that I recognize that this is one more example of the oldest child taking care of things. Thank you for caring so much for so long. Thank you for creating a little bit of space where things were safe and less crazy . . . Thanks for paying attention and for reaching out. Thanks for being my sister!

I am so overwhelmed by the letter I can't absorb it in one sitting. It triggers so many flashbacks—wonderful memories, and sad ones, too. I had no idea Mum worried about our relationship or that she cared so much she was constantly asking Chris for advice. I take the letter upstairs with me and reread it before I go to bed. Chris often criticized Mum for what he called her "triangulated" relationships: where she would speak to one of us about the other, instead of going direct. But I saw her habit in a positive light; it caused us to consider each other. I think she was trying to keep us connected.

The following morning, I read it again and find the part where Chris reminisces about our Christmas parties, *especially that giant wooden bowl filled with nuts . . . It had a honker of a nutcracker attached in the middle . . . remember?* He used to marvel at its "cracking triumph" when the machine finally broke open the shells to reveal "the strange pulp" inside. He feels that the death of our parents is similar: *The great big nuts have finally been cracked wide open.*

Two days later, as I'm shivering in Dad's workshop, stirring Mum's eggnog with the wooden spoon, my eyes glance over at the debris of bolts and nails strewn across Dad's worktable. There—in the mound of brass and iron—I see the top of the "honker." Dad has conscripted the wooden bowl to hold miscellaneous screws. It is nowhere near the size Chris remembers as a child, but I rescue it, package it, and send it to him in B.C.

Victor and I hold a New Year's Eve party, which we know may be our last in this house. Food is prepared, family members gather, and friends of all ages are invited. Nobody much likes my eggnog. Tastes have changed and eggnog has gone the way of suet and Christmas pudding—stodgy recipes better remembered than served. A few neighbors arrive, laughing, through the garden gate at midnight, fumbling with the fox latch in the dark, holding out a bottle of champagne. We decide to walk along the lake to the end of the pier. The sky is so clear I want to see the stars in all directions. When we get there, the horizon is popping with fireworks displays.

I stand on the end of the pier, thinking about all the things we've inherited, all the carefully saved fragments from another time—George's Napoleonic pardon, Great-grandfather's family Bible, Mum's World War II identity card, Dad's Hong Kong newspaper, our "Wowance" book, even the beads from Sandy's baby bracelet—each generation preserving them in turn, wanting future generations to know of this long, braided chain of genes, habits, and attitudes that binds us together as family: our history and stories. I think about something Pat once said to me: "You didn't just inherit from your mother—you inherited from your father, too. You and your brothers are the best part of them."

New Year's Day is gray, misty, drizzling, and warm. People are carrying umbrellas as they walk their dogs along the lakefront. Tiny sparrows flurry up from the grass to settle on the uppermost branches of a bare tree, giving it what looks like instant leaves. Commingled ducks and geese quack and squawk in high and low registers as their wings flap through the water at liftoff.

Will this be my last winter in this house? Conflicting thoughts—wanting the house to sell and not wanting it to sell—clang around in my heart. It feels unsettling that the timing of my "moving on" is in the hands of a stranger. I could, of course, move on now, hire someone to house-sit, and dictate my own future. But why would I give up a moment of this? I try to live in the here and now, to embrace the unpredictability, to feel gratitude for this chance, to make the most of every day. If everything has a purpose, then there's a reason the house hasn't sold yet. There's still something more I'm meant to discover.

Separation

Some days, the waves on the lake dance forward in pairs, as if they're holding hands, flirting and flashing white petticoats. Other times—more ominously—the waves don't break at all; they just roll under the surface, heaving up and down, going nowhere, like a suspenseful blanket. This is when the ducks flock in and huddle in groups, taking cover, resigned. Mum said the birds know everything. Tonight, they seem to know a storm is coming.

On TV, weather stations are mapping a raging monster—a swirling orange eye surrounded by blotches of white and blue—churning angrily up the Eastern Seaboard, heading straight for Toronto. They're calling it "the mother of all storms." Like everyone else, I go to the hardware store to buy a new shovel and a bag of salt and to the grocery store to stock up on necessary food: coffee and chocolate-mousse cake. I'm going to stay home, warm and cozy, and start reading Mum's letters. I've been waiting all year to finish the task of clearing this house, saving Mum's letters as my reward. Now it's time.

I dive into the binder marked "1941 Working Girl NYC"—when Mum is twenty-five years old and describing her new job as advertising copywriter at Macy's. Although war had been raging in Europe for more than a year, Mum's life in New York seems like a nonstop party. I find tearsheets from the fashion ads she wrote: "Dress for one man, not for many!" . . . "Live on a budget but look as if you didn't!"

She describes her apartment on East 52nd Street that she shared with three other girls: the rent they paid, the full-time maid they hired to cook for them, and her many dates with handsome young men who had names like Bass Bridgeforth, Truman Welling, Rucker Ryland, and Howze Haskell. They take her dancing to places like the Rainbow Room, the Stork Club, El Morocco, and the Cloud Club atop the Chrysler Building. She describes paying the exorbitant sum of $1.50 for scrambled eggs at four-thirty in the morning at Reubens, where she runs into Lana Turner at the next table. I read about Noël Coward's wonderful new play *Blithe Spirit* and the movies Mum watched, like *That Hamilton Woman* and *Target for Tonight*, a documentary showing an actual bombing raid over Germany. I smile as I notice that at the end of every letter Mum delegates a task to her mother: *I sent you my laundry two weeks ago but it hasn't come back! Where is it? . . . We're having a house party next weekend so if you could get Edmonia to cook us some food and send it up by train, it would be much appreciated!*

Then, on December 9, 1941, two days after the attack on Pearl Harbor, she describes New York City's first air-raid warning. Instead of diving for cover, as I would have done, she runs up to the roof of her office building to scan the skies for German bombers because she doesn't want to miss any of the action. Within a month the streets of New York are filling up with men in uniform. Mum decides to join the American Red Cross, but they tell her she isn't a suitable candidate. Instead, she's accepted as a Junior Hostess for an Armed Forces program that operates out of the Hotel Delmonico on Park Avenue. Her job is to entertain officers in transit.

In her letters home to Rokeby, Mum complains of being "danced off her feet": *On Friday, I went to Radio City Music Hall with a Navy flier who has just come back from Pearl Harbor. They all say, "This might be the last time you'll see me," which is a pretty worn-out phrase by now, if you ask me.*

With America's entry into the war, and to Mum's delight, the Red Cross now tells her she's exactly the kind of candidate they want. She signs up, but it takes a year before she's finally deployed. During that year she continues to work as a Junior Hostess—being danced off her feet.

I switch to the binder marked "1942 Falling in Love" and find the letter she wrote to her mother the night she met Dad—the letter the boys and I had already read.

I know you probably think I've lost my mind, but it's only my heart! Nothing like this has ever happened to me before & I still don't believe it's real . . .

Now that she's met Dad, she's determined to be sent to England, so she gets her brother Langbourne to make a phone call. He's friends with Norman Davis, who had once been President Woodrow Wilson's undersecretary of state and is now chairman of the International Federation of the Red Cross. A few months later, Mum is sailing happily for England aboard the Cunard liner *Queen Elizabeth.*

I read hundreds of letters and cables documenting her war years: how she became program director of the Aero Club for the famed Eagle Squadrons of the American Air Force 4th Fighter Group stationed at Debden and how she later organized entertainment for convalescing officers at Rest Homes in the countryside, getting to know "the Clivedon Set"—influential friends of Lord and Lady Astor, many of whom had contributed the use of their country homes to the war effort. She describes greeting Bob Hope and Ike Eisenhower; having tea with the famous political theorist Harold Laski; "bumping into" Field Marshal Montgomery at Claridge's; chatting to Noël Coward in a pub. War highlighted her resourcefulness: she had a talent for putting herself in the right place at the right time—and then making the most of it. She reassures her mother that although her fighter base is only about forty miles from London, the Germans don't know where it is: *Don't worry—I don't like bombs any more than you do. We haven't been bombed yet.* Her letters are full of enclosures: maps, pub menus, local leaflets, advertisements, and autographs and snapshots of famous pilots like Don Gentile and Johnny Godfrey. In one letter, she describes a gift that I recognize, the galoshes she wore to my grade-two Christmas party:

> *Col. Malone has given me some RAF escape boots—They are fleece-lined and warm as toast—only they're about size 20, so I look like a cartoon. Whenever I wear them everybody laughs, and all the dogs start barking!*

The first Christmas at her base she organizes a party for local children—evacuees, whose fathers have gone off to war. She scrounges a Santa suit and carol music and asks the GIs to play "daddy for the day," donating their rations of food and candy. Toys have become scarce in England, since most factories have been retooled to produce munitions, but Mum drives a truck into London where she manages to forage masses of toys from a wholesaler. Word spreads throughout the county, and on Christmas afternoon more than four hundred children show up.

> *We had a grand time. They looked more like 4000 than 400 but the GIs grabbed one each, and were so attentive*

and the kids so responsive that there was a wonderful festive atmosphere. Many of the kids had never seen ice cream. One little girl said she'd give anything to have that party over and over again, if only in a dream.

There is a slew of letters from strangers to the family at Rokeby—introducing themselves and announcing their upcoming arrival. It seems Mum's habit of welcoming waifs and strays to Oakville when we were young was nothing new. She casually suggested to many GIs that they go stay with her family whenever they went back to America on leave. Nonplussed, Granny always welcomed them in. One letter describes "a nice Minnesota farm boy, who looked after the guns on Annie's Post."

By early summer Mum has still heard nothing from Dad, but she manages to commandeer army jeeps on her time off and enjoy an astonishing social life with various boyfriends. One night, she's invited to dinner by the editor of the *New Statesman*, Kingsley Martin, and the author Dorothy Woodman.

They live in the cutest house out in the country—a 300-yr.-old pub, practically all thatch roof with a lovely lawn and garden, full of beautiful old furniture—all very simple. They're both fascinating people, terribly intelligent, though in the middle of a heated discussion on Japan's economy or something, one of them would suddenly grab a pair of field glasses and shout, "Look—I do believe that's the little woodpecker we were looking for!" Before I left, K. asked how I had managed to get a jeep . . . was my visit "important business"? I told him I thought anything was important, if it helped you to survive. He pondered this, picked me a lovely bunch of flowers from his rockery, and said "I think that is a very profound remark!"

Then suddenly, just before closing time on Monday night, June 6, 1944, the whole base is put on lockdown: no one can go home or use the phones; everything becomes "strictly business." Mum is suspicious—she's seen the boys painting the planes all afternoon. By midnight she's convinced something's up—that this could be D-Day. Determined not to miss such a momentous event, she stays up to watch. Soon she hears the concentrated engine noises of dozens of planes and rushes outside to watch them zoom off. This is the event that they've been waiting for, and planning, for three long years . . . *our Allied Air Armada, disappearing into the vastness of the sky until they just became part of the huge roar overhead. I wouldn't have missed being here for anything in the world!*

The next morning, ground crews are racing around the clock. Pilots are looking tired and haggard from continuous flying. Now they're dashing in and out, dressed in gear, grabbing a sandwich, and boasting about the thirty-six-hour stretch they've just put in. To Mum, all activity prior to D-Day seems like child's play. *The awful waiting is over. It's as though you've been treading water in the surging seas for hours on end and suddenly you're picked up and rescued—and life begins again!*

The awful waiting was over in a more personal sense, too, because that very evening she's called to the front gate. A man, claiming to know Mum, is being held in the guardhouse, and needs to be identified. It's Dad. She hasn't seen him since they first met in New York, two years earlier, but their life together is about to begin again—prophetically, on D-Day.

Separation

He looks a little yellowed from Quinine, but otherwise much the same. He wants me to spend a week with him at his sister's. Will let you know what I think of him after that!

She slips up to London with Dad and stays in a hotel. As the bombs start falling, she calmly tells Dad to "have faith in God." He replies, "I think God would tell us to go to an air-raid shelter."

A week later, I notice with relief that she's finally spelling his name correctly. *Alex and I want to get married—OK? I know you will think we should wait till after the war but I hope you understand how impractical that is. You'll think I'm nuts, but it's a screwy world anyway!*

They plan their wedding for September. Mum delegates her trousseau to her brother's secretary in New York, asking her to buy and ship over "the most impractical clothes you can find," one of which is a wedding dress . . . *something simple—maybe organdy or taffeta—I don't really care. Also I'd like a pretty afternoon dress—possibly navy blue with white fluff and a hat to go with it. I need some perfume, a slip that swishes, and two or three risqué nightgowns . . . I'm pining for frills.*

Then she delegates the wedding announcements to her mother: *I wonder if you could get them printed over there and send them out. I've forgotten most of my friends' names, so will you be thinking up a list? Also, can you suggest something for me to give to Alex? My mind is a blank on the subject.* She apologizes for being such a "screwball daughter." *If only someday I could come near to being the kind of mother you are, I'll be satisfied.* She encloses a letter from Dad, which she says took him several stiff drinks and six pipes full of tobacco to compose.

In it, Dad asks permission to marry Mum, even though he

warns that the first year or so of married life will include long periods of separation and no definite home. He says he has tried "in not too gallant a manner to put Anne out of my thoughts the past two years, and failed." Then he adds his own P.S.: *I shall never be anything but English, but then, thank God, Anne will never be other than American, and if we don't always understand each other that's probably what we love about each other.*

With Dad's weeklong leave ended and their wedding still three months away, Mum busies herself opening a Rest Home for American pilots at Eynsham Hall, a colossal, Jacobean-style home in the country near Oxford. In peacetime, she says, it needed 240 servants to run it. Now it's known as the "Flak Shack." Mum describes the grounds as particularly lovely, with lake and boathouse, swans and wild ducks, indoor and outdoor tennis courts and a house that can easily accommodate a hundred people. She also describes the fragile emotional state of the men, who "wake up in beds soaked with sweat, describing their nightmares."

There are interleaved letters and cables from Dad, as well—most of them written aboard destroyers in secret locations and heavily censored. They are full of love and longing. If Mum was missing Dad, there is little mention. She's sketching portraits of the pilots, tagging along with the recently widowed war artist Frank Beresford, whose famous painting of George V lying in state has just been bought by Queen Mary, and she's still being feted by admirers from her old fighter base. *I've been jitterbugging till 3 am . . . and playing "Sardines"—you should have seen me and a Colonel hiding on a shelf in the broom closet . . . whattanite!* By now the owners of Eynsham Hall, who have relocated to a smaller house on the property, are fans of Mum's, too, so Mrs. Mason offers to host her wedding reception there, putting kitchens and cooks at Mum's disposal.

Mum's descriptions of her wedding sound like the original blueprint for my own wedding, which she organized thirty years later. Her dress arrived with shoes that didn't fit, so she wore her old tennis shoes; she asked friends to donate booze and hitched a ride in an army truck to get to the church on time. Dad arrived at the last minute.

I also discover that we've inherited Mum's genes for altering church services, as we did at her funeral: *The cute old vicar told Alex that I had made history by insisting my bridesmaid precede me down the aisle (apparently it's the reverse here) and cutting out most of the service (he was referring to the C. of E. stuff) and tho Alex insisted on putting back in the word* obey, *the vicar said, "I don't believe this could have been done snappier in America!"*

Once she's married she gushes about her new husband, in ways that take me by surprise:

> *He's so wonderful, Mum, I don't see how one man can have so much of everything. He's the only person I've ever known who completely fulfills all the principles you've always taught us to live by. All the girls are crazy about him, saying they'd marry him, even if he was a Russian! I certainly never expected to marry a man who takes such complete charge of me. He's a combination of stern mother, indulgent father, and loving husband, all rolled into one. He reminds me a lot of Daddy in his desire to help others. He even picked up an old hitchhiker in our dash from the reception to our honeymoon, and threw him in the backseat, atop our rice-covered luggage!*

I certainly recognize Dad's generosity toward hitchhikers, but "indulgent father" is news to me. She writes, *We will only have two weeks together—but however long or however short, I'm grateful.* Then she adds a curious afterthought—one that we'd seen her put into practice the whole time we were growing up: *How do you build up an impression of bold indifference to a husband like mine??? That's what he needs!*

After their brief honeymoon, Dad was ordered to Belgium and they were separated once again. Mum went to work at a second Rest Home—Knightshayes Court—where she came down with a chest cold and developed full-blown pneumonia, apparently turning blue and spewing streams of nonsense for ten days while delirious. *I'm told everyone came by to listen. Isn't that funny? I was the main entertainment again, even tho I was unconscious!* Dad was given leave to visit his dying wife—an event that saved his life since, during his brief absence, the rest of his unit was blown up in Antwerp. At the eleventh hour Mum received rare penicillin reserved for U.S. troops, and now both their lives had been spared.

Almost immediately Dad was posted to India and the Far East, possibly for a two-year stint, and Mum's strategy, "to build up a bold indifference," crumbled. She was losing her hair as a result of the drugs—*They're calling me Baldy*—and she melted into melancholy. As the glamor of war wore thin and 1945 dragged on, her letters to Dad swing from love and longing . . . *I must have been born loving you . . . If you do stay two years, I think my heartstrings will be plucked clean by then . . .* to anger and resentment . . . *I don't want to be the widow of a hero! Dammit, this makes me maddernhell—you don't have to fight every battle in this damn war!*

But her letters aren't all so feisty; they also include her unique observations: *I was glad to read where the Allies are forcing German civilians to tour the awful concentration camps and see them while the pitiful victims are still there, but I believe only God can bring justice to the criminals. Somehow it seems kind of egotistical for us to be talking of giving justice—don't you think so?*

When Dad describes landing in Burma and witnessing "the ragged, starving natives" and the "awful sacrilege" committed by the Japanese forces against the "beautiful cathedral in Rangoon," which has been gutted and filled with pigsties, he draws a sketch of what he's seen and writes that he can never look at a Japanese soldier the same way again. But Mum tells him, *It's not the Cathedral that's been desecrated—the Japanese soldiers have desecrated* themselves.

Reading Mum and Dad's letters makes me feel that I, and my whole generation in North America, have only experienced "life lite"—with none of the sacrifice and courage demanded of theirs. No wonder Dad thought we had it "too soft."

When the war ended in Europe, Dad's unit remained in the Far East—in what they referred to as the "other war," the one that hadn't ended yet—waiting for the Japanese surrender. One of Dad's letters calculates the amount of time he's been able to spend with Mum since they first met—twelve percent. Mum returned to her family in Rokeby, where, after seeing Dad the following spring for a brief "second honeymoon," she discovered she was pregnant with me: *I'm filled with more than just promises now!*

Mum's letter to Dad describing my birth reached him aboard ship, off the coast of Manila in late November 1946. She had inked the soles of my feet to the paper and taped a snippet of my hair. Dad cabled back, *Always wanted a daughter.* He suggests naming me Victoria, but Mum doesn't like it—she says it's way too British-sounding. She's willing to compromise, though; if he wants to name me after a plum, it should be a sweeter variety than the Victoria—so how about Sugar Plum?

Dad had finally returned to his prewar civilian job in the Far East, and he sent for us. Mum took me in a bassinet by train from New York to San Francisco, where she boarded a ship for Hong Kong.

She wrote daily to her mother.

Dearest Mum, They call the General Meigs *a converted troop ship, but they forgot to convert it! There are eighteen of us to a cabin—all in bunk beds. Plum has been so good— she just sleeps and smiles.*

After a month on board ship, she docks in Shanghai, tantalizingly close to her final destination: *I feel like I'm serving a sentence in a girls' reformatory & am coming up for parole—praise Allah.*

She describes traveling up the Yangtze River and docking in the harbor where milling, screaming people are holding up banners lettered in Chinese, trying to locate friends and relatives aboard ship. Dozens of sampans and junks besiege the ship, hawking carved boxes, vases, and kimonos. With long-handled nets, they hand up a ball of string to the passengers, who tie money to the string, drop it over the side, and hoist up their purchases. The ship keeps its fire hoses over the side, periodically turning them on full blast to scatter the hawkers, but it doesn't keep them away for long. When police boats appear, looking for opium smugglers, the sampans "vanish like mist." Mum didn't go ashore—she'd heard too many stories about vandalism and robberies and didn't want to risk it so close to the end of her journey. She set sail for Hong Kong in the afternoon.

April 4, 1947. Dearest Mum, I still can't believe that I'll be seeing Alex in 2 days—I feel as tho I've been on this damn ship for years. It's been a nightmare . . .

I hadn't realized the gargantuan effort it took to travel with me or what guts it must have taken for Mum to leave behind her family and travel into the unknown to be with Dad.

In Hong Kong, Dad was anxiously awaiting us. He'd found an ideal piece of land on Coombe Road, high on The Peak with spectacular views of the harbor and mountains, and here he built a spacious, sprawling bungalow with separate servants' quarters. My amah, Ah Kan, spent every waking minute with me, and when my brother Sandy was born in 1948, he got his own amah, too.

Now that they've spent their first two years together, Mum's descriptions of Dad aren't quite as glowing as they were when she first married him after knowing him for only two weeks:

When he gets his mind set on something, there's absolutely nothing I can do—it's hell! For the first time in my life, I've run into a stone wall. Alex, like Daddy, doesn't know what rest means, can't stand being idle, highly disapproves of sleeping in late even if he has to concoct things to do; thinks milk is far better for his health than Scotch whiskey; and that it's a sin to take a taxi instead of a bus when there are so many starving people in the world!

She'd been more hard-hitting when she'd earlier put her feelings on a piece of paper for Dad: *I don't think you'd listen to all this in conversation, tho you might absorb it in writing—am I right? We'll have to make a start toward agreeing with each other, for we are forever being childish and stubborn and taking opposite views, just to annoy. That gets us nothing but unhappiness and it's time we matured. I've always had the feeling that you didn't respect my opinions, from the way you instantly discard them, and I don't give you the cooperation you frequently want & need. I know you're interested in talking to me, but I've never had the feeling you were in the least interested in what I have to say. I resent being slapped down! Believe me, nothing can separate 2 people as quickly or completely as that lack of mutual support, and nothing conveys itself so quickly to children—as you should well remember.*

It's a revelation to me to discover that their marriage had been so conflicted from the start. I'd clung to the illusion that their early years were supportive and romantic, but it seems that was only because they were kept apart. Oddly, I find myself feeling humbled that despite their ongoing battles they stayed together because of us; mindful of the personal sacrifices they made; grateful that I'm allowed to see the private, inner workings of a marriage of great longevity—not something to be ashamed of, but a hard-fought achievement, an investment in *love*—a union that left us *all this*.

In 1949, we left on a big boat to go see Granny, but I didn't want to leave Ah Kan. *Please don't make me leave Ah Kan. Please, please, please . . . Ah Kan! Ah Kan!* Daddy unhooks my fingers. Ah Kan is crying. Through the railings on deck I see her getting smaller and smaller until I can't see her anymore.

April 21, On board ship: Hong Kong to London. Dearest Mum, We've been thru absolute hell on this ship—in a cabin so tiny, there's not even a spot to put the baby's basket & not any soul to watch the kids. We spend all our time nursing, washing & feeding. Dear little Plum has suffered absolute heartbreak with everything she's ever known vanished from her life—she won't let us out of her sight. We had to leave her alone, screaming in terror several times, in order to get food. She misses Ah Kan unmercifully & says hopefully, "maybe tomorrow I go home?" She has tried so hard to be brave, but all sparkle has left her. I leave Sandy in his pram on deck and hope that if he cries, somebody will tell me. When Alex yells at me, Plum says, "Sorry, Mummy." We arrive in London a month from now . . .

Although Mum and Dad took a six-month leave, the trip took more than two months by sea, each way, traveling via the Suez Canal to Portugal, London, and New York City; then back via San Francisco, Hawaii, Japan, and Singapore, so that once they arrived in Virginia, Mum had only six weeks to spend with her family.

She describes the ship's cabins as being "the size of a telephone booth," with no bath and few facilities for drying diapers or mixing baby formula. Adults were required to dress formally for dinner and children weren't permitted, so they had to be left behind alone in the cabins. Switching ships at various ports often meant organizing the transfer of luggage—trunks, suitcases, cribs, and pram—remembering to keep on hand enough formula and diapers for emergencies because there were none to buy in the ports.

She's saved a dog-eared pamphlet: *If You Must Travel with Baby During Wartime.* One of its helpful hints is that you can wrap soiled diapers in waxed paper and then tuck them back into your suitcase.

On our return to the Far East, in December 1949, we left the beautiful home that Dad had built on The Peak in Hong Kong and moved to Singapore, where Dad became manager. Mum was now pregnant with her third child—my brother Robin.

The house was bigger—it had its own tennis court—the climate less humid, the stores better stocked, the social life easier, and the pace more relaxed. In the Malay countryside expanses of paddy fields were plowed by water buffalo, and bullock carts with steep attap roofs lumbered past doll-like teak houses built on stilts with hand-carved fretwork designs around the windows. Fowl and goats roamed under the palms, and monkeys were trained to clamber up the trees to bring down the coconuts. In summer we flew to Fraser's Hill, high on a peak near Kuala Lumpur, to find relief from the heat of the lowlands. It was surrounded by jungle and ancient forest, and the colonial government maintained a country club and golf course there.

Mum had a full-time Malay chauffeur, Soho. He dressed in a white uniform and took her to the American Club in the morning for swimming and mah-jongg, the Botanical Gardens for tea, and the Tanglin Club or Raffles Hotel for dancing in the evenings with Dad. I read about their friends, an interesting mix of journalists, authors, and influential politicians. Mum seemed happy that she could still get "the inside scoop."

The political climate, however, began to heat up. One month after my brother Robin was born in May 1950, North Korea attacked South Korea and there was growing talk of a new war between the United States and China. As the year progressed, tensions between East and West drifted toward Singapore, too.

There were curfews at night. I read that whenever we drove up to Malacca, we went in convoys for fear of armed bandits. I have another flashback: a memory of taking a car ride down a winding mountain road. Daddy is in the front seat beside our driver and Mummy is in the back with Sandy and me, holding Robin in her arms. Suddenly Mum shouts, "Oh, God, Alex!" and shoves me down onto the floor. But I've already seen the burned-up car in the ditch with an arm sticking out. Daddy shouts, "Faster!"

In September, Mum writes that intruders attempt to smash through our living room shutters late one night, and Mum and Dad begin sleeping with a big stick under their mosquito net—along with glass bottles of soda water that they're told will have "a fine explosive effect" when dropped out the window onto the brick path below. But when a British soldier is dragged unconscious from a bus into a ditch and set alight by an angry mob, Mum becomes anxious to leave. Dad reluctantly agrees, thinking of it as a "temporary solution to safeguard the children until everything blows over." He books passage for Mum on a ship leaving in January.

By November, however, tensions between Muslims and Christians have escalated, sparked by the famous Maria Hertogh case: the thirteen-year-old Dutch girl whose parents had been trying to retrieve her from her Muslim foster mother since their release from internment camps at the end of the war. Malay and Chinese mobs start killing Europeans on sight, and troops are called in. By December 12, 1950, eighteen people are dead and almost two hundred wounded. Hundreds of vehicles are damaged and many buildings set ablaze. The American consul advises all American citizens to leave immediately, but Dad tells Mum the evacuation order doesn't apply to her: she's *British* now, he reminds her, since she's married to him.

Mum pays no heed to Dad. The very next day she packs hastily and bundles us onto the last plane out. With stopovers, the flight takes four days. This time she's traveling alone with three young children, including Robin, who's just an infant.

Dad was left behind. He spent Christmas alone in the big house, surrounded by unopened toys. Enduring two weeks of twenty-four-hour curfews, he had two servants sleep at the bottom of the stairs during the nights to guard against intruders. His letters are full of longing, enough to break my heart. He begins each one "To My Own Precious Wife" and signs them "Your Devoted Husband." The following October, the British high commissioner, Sir Henry Gurney, is assassinated at Fraser's Hill.

Mum arrived in Virginia just in time to see her ailing mother, who died shortly after. The large redbrick mansion at 500 West Franklin Street that had always been their city home in Richmond had already been emptied and sold, and the family traditions continued at Rokeby Farm.

It's obvious from all her letters what a close relationship Mum had with her own mother—she tells her everything—and I'm envious. This must have been her expectation of me, too. It makes me wonder what Granny was like as a mother. She supported all Mum's choices, like going away to college, going overseas during the war, and moving halfway across the world to live in the Far East with Dad. Mum was so independent and adventurous, in ways I had never imagined. How do I square this with the mother I knew, who was so intrusive, demanding, and possessive of me? Then I notice how many letters were written by Granny to Mum *when she was a child.* There are many letters written to Mum on her birthdays—her eighth, her ninth, her tenth—and it dawns on me: perhaps Granny was an *absentee* mother! Since Mum was her eighth and last child, I conclude that Granny may have spent much of Mum's childhood away—traveling to doctors in New York and Boston, trying to find a cure for her eldest daughter's diabetes. On these occasions, Mum would have been left behind with her father and siblings, achieving independence from her mother early, an independence that even allowed her to hold her wedding in England—without her mother there. Their relationship would have developed almost exclusively through letters.

Maybe Mum hadn't wanted independence! Maybe she tried to reconstruct a relationship with me like the one she wished she could have had with her own mother. I always felt that I instinctively understood Dad, but these letters are helping me understand Mum, after pushing her away for so long. These are the puzzle pieces I had hoped to find. This is her *diary.*

My heart stops when I find this: *My Darling Anne, I'm saving all your letters because I know your biographer will one day want them . . . your devoted Mother.*

Am I my mother's biographer? Do all daughters become their mother's biographers, taking her history and passing it on to future generations? Writing letters was one of Mum's greatest talents, and here is the record of her life. At the end of our lives, we become only memories. If we're lucky, someone is passing those down.

All night the lake roars like a freight train. When I go to bed the waves are racing, flat and sleek, competing with each other for speed. The surface of the lake looks like a Venetian blind, with only the horizontal white lines of surf visible in the blackness of night. By midnight, ice pellets have started to fall and the waves become wide shovels, slamming the ice up against the shore with a thunderous force and spectacular spray. The waves shovel all night and are still working slavishly in the morning. There's an ice shelf forming—an amazing phenomenon. It feels as if I'm in a bowl of white ice. From the veranda, I'm looking out at the lip, which curls over in front of the house like a prehistoric iceberg. It's about eight feet high now and thirty feet deep and still growing its crystalline wall along the shoreline. Mum would have been clapping her hands. "Come see! Come see! It's the best show on earth, and it's free!"

Frosted beards of icicles grow from the windowsills and freeze-frame my views. When I describe them to Robin in an e-mail, he writes back, "I hope they're on the outside!" Later in the week, when the sun melts their roots, I hear the giant ones plummet and shatter onto the brick path below.

Outside, the water in the lake is a deep viridian green. It's lapping at the ice shelf and licking it away. Splotchy chunks of ice, glittering with crystals in the early sunlight, are floating away from the jagged-edged crust and a few brave ducks are paddling among them. The sky is sliced apart with white contrails and wispy, long-legged clouds are drifting past in the shape of dancing camels. I can never go back to being surrounded by buildings again, hemmed in and confined by man-made structures.

This house and its setting, Mum said, were "in her bones" . . . and they're in mine, too. But I've spent so many of the past twenty years feeling trapped here and wishing for release that I hadn't stopped to imagine what it would be like when it was all gone.

Now I want a reprieve. Why do we have to sell it? Why can't I dr
here like everybody else?

I speak to my friend Lesley on the phone, lamenting my pending loss of this beautiful landscape with its limitless horizon. She understands only too well; she grew up in similar surroundings.

"When you have an unobstructed view," she muses, "something happens to the mind . . . it expands, doesn't it?" Then she adds, "But if you look up, you'll see the clouds. The thing about clouds is that they tell you how to live."

"What do you mean?"

"They're always *moving* . . . and that's what we're supposed to do, too."

Hong Kong Farewell

In early January, I find myself in the doctor's office: Dr. Breen, my mother's doctor. She gives me a warm hug, and her thick brown curls brush my cheek. She asks how I'm doing. I haven't spoken to her since the night Mum died, although once or twice I've seen her youthful figure walking briskly along the lakefront path in front of the house. I have a small blemish on my leg, I tell her, so I need a referral to a dermatologist in Oakville. She takes a look and decides it's unnecessary; she thinks the spot will go away on its own.

"But let's take a little social history," she says, and turns to her computer.

I answer questions like how old I am, when did I divorce, how many children do I have, how much exercise do I get, how much alcohol do I consume, and then: am I still smoking? Yes, I tell her, I've quit in the past, but now cigarettes are my friends. Then I blurt out, "Of course, it's a slow suicide—I know that." Dr. Breen has her back to me, typing, but when I say this, she stops. "Do you think about suicide?" she asks.

I tell her no, but I don't want to live long enough to get dementia, like Dad. I'd rather die early, of a heart attack. Then I tell her that this past week I've been feeling a little depressed. I've been second-guessing my motivations for everything. Maybe isolating myself in Mum's house is unhealthy, akin to pulling blankets over my head. I've been cutting myself off from family and friends. My world is shrinking and I'm strangely okay with this. But maybe I shouldn't be?

When I leave her office I'm clutching a referral, not to a dermatologist, but to a therapist. I'm told that the intake secretary from the Adult Mental Health Office will call me to schedule it. When I get home, I vow to cancel. The thought of having to bring some shrink up to speed with what's been going on in my life over the past twenty years fills me with fatigue. Besides, I think, I'm hardly worth their time: until recently, I've been feeling wonderful. Am I really depressed or just "lying fallow"—an artistic condition that usually precedes a period of great creativity for me. *How can I tell the difference?*

When Halton Healthcare finally calls, they tell me I'm in luck—there's been a cancelation and they can see me tomorrow. I'm about to say "No, thanks" when my brain stalls: *Wait a minute . . . why does that date have resonance for me? The anniversary of Mum's death! How could I have forgotten?* No wonder I've been feeling low this week. It seems too coincidental—almost preordained—so I decide to go.

The intake secretary, a soft-spoken woman in a lavender sweater, asks me a variety of in-depth questions, smiling as she speaks. She has a ten-page printed questionnaire on her desk, and she circles things and puts checkmarks or lines through boxes. Her bright, lively eyes give no hint of judgment. She asks me about my physical health: whether I've ever had a head injury, any serious accidents or operations, and expresses surprise when I tell her the only things I take are vitamins.

"We rarely see someone your age who's not taking any medications," she says.

She asks me whether I've ever taken drugs (no), how much alcohol I consume (not much), and how much exercise I get (lots). Then she asks whether there's a history of suicide in the family. I answer yes—my mother's brother Frank—although no one was ever sure whether he jumped or was pushed, and this was eighty years ago. She asks about my childhood: What kind of child was I? Shy? Happy? Gifted? What about my past careers, what I do now? When I tell her I'm an artist and a writer, she asks what I live on. I want to say "hope," but instead I confess that I'm burning through savings from my earlier career in publishing. It's a big stressor in my life. When I decided to follow my bliss ten years ago, I knew I'd have to give up luxuries. Dad was right: society doesn't value artists, even though, when a civilization disappears, artwork is the only thing that survives. We dig up pots and statues and ancient wall murals and put them in museums. If it hadn't been for Mum and Dad's frugality, and what they've just left us, I'd be really worried about my future.

The secretary probes my parents' marriage. "How would you describe it?" she asks.

I stumble for words. "Well . . . it was passionate . . . passionate in both directions."

"Was it violent?"

"No," I say, "I wouldn't describe it as violent . . . I would say . . . um . . . emotionally intense." I didn't recall any physical violence between my parents, but I find myself making a conscious effort not to defensively cross my arms, remembering the letter I read only last night.

Sept. 28, 1949. Honolulu, aboard the ship S.S. President Cleveland. *Dearest Mum, The other night, Alex got very irritated & started pushing Plum around for no reason, so I smacked him. He got so mad that he hit her very hard & she cried and cried. I tried to comfort her & explain that he was tired. Later, full of remorse, he told me he was sorry. I told him he should apologize to Plum, not to me. So he did—whereupon she looked up sympathetically & said, "That's awright, Daddy, you didn't mean to."*

"Did your parents drink?" she asks.

I find myself minimizing Mum's alcoholism. After all, it started in the fifties—women in frilly aprons, evening cocktails, and all that. Besides, she quit drinking when my brother Sandy asked her to. My memory flashes to all the empty gin bottles Dad had stacked up in the garage to make her feel guilty.

"She had a will of iron, my mother," I tell her. "She smoked until she was eighty-five, but she gave it up each year during Lent. She chewed an empty corncob pipe instead."

"Were there any weapons in the house?" she asks.

"Only Dad's bamboo cane," I say. "The one he disciplined my brothers with . . . I think one of them took it away to be framed."

She asks me if I have hallucinations, hear voices, or see things that aren't there, and rapidly strikes through the remaining boxes. Then she caps her pen and turns to me, smiling sympathetically.

"Do you think you need to talk to a grief counselor?" The thought that I might be finally grieving had never entered my head until now.

As I pull out of the parking lot and head south, I look up into the cold, clear sky. Two large flocks of Canada geese are flying high above in their V-formation, one on either side of my car. They escort me all the way down Dorval Road, east along the Lakeshore, down Trafalgar Road, and straight home to the lake. Am I seeing things that aren't there? I wonder what the psychiatrist would make of this?

As I drive into the boathouse, I think of how I've been navigating memories of the past, like stuffing myself in the hull of Dad's boat again—looking for ballast. It's been a necessary process but now I know I'm ready to move on.

A few days later, in my old bedroom, I awaken with the gift of dawn. The radiant light warms my cheeks, and when I open my eyes, the whole room is filled with an orange glow. To have a perfectly round sun lift up over the horizon, directly outside my bedroom window, and pour gold into my lap fills me with hope and optimism.

In February, Alex phones to say she has some people who want to come back for a second look. They'd seen the house before Christmas and they can't get it out of their heads. Once again I spend hours vacuuming and mopping floors, and once again I leave for the prescribed hour. But when I drive back their cars are still in the driveway, so I pull up on the street and wait. I wait and wait. After an hour, I think, *Okay, that's enough,* and barge in through the boathouse door.

"Time's up!" I shout.

Alex greets me in the pantry and introduces me to Clive and Hilary. Hilary is a pretty, petite blonde with a warm, engaging smile. Clive is a tall, dark, ruddy-faced Welshman with a black mustache and bushy eyebrows. His eyes are dancing, and I think,

Uh-oh, this could be serious. He's marveling at the old built-in glass cabinets in the dining room and the wide wood-plank countertops in the pantry, and he wants to know the history of everything. By mid-afternoon we have an offer from Clive, but it's too low. Victor doesn't even want to respond.

"We have to view this as a conversation," I reason. "It would be insulting not to respond."

"We're miles apart," says Victor, "and I'm not prepared to give it away."

"Let's just shave a hair off and see what he does."

Over the next twenty-four hours the offer goes back and forth, with Clive inching up and us inching down. Victor polls Chris and Robin to find out what their bottom line is. When Clive delivers his final offer, it's tantalizingly close. We have no way of knowing whether he'll move in or resell it, but the clincher for me is knowing how well Clive will care for this house. Alex tells us he has a reputation for beautiful restorations. More importantly, I feel Mum and Dad would have approved. We accept Clive's offer with a long closing—June. This gives us four more months to say good-bye to Point O' View. I paint another portrait—this time of Clive—but not until the deal is inked. One day, I take down Mum's portrait in the pantry and hang Clive in her place: I'm finally pressing the eject button.

When I speak to Chris on the phone in B.C., I tell him I won't feel sad to leave; it's time for a new young family to cherish it. It feels right. We're at the end of a life cycle and a new one is beginning. I tell him how happiness has flooded me in this house this past year, how creative energy has rushed through me the way it did in childhood.

"Maybe that's Mum's gift to you," he says. "Maybe she wanted to give you this while she was alive; she just didn't know how."

It's been just over a year since Mum died. The lake is gently stippled by a soft breeze, and even though it's the end of February, which I'd normally describe as the depths of winter, it looks as beautiful as spring. Black squirrels are running along the fence and jumping between the bare branches of the maple tree, sparrows are pecking at the lawn, geese float quietly on the surface of the water, and the swans are back.

We've finally untangled the mess—and given everything a new home, a task that turned out to be much harder yet much more rewarding than I ever anticipated.

I come eyeball to eyeball with a tiny mouse in the kitchen cupboard this morning. His head pops up beneath a grimy paper towel in the garbage, and his tiny nose twitches. He eyes me sideways. Instead of shrieking and rushing for a mousetrap, I feel tender toward him. Shouldn't he eat, too? I close the cupboard door to give him some privacy. I hear him scurry back down the hole by the sink pipes to his family.

I go out on the veranda with my coffee, leaving the door unlatched, and when I come back inside I find the stray black cat by the table, crouched below the picture of the smiling girl. The cat's eyes freak me out: they seem to pull me into orbs of infinity, and I'm reminded of Mum's look on her last day. Has she come back already—as a cat? I follow the cat's gaze to the girl's impudent, gutsy expression.

Of course this is Mum. Who else could have jumped off the

Eiffel Tower? Why did it take me so long to recognize her? Was I afraid to see that she looks like me?

I think of all the adventures Mum experienced in her life and the richness I absorbed by extension. I remember her exuberance, how much she loved life. She valued every second. Not a detail of her amazing life was wasted—she could recall it all, until the day she died. The crankiness during her final years is receding from my memory. I have replaced the lens through which I view her. I have more empathy. I'm experiencing some aches and pains myself, and I see now that old people are simply young people locked into aging bodies. No wonder she was cranky. Now I view her with more understanding and gratitude. I can remember all the enthusiastic support she gave me throughout my life. I'm beginning to wish I could have been more like her. I wish I had her derring-do.

I call Pat. "I know why I needed to spend so much time in this house," I tell her. "It wasn't about untangling the stuff—it was about untangling myself from Mum. The clutter wasn't hers . . . it was mine."

"Yes!" she says. "We all need to make the break at some point, and it takes courage . . . you just waited until the end."

"Why couldn't I find the courage earlier?" I say, shaking my head sadly at the memory. "Why didn't I break away as a teenager, like most smart people?"

"Your mother was too powerful. Mine was, too—it was impossible to break away from my mother until the end, because she wouldn't let me."

"I was too obedient," I say.

"Of course! We have no one to blame but ourselves."

"But where was my compassion in her final years? Why couldn't I handle her crankiness?"

"Mothers are always 'The Nurturer' and 'The Witch,' whether we like it or not," says Pat. "I'm both to my children . . . and you're both to your children—just as your mother was to you. We have to accept both in the same package." Then Pat laughs as if she's just discovered the joke. "It's all projection, anyway!" Her delightful high-pitched laugh tinkles away like a run of musical notes.

Before we hang up, Pat says, "There aren't many people who could have gone on your journey. You may be more like your mother than you think!"

For the first time in my life I take it as a compliment.

It's been a long spring, moody and wet, but the torrential rains have produced a silver lining: the lawns are emerald green and the gardens lush. Dad's daffodils are blooming, their sunburst yellow heads poking out of deep lumpy blankets of blue forget-me-nots. Lake breezes shake the tall stalks of purple phlox and carry to the veranda waves of perfume from the lilac hedges.

I tell Robert Baines that he can have the big old dresser with the secret drawer, so the following week he rushes out with a moving van. While he's here, I give him the remaining dining room chairs and anything else we can find that once belonged to his great-grandfather. There's one more item that came with the house, but I doubt he'd want it—it looks like a coffin. I take him up the back stairs to the now-empty trunk room and point to a narrow, ten-foot-long box cowering in a corner under the eaves. He drags it into the light. The hinged lid is covered in a padded green material.

"Do you mind if I peel back some of the cloth?" asks Robert. He takes a key out of his pocket and rips a slit in the lining. The material is rotten, and when we give it a tug the whole sheet tears away in a cloud of dust.

"Well, what do you know!" he says, shaking his head. Scribbled in pencil on the inside lid is a row of Christian names. "Those are my aunts and uncles . . . this must have been their toy chest or something!"

Happily, he hoists the box into the van and drives his treasures back into the city.

Our neighbor Dick Rampen brings me the plastic mold he's made from the fox-head gate latch and we send it to a factory in China to make replicas in cast iron. Everyone seems to want one, including the new owners. The Baines family orders five.

We put all the dregs in the garage, and I write an ad for exactly the kind of garage sale my mother would have loved to attend:

> Antique furniture, collectibles, lamps, vintage steamer trunks, 1950s magazines, Telefunken stereo, LPs, wicker rocker, framed prints & original art, dishes, glassware, cutlery, Persian rugs, old tools, vases, mini-fridge, etc. All priced to sell.

Grandchildren come out for the day to help do the selling. Dealers arrive early to scoop up the good stuff. A neighbor buys Dad's old wicker rocker and carries it around the corner, where she puts it on her back porch. I can see it from the kitchen window and it fills me with happiness. The next shift—women on walkers, younger than Mum but older than me—buy up all the picture frames, salad bowls, and out-of-date atlases. We even manage to sell a naked Barbie.

Dad's 1912 Nordheimer piano is a collector's item and still

carries a tune, but we have trouble finding a buyer. I resist the temptation to take it apart and hang its beautiful cast-bronze, harp-shaped guts on the wall of my house as a piece of art, but I do rescue one of the steamer trunks—the small black metal one with Mum's maiden initials painted in gold under the lock, the one she took to war.

My six-week plan to sort through clutter has taken sixteen months. On a sunny May afternoon, my brothers return and we hold a tea party on the veranda for friends—including the Baineses—to say good-bye. After they leave, my brothers and I hold our last Sibling Supper. In the big, empty house, with the dining room table gone, we sit around a card table, nibble on pizza, and disperse some final odds and ends we've found: a lock of blond baby hair in a box (but whose?), a Victorian watch fob, and a rolled-up aerial photo of Oporto, Portugal, showing Dad's family home before it was torn down to make way for the main bridge across the River Douro.

At the end of the evening, we go outside in the twilight to stumble backward around the outside perimeter of the house. Robin calls it the "Hong Kong Farewell" and reminds us that all departing governors general used to do this—drive backward three times around Government House in Hong Kong to say good-bye. Robin says it realigns the feng shui.

Victor refuses to participate. He reminds us that Robin always makes up stuff like this, and he sits huffing impatiently in his car with the headlights on in the darkened street. Laughing, Robin, Chris, and I, holding hands, stumble backward single file through the garage and down the path beside the old sandbox; past Dad's hollyhock beds, the outdoor clothesline, and the laundry room door; then across the side of the pool, up the hill to the veranda, through the garden gate to the front door, and back to where we started. We pretend Sandy is with us.

As we pass the streetlight, Victor leans out of his car window. "Hey, just for the record . . . in case anybody comes by . . . I'm not related to any of you—okay? You're all out of your friggin' minds! And did Plum tell you she hears the walls humming? I swear to God, she's been living here way too long!"

We look up at the flag: it ripples and snaps. We had decided not to lower it tonight; neighbors might think there's been another death in the family.

It feels like that.

This house with its setting is part of me, seared into my bones like fossil on rock. It's more a true ancestor than any of those we never met. It's held our blood in its veins: some of us have been born here, married here, and died here. Nothing can ever take it away.

I can't resist taking one more walk-through.

I am now seeing the house empty, exactly the way my mother first saw it all those years ago when she was thirty-six years old, standing here, imagining all its possibilities and the love she could breathe into a life for us here. I realize that Mum *was* the house, and all this time she's been speaking to me.

I listen to the waves lapping rhythmically against the shore, like the beating of my mother's heart, and I hear, "Nothing lasts forever, *Darling*, but this . . . this is *everything*."

One Last Look

The house has new owners and I've moved back to the city. The contents—and the memories they hold—have been dispersed like seeds to the wind: some to strangers, some to friends, most to family. I've hung the fox-head latch from the garden gate—with the familiar *chink-chink* of its ears—on the wall beside my bed in Toronto, and I've cleared a room on the third floor for my most treasured possession, Mum's letters.

Robin has sent me his self-published book titled *Point O' View Books*. The preface begins "This catalog is a partial listing of the more than 2,000 books . . ." I notice with satisfaction that Mum's cookbooks have their own section, even though it's an addendum in the back. I've sent each of my brothers a self-published book, too: a photographic record of every nook and scratch mark in the house. They seem glad now that I was so obsessive in my mission to catalog the memories.

A month later I can't resist going back to Oakville and driving by the house. The new owners have wasted no time in taking a crowbar to the interior. I peer in through the front door. They've gutted the house to its studs, scraped it to the bones. All that remains downstairs is the shell of the staircase, with an ancient, unfamiliar green milk paint revealed on its now-naked underbelly. It's disorienting—the house is a maze of studs and joists, with holes where once there were windows—but it doesn't feel sad; it feels hopeful.

The contractor sees me and comes running, asking me to please not come in too far, since I'm not wearing a helmet or steel-toed boots.

"You won't believe what we found above the dining room ceiling," he says.

"A million dollars?" I ask, hopefully.

"No!" he laughs. "A gigantic hornet's nest, running the whole length of the room! Didn't you ever hear the humming?"

Acknowledgments

This book took me two years to write—slightly longer than it took to clear out Mum and Dad's house. I used to think parents should clean up their own mess before they depart this world; now I think just the opposite. Don't die early. Wait till your children are old enough to appreciate it, and then leave them everything.

My children—Virginia, Carter, and Jessica—were empathetic and loving, as always. They let me slip away for sixteen months to reconnect with my childhood memories. They said "Yaay!" when I told them I wanted to write about it, so I fear one day they will write about me.

I thank my brothers for their love, loyalty, and laughter as I dug into the family home. They were right: most of the clutter was in my head.

The clutter has been replaced by regret—something I swore I'd never have. I wouldn't have traded Mum; I just wish the last twenty years hadn't been so thorny. Because then I wouldn't have felt the need to put her back up on a pedestal—which is where she sits now.

I thank Pelmo and her husband, Tashi, who, along with their nieces, Wosel and Tinley, lovingly helped us care for Mum and Dad in their final years; Michael Nightingale, faithful friend to us all; Patricia Goss, who listened to my many confessions and dreams and offered wisdom repeatedly; and my best friend in childhood, Diana Caldwell-Taynen, who shared many of these experiences with me, back then. She tells me Mum was one of the women she admired the most.

Acknowledgments

Many friends helped me declutter. Heather Chappell, Lesley Fairfield, and Jan Quinlan helped me do the heavy lifting; Peni Patrick and Amelia Farquharson read early drafts; and other loyal friends checked in regularly, just to make sure I hadn't fallen through a floorboard: Lola Rasminsky, Janine Kroon, Chris Hornett, Joan Vanduzer, Roger Middleton, Isabel Mitchell, Dennis van Dyke, Charlotte Carter, Trevor Collier, Corinne Ong Tan, Judy Hatcher, Fran Bennett, and the "Swim Frantastics."

A special thanks to the neighbours in Oakville who reached out to me, especially Gloria and Michael Niblok, Phil and Lesley Weingarden, Dick and Cathy Rampen, Rudy Bauer, Sarah Rochon, Brock Mason, and Hugh and Sue Wilkinson. Sybil Rampen kindly invited me to join the Flying Pigs Arts and Letters Club, which meets monthly at her Joshua Creek Heritage Art Centre; and Dale Stapleton, Nancy Schock, Marvyn Roseland-Barnes, Fenela Townsend, and the rest of the "Real Swimmers of Centennial Pool" who warmly welcomed me in the mornings for a needed shot of exercise and frivolity.

I am indebted to Mary McQueen, John Dixon, and John Sewell, who spent time at the house advising me on the many artifacts.

No book is written without an editorial support team, and I had a great one. I thank them all, especially Edith Beleites, who generously gave me hours of advice on early drafts, often via Skype from Germany; Tracy Bordian, who took my unwieldy manuscript and masterfully sliced it into shape; Diane Turbide, publishing director at Penguin Canada; Sara Minnich, editor at G. P. Putnam's Sons; and most of all my amazing agent, Samantha Haywood, who wore many hats during the process: friend, confidante, cheerleader, editor, and adviser. She is the best in the business and I couldn't do any of this without her.

On a cold day in January, shortly before the book went into production, Samantha and I drove to Oakville with Diane Turbide so she

Acknowledgments

could see the house and get a feel for the setting. Mum's geese were visiting and two swans were testing the icy waters. Restoration on the house by the new owners hadn't finished yet, but the hornets were gone. The date Diane had picked, by pure coincidence, was the anniversary of Mum's death: January 17.

Then the production team gave me the book's final "birth date"—August 12—Mum's true birth date, another shivery coincidence, and I took it as a sign: the whole process had come full circle, from death to rebirth: Happy birthday, Mum (despite what your plaque says); you always said you wanted to come back as a tree!